GOLF
THE
WINNING FORMULA

Nick Faldo

WITH VIVIEN SAUNDERS

Stanley Paul

LONDON   SYDNEY   AUCKLAND   JOHANNESBURG

Stanley Paul & Co. Ltd

An imprint of the Random Century Group
20 Vauxhall Bridge Road, London SW1V 2SA

Random Century Australia (Pty) Ltd
20 Alfred Street, Milsons Point, Sydney, NSW 2061

Random Century New Zealand Limited
191 Archers Road, PO Box 40–086, Glenfield,
Auckland 10

Century Hutchinson South Africa (Pty) Ltd
PO Box 337, Bergvlei 2012, South Africa

First published 1989
Reprinted 1989, 1990 (four times), 1991

Copyright © Nick Faldo 1989

Illustrations © Albany Wiseman 1989

Typesetting by
𝐅\ Tek Art Ltd, Croydon, Surrey

Printed and bound in Great Britain by
Butler & Tanner Ltd, Frome and London

British Library Cataloguing in Publication Data

Faldo, Nick *1957–*
    Golf – the winning formula
    1. Golf. Faldo, Nick, 1957–
    I. Title
    796.352'092'4

ISBN 0 09 173699 4

Acknowledgement

The author and publishers would like to
thank David Cannon of Allsport and Jim
Moriarty for the photographs in this book.

Colour section: driving and playing out of
sand

Contents

Foreword

WHEN I MET Nick Faldo at Sun City in 1984 he was a highly successful golfer, ranked number one in Europe at the end of 1983 and with one of the prettiest swings in the game. There were just two things wrong. The beautiful swing concealed ugly faults that would never stand up under the ultimate pressure, and Nick had to face the ultimate pressure, because he wanted to be the best golfer in the world. When he consulted me, I told him what I thought, and that if he seriously wanted to transform his game from what it was then to what it would need to be, I'd be happy to help. But I warned him that there would be no half-measures. He'd be risking the lot.

It takes a brave man to come back to you after that, as Nick did at the Memorial Tournament in 1985, and say, 'Come on then. Throw the book at me.' With character like that, a sportsman already has the word 'champion' written on him somewhere. So we went to work. We had to make many changes. I told him they would feel weird to start with and that his game would suffer. But, if he wanted to achieve his goals he would have to go through the pain and give the swing changes two years to become natural and instinctive.

Nick never doubted me, despite umpteen unbelievers telling him that he was making a big mistake. It was no mistake. We started with a new rotation of the arms on the backswing, which made him learn to turn his body rather than tilt it. We worked on a completely new leg action to stabilize his swing. He learnt the setting action of the wrists, and how to follow-through by releasing the left arm and pulling left. Following these major alterations, we made countless small adjustments to establish a whole new sensation of feel and consistency. And although I was there to help and advise, it was Nick who sweated and worked and drove himself as few successful golfers would have done, taking his career in his hands.

What Nick learned, he wants to tell you. This is no ordinary instructional book. It was written while the whole agonizing, transforming process was fresh in his mind, the one that led to triumph in 1987 as Nick won his well-deserved British Open and went from strength to strength. What it says, in hundreds of beautifully helpful photographs and clear, magical words, is 'This is how it's done. If you really want to change your game and aim for the top, risk everything, and you can win it all'. Why not let Nick Faldo throw the book at you?

DAVID LEADBETTER

Introduction

As a youngster, Nick Faldo tried most sports. He was a gifted all-round games player who seemed able to turn his hand to most sports and succeed. He looked set to be a first-class cyclist. His parents bought him a racing cycle to help him on the road to success. His father was horrified when the first thing Nick did was to dismantle the whole machine because he wanted to know exactly how it worked and to ensure that it was put together with 100 per cent precision.

Some ten years later Nick was a golfer of world-class calibre with, in 1983, five wins to his name in Europe. In much the same way as he had done with his bicycle as a boy, he decided to take apart his golf swing, learn about it in much greater detail, put it together with 100 per cent precision and then tackle the task afresh knowing his 'machinery' was perfectly built.

His father had been none too pleased when the bicycle was dismantled and reassembled. His friends, relatives and the golf critics were equally unimpressed at the thought of Nick's elegant, fluent and apparently faultless swing being demolished and rebuilt. But under the guidance of David Leadbetter that is exactly what Nick did. Systematically they went back to the drawing board till Nick knew precisely what should happen in the swing, what did happen in the swing, why it happened and how he was going to get it right. His form deteriorated and his once majestic swing began to look mechanical. Some of the press didn't go a bundle on Nick's results during this rebuilding process. But he and David soldiered on, patiently watching videos, working on the key moves for the reassembled swing and finally honing the method ready to stand up to the pressures and demands of major tournament golf.

In 1987 Nick emerged from the wilderness a new man. First came victory in the Spanish Open and with it the belief that he was on the winning track again. Not for himself, you understand. There was no doubt in his mind that the rebuilding would pay off. But his fans, the press and the connois-

Nick, aged fourteen, cycling in the Hemel Hempstead Road Trials

seurs of golf swings knew it too. Then came victory in the British Open at Muirfield followed by the historic European win in America in the Ryder Cup and England's win in the Dunhill Cup. In 1988 he sadly lost a play-off against Curtis Strange in the US Open, finished first or second in eight other tournaments and was voted by his rivals the world's most consistent golfer. The rebuilding had paid off.

In this extraordinary book, Nick Faldo talks about the golf swing with a clarity and precision very rarely encountered in sports instruction books. Not since Ben Hogan's *Modern Fundamentals of Golf* has a leading player described so thoughtfully the feelings which he and the good golfer and the club golfer need to master the game. Many of Faldo's revelations about the game will prove as enlightening for the professional and scratch golfer as they will for the novice. Others of his ideas and techniques are by no means revolutionary. But nowhere will you have read in such detail the precise movements which go to make up the swing or are used in a full repertoire of golf shots.

Nick Faldo is not only a great student of the game but also, like his great friend and rival Ballesteros, one of the finest teachers of the game. Sadly, until their playing days are over, Open champions very rarely have the time to stand on practice grounds giving lessons. Faldo's ideas, however, are all here, with his key thoughts and movements for executing virtually every shot in the game. Whether you want to achieve a drive of maximum length with just the tiniest bit of draw, or the softest, most delicate little wedge shot, the mechanics and feelings for producing each are set out ahead of you.

Don't be impatient with the game. It takes far longer to learn than most but on the other hand it is a game which will last a lifetime and is not all spent in a few summers of youth.

Faldo's thoughts and methods may revolutionize your game. They revolutionized his life.

VIVIEN SAUNDERS

The grip

A perfect grip must produce power. It must also return the club face squarely to the ball. Start with this feeling of aiming it on target before setting it on the ground behind the ball

GOOD GOLF begins with the way in which you hold the club. Unfortunately very few golfers hold the club really well, and are therefore hampered with the rest of the swing. The grip is your only contact with the club and it needs to be absolutely correct. I am sure the average club golfer does not understand what the grip does and why you cannot simply hold the club in a haphazard way and get away with it.

Let's start by seeing what we are trying to do with the golf ball. The object of any full shot in golf is to hit the ball with the right sort of height, maximum distance and to get the ball flying predominantly straight. The dimples on a golf ball are designed to make it easy for the ball to take up backspin and so get airborne. But just as the ball takes up backspin so it will very easily take up sidespin. In order to hit a ball straight, the club face has to be square at the moment of impact. For the uninitiated, this means that the club face must be aiming in the same direction as the swing. If the direction of the swing and the club face are at odds with each other, this puts on sidespin and the ball will tend to slice away to the right or hook away to the left.

The aim of the grip is therefore to return the club face squarely to the ball, while being able to produce maximum power and good height to the shots.

The key point which I am going to drum into you right from the beginning is that the right hand is going to be set behind the shaft of the club aiming towards your target. In fact the whole simple principle of golf and of this book is to teach you how to hit a ball from A to B repeatedly with guidance and control, in the main, from the right hand.

To many good golfers this in itself may be revolutionary because so many of us have had it drilled into us for years that golf has to be a left-handed game to enable a good player to hit the ball without hooking. As you will see, however, correct use of the right hand is going to be the key for much of what you read in the book.

Having said that, we obviously have to start with the left hand. It goes on at the top of the club, its positioning has to be done first and its precise placement will make the setting of the right hand both possible and logical.

There are three preparatory things we have to get right before even setting the left hand. First, you need to have grips which are set on the club with perfect alignment. Tournament professionals are meticulous about this. Club golfers will often unfortunately buy a set of clubs where the alignment of the grips is far from perfect. Get the professional who sells you the clubs to check the grips and to set them accurately. The majority of grips are egg-shaped, not round. If the grip is set correctly a professional golfer should be able to pick up the club, close his eyes, twiddle the club round in his hands and hold it with the club face perfectly square to his own grip. Check the grips and get them right or you are making life impossible.

Second, as preparation for the grip, you need to be able to set the club face squarely behind the ball so that it aims at the target. For the long-handicap player let's get it clear that it is the leading edge of the club, the line along the bottom of the club face, which you are concerned about. Forget about the top of the club. We are going to talk a lot more about aiming and general alignment in the chapter on the setup, but at this stage practise setting the club face square to your target with your right hand, pre-

1

2

Above As preparation for gripping the club correctly, you need to adopt good posture, bending from the hips, bottom out, and arms hanging loosely. This encourages the correct angles in the wrists, wrists down, not arched. If you wrongly try to hold the club out in front of you and grip, then dropping the club, the wrist angle gets locked, and the arm and club shaft wrongly form a straight line

Middle and right Steady the club at the end of the grip with the right hand in preparation for setting the left hand on the grip, club face square. Right from this moment, posture is important, bending slightly from the hips to encourage the arms to relax and the wrists to drop

ferably with some right-angled reference on the ground – whether a club shaft or some other line.

Third, before you grip the club you need to understand a little about posture and the way the hands and wrists are going to work. When you set up to a golf ball, viewing the setup from directly behind the line of the shot, the body bends over by sticking out the bottom so that there is always an angle between the arms and the club shaft. You need to get the beginning of this type of posture before you ever grip a club. This gets the angle in the left wrist correct with the wrist a little down and never arched. There are two places you can correctly learn to grip a club. One position is that you can hold the club up in front of you and pointing vertically upwards, again so that you get a cupping in the left wrist. The second position is to set the club face behind the ball and then make sure that you bend over slightly before taking up the club. Never stand up erect, arms and club straight out in front of you, and expect to hold the club properly.

THE LEFT-HAND POSITION

Although I am going to teach you that golf can be very much a right-handed game we are going to start with the left hand. You need first to understand that

there are two ways in which you can actually take up the grip on a club. A top-class player can pick up a golf club and automatically put his hands on the club in the right way, with the club face square in relation to his hands, whether holding the club up in front of him or whatever. In fact our feel for the balance of the club head and the shape of the grip is such that we should be able to do it with our eyes closed. But the club golfer usually needs to take up the grip by reference to having the club set on the ground behind the ball, club face square. Let's therefore start from that point. The easiest thing is to set the club face squarely behind the ball, standing in much closer than you might in a full setup, either just steadying the club at the top with your right thumb and index finger or, as you may prefer, by holding the club virtually at the bottom of the grip with your right hand facing the target. Now let's start with the left hand.

The feeling you should have with the left hand is that the hand and fingers are set diagonally against the shaft of the club as you take hold of it. Providing you have the club sitting squarely, with the sole on the ground and therefore taking up its natural lie, you should simply be able to hang the left arm and hand down, fingers pointing to the ground, and then fold the left hand over to take hold of the club. This

Set the left hand beside the grip, fingers hanging more or less vertically downwards and so diagonally against the club

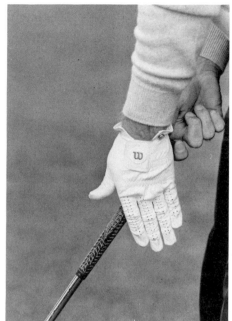

1

2

The left thumb is now put in position just to the right side of the front of the grip and the hand folded over, the index finger slightly triggered away from the second finger. The club is in the fingers far more than the palm, running diagonally through the fingers

1

2

should set the club diagonally in the hand. If done correctly your hand should look fairly long and elegant, with the thumb seeming to be pulled up well and the first joint of the index finger a little below the left tip of the thumb. The left wrist should be slightly dropped and if you open up and extend the fingers again you should have the impression that they point diagonally along the shaft of the club, never with the feeling of being wrapped straight around it. My hand can fold up to grip something in two ways.

It can curl diagonally as though holding a hammer or shaking hands – correct for the golf grip. Alternatively it can fold to form a fist, quite wrong in the golf grip.

Club golfers often make too much effort to get the hand straight round the club and so get this second, wrong kind of curl. This sees the left thumb incorrectly extended down the shaft of the club, with the left wrist arched, locked and powerless. If you still have difficulty in feeling this correct finger curl on the club, get someone to hold the club out to you and learn to grip with the left hand out at waist height. Now the fingers should very definitely follow the overall direction of the arm and take hold of the club in the correct manner – just like taking hold of a hammer.

With the correct preliminary positioning of the left hand, look down at your own grip, or lift the club very slightly off the ground to check the exact positioning. As the good player will know, we talk about grips in terms of whether they are strong or weak (that doesn't imply that strong is good and weak is poor) by reference to the

line which you will see between your thumb and index finger. As a starting point and what I would describe as a perfectly orthodox grip, that line should seem to you to point up to a point somewhere between your right eye and right shoulder. And it should be a line, rather more than a 'V'. Certainly the bottom of the thumb stays in contact with the bottom of the index finger, even though the tip of the thumb may spread away from the first joint of that index finger. This means that the left hand is slightly on the top of the club.

We also talk in terms of how many

The completed left-hand grip shows the back of the hand facing the target, with the line formed between thumb and index finger pointing towards my right eye or ear, showing the first two knuckles

1

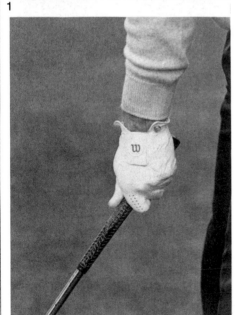

2

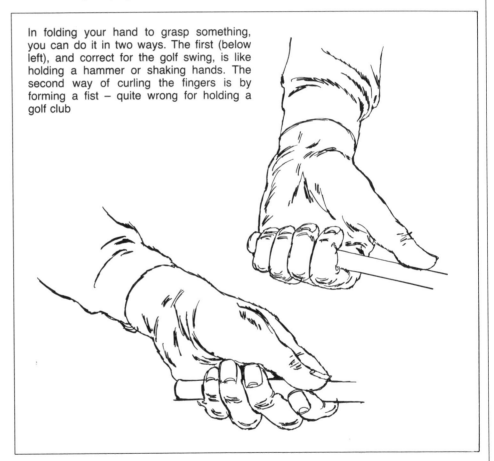

In folding your hand to grasp something, you can do it in two ways. The first (below left), and correct for the golf swing, is like holding a hammer or shaking hands. The second way of curling the fingers is by forming a fist – quite wrong for holding a golf club

knuckles of the left hand you can see as you form the grip. This can be slightly deceptive, varying according to the exact position of your head. As a starting point you should see the first two knuckles of the left hand, possibly with part of the third but not the fourth. The line between the thumb and index finger I find a more helpful guide. When judging your own grip in this way you need to keep your head central, correct angle in the left wrist.

THE RIGHT HAND

I am going to look at the Vardon grip. Almost all the world's top players use it and although there are two alternatives, I believe most of the world's leading teachers agree that this is the best. For some, unfortunately, the Vardon grip is far from easy.

There is one important key which determines whether or not you can achieve a really good grip. Your right hand needs a specific flexibility with an ability to spread and separate the fingers as shown. What you are going to do is to set the right hand predominantly behind the club facing your target. The club is going to rest in the middle of the fingers of the right hand with the little finger hooked around the index finger of the left and the right index finger triggered away from the next finger for power combined with control. In order to check this important separation, hold your right hand up towards you, palm facing, and spread both the little finger and the index finger as wide apart as possible, keeping the middle two fingers together. Without sufficient spread in the little finger in particular you are going to find difficulty with the grip and may have to go through hours of patient work. I am going to assume that you can spread your hand like this; if you cannot then the separation needs working at.

To form the grip, start by holding your right hand behind the shaft of the club, fitting the base of your left thumb snugly against that fold or pocket at the bottom of your right hand. Just as with the left hand, your right hand should feel as though the fingers hang straight downwards or almost point along the shaft of the club. At this point very definitely separate the little finger

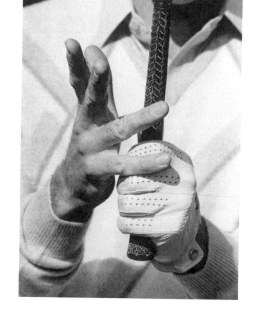

To set the hands in an orthodox Vardon grip the fingers of the right hand need to spread. In particular, the little finger must be clearly separated from the third finger, positioning the tip of it in the little space between the joint of the left index finger and second finger

Right The second and third fingers then fit into position, setting the club against the middle joints of the fingers with a feeling of holding it towards the tips of the fingers and never in the palm

The right index finger is distinctly separated from the second finger. The second and third fingers wrap round the club in harmony. The index finger is going to be triggered away to produce leverage and power

Right Here we see the completed trigger position of the index finger. Note that we no longer see the fingernail of the second finger. It is around the side of the club. The index finger does something completely different. The feeling is of pointing the finger almost along the shaft and then triggering it back again. The right thumb then rides down the side of the grip and most definitely not the front. Its role is to steady and counter the leverege in the right index finger away from the next one. Fit the little finger around the knuckle of the index finger of the left, rest the club in the middle joints to tips of the middle two fingers, and fold the right hand over so that the fleshy pocket at the bottom of your thumb snuggly covers and envelopes your left thumb. Your right index finger should now form a definite trigger position behind the club shaft with a very obvious separation between it and the second finger.

Now for the positioning of the right thumb. Club golfers are often under the mistaken belief that the right thumb should point straight down the shaft of the club. It shouldn't. The right hand is in a powerful position behind the shaft and in particular the right index finger is set behind the club to provide leverage and control. If you incorrectly set the right thumb straight down the shaft, there is nothing to steady the power in the right index finger and there is a gaping gap on the other side of the shaft. You are either likely to grip far too tightly or to lose control. The right thumb must run slightly down to the left of centre of the grip so that the two balance each other. When we look at the grip from underneath, the separation of the fingers is obvious. What is also clear is that for my full shots perhaps half an inch of the club shaft protrudes from the end of my left hand.

The positioning of my right hand is vital. I am going to teach you to play golf in a way where the right hand, even for the good player, can be seen to be more important than the left. The palm of the right hand has to face the target and again we can get a good idea of the suitability of the grip by looking at the line, or this time more of a 'V', between the thumb and index finger. Once more this line or 'V' should point up to approximately the right eye or the right shoulder. In general terms, though this is not an absolutely hard and fast rule, the top professional golfer's 'V' will point towards the right eye, and the club golfer's towards the shoulder. If you put the hand in this position and open it up you should find the palm of the hand very naturally facing the target and not facing down to the ground or opened up towards the sky. This should be your natural hitting position

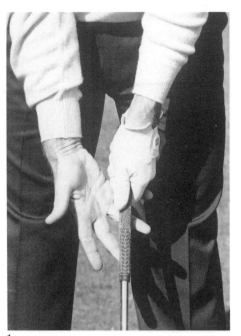

1

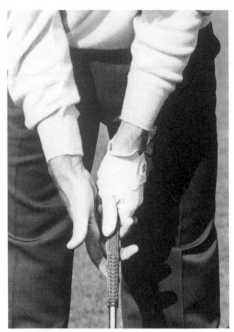

1

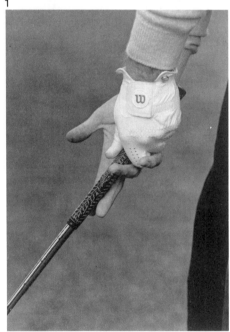

2

From this angle we see again the club being brought into the fingers of the right hand, the grip being formed with a feeling of getting the club into the fingertips

2

The right hand is going to generate power through impact, on target. With the club correctly in the fingers, the palm of the right hand now faces the target down the fairway. The hands are connected for power and control by setting the base of the left thumb snugly into the pocket in the palm of the right hand

as though actually driving the ball out towards your target with the hand itself, the right wrist slightly angled, never flat. As you open up your hand, again check that the fingers seem if anything to point down the shaft of the club and that there is no question of the hand being incorrectly put straight round the club. The finger curl is very similar to that of the left hand, again with a tight curling of the little finger and a more gradual curling of the other fingers.

THE STRONG AND WEAK GRIPS

Let's repeat that the main object of our grip is to return the club face squarely at impact so that it faces the target. The grip I have shown you above should help you do that. Broadly speaking, if you turn either the left hand too much on the top of the club or the right hand too much underneath or you have a combination of the two then this grip is likely to hook the ball, in other words sending it bending away to the left. This is known as a strong grip, but again don't let the word 'strong' make you think it is ideal. There are some

There are some professional golfers who grip with a comparatively strong left hand so that the hand is well on the top. Bernard Langer is one who springs to mind. But if you do see a professional with a strong left hand you will nearly always see the right hand not quite matching this. Instead of the right hand being under the club, the right hand is usually again set very much behind the shaft and so set on target. If on the contrary you let the right hand get too much underneath it will turn into a position where the palm faces the target through impact and so closes the club face through impact, resulting in loss of height and shots that bend away to the left. Very often players who grip in this way learn to hit the ball relatively straight and so don't notice the sidespin, but they do usually find considerable difficulty in getting height with their long irons and their fairway woods.

The player who has a very strong right-hand grip beneath the club often feels that this is a good grip because the right hand supports the weight of the club instead of aiming towards the target. It almost feels as though the player is going to be able to lift the ball more into the air, the right hand giving the impression of an upward lift. In fact it actually has the opposite effect and reduces the height.

For these players there needs to be a definite feel of the club resting almost on the ends of the fingers of the right hand with the hand set very much on target. Here I will touch on a point which we will mention again later in the book: the player who gets a strong right-hand position will often gradually learn to correct this with the long game but will then revert to his or her natural bad grip when trying to get height on the ball with pitching or bunker shots.

The other error which is likely to occur is what is known as the weak grip. The weak grip produces weak shots which tend to curve away to the right with excess height. In this case the left hand is put far too much round to the left, often with only the first knuckle of the left hand showing, and the hand almost under the club, again possibly feeling as though it supports the weight of the club. A weak grip is likely to take two forms. First of all there is the relative beginner or long-handicap player who may use grips which are too thick or may simply not get the left hand sufficiently onto the top of the club. The left hand supports the weight of the club from underneath, the line between thumb and index finger probably pointing away out towards the left shoulder. Combined with this is often a right hand which is behind the shaft or may come

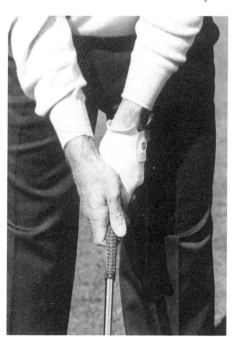

1

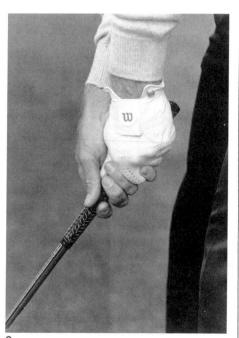

2

In the completed grip the right hand is behind the club, aiming on target. A good guide is to look at the line between thumb and index finger of the right hand, which should point up parallel to the corresponding line in the left hand – to approximately the right ear. The trigger position of the right index finger is now very clear. It is separated from the second finger and quite definitely the lowest point of the grip, the thumb in a relaxed position to the side of the club. Turn the book upside down and follow the first sequence to see my view of my own grip

a little too much on top of it. Whatever the positioning of the right hand, the left-hand positioning usually means that the club face will be twisted into an open position through impact, seeing the ball trailing away to the right. The reason for wrongly adopting this type of grip is often an attempt to put the left hand on the club from underneath instead of from the side or above.

Lastly, on the subject of strong and weak grips, a word of caution and further explanation for the aspiring tournament golfer. In theory a slightly strong grip hooks or draws the ball, and a weak one fades it. In practice, for the good player in particular, this isn't always the case. Most good young golfers – teenagers – will if anything adopt a strong grip and hook. If they persist with a strong grip, in time the tendency is to counteract this by holding the club face a shade open through impact, just manipulating the club face by feel in the hands. Subconsciously the player probably always thinks of himself as being prone to hooking – and yet in reality resists this and is far more troubled by shots to the right. 'Weakening' the hands into an orthodox grip may, by contrast, allow him to hit the ball more reliably.

The reverse can happen. One way in which a weak grip is likely to occur is where a relatively good player, and possibly even a very good player, tends to hook the ball and instead of learning to use the right hand in the correct way as I am going to show you, assumes that the way of eliminating any tendency towards hooking is to weaken the left hand into a one-knuckle grip. Youngsters often start out by hooking the ball with the left hand too much on top and possibly the right hand too much underneath. They are taught to weaken the left hand by gradually moving it more round to the left, but instead of stopping in the correct neutral position, go on and on with this adjustment, still possibly tending to hook, until the left hand moves too far round and the line between thumb and index finger points to the chin or even the left of it. Often the right hand is brought up too much on top of the club as well and the player has real difficulty in squaring up the club face. I am sure many top-class amateurs and non-tournament professionals believe that the world's top golfers use a weaker grip than we really do. What you see amongst the world's top golfers is a right hand which aims at the target and is therefore well behind the shaft of the club, but what you possibly don't realize is that the left hand certainly isn't in this one-knuckle grip. For preference, a grip tending to be strong is far better than one tending to be weak. At least it retains good power.

GRIP PRESSURE

It is very, very difficult to get a club golfer to hold a golf club loosely enough. My whole emphasis when we get to the address position and swing will be on relaxation and a feeling of freedom. This starts right from the grip. The feeling you should have is of the tips of the fingers, or the end two joints, holding the club firmly so that you aren't going to let go and it isn't going to move. But the rest of the hand needs to be loose and free, with real emphasis on getting the wrists relaxed and able to generate speed. If you were able to feel my grip on the club and to come up and move my right thumb, the odds are you would be surprised at the way it just sits there. Obviously my hands are large and very strong, but the grip that I use is so much looser and so much freer than that used by the club golfer. I have played with pro–am partners with faulty grips where I have tried to help by making a grip adjustment, to find that the guy is holding the club almost so tightly that I can't prise his hands off the shaft. I don't think it is fright at me; I think it is just fright and general tension with the game!

Grip the club lightly and loosely, perhaps feeling a little extra effort in the last two fingers of the left hand and the middle two fingers of the right. But remember that it is the fingertips that hold that club, with the rest of the hand relaxed. It is like holding a violin bow, a pencil, a small paintbrush or even a squash racket. You have to get mobility in the wrists and produce sensitivity without letting go of the thing.

Learn to make friends with a golf club, most importantly feeling the club

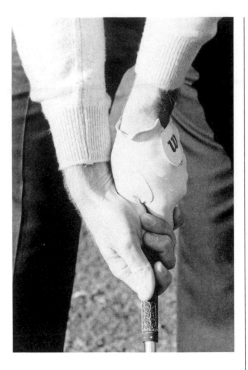

A 'strong' grip – left hand excessively on top of the club and right beneath. Don't be fooled by the description 'strong'; it doesn't mean this is a good grip. It tends to produce shots that hook to the left with loss of height, and shots that hold poorly into the green. The good player fearing the hook will then in fact often block shots to the right with this grip, completely failing to accelerate and release through impact

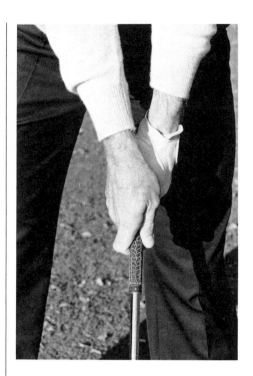

A weak grip, with the left hand almost beneath the club, right on top. Here the lines between thumb and index finger of either or both hands point left of the chin. The usual result is an open club face through impact, giving high, weak shots fading away to the right. It also causes problems in the takeaway, making it difficult to take the club away on the inside and in the correct plane

head. Learn to make it feel like a workshop tool or kitchen implement, where you make the object move and do a specific task without having to think of the arms, hands and movements involved. Pick up a hammer to knock in a nail. You feel the hammer head moving, not what you do. Ladle soup out of a pan and you make the ladle do the job. The golf club will respond in the same way. You need to transmit feel from hands to club head, from club head back to hands. In a really good grip the palm of the right hand should be so perfectly aligned with the club face that it *is* to all intents and purposes the club face. They work in harmony: feel the right palm doing something and the club face will follow. Ultimately, the good golfer imagines the club face working in a specific way, and the right hand instinctively and subconsciously moves accordingly.

So, let's try to get club head and club face control straight away. First, let's get the club head responding. Grip the club in mid air, wrists dropped, and 'write' your name or go through the alphabet with the club head, loosening up the wrists and concentrating on the club head, not on your movements. To learn club face control, practise gripping the club, eyes closed, to feel its position relative to the hands – not so obvious for the perfectly round (as opposed to egg-shaped) grip. Hold the club out in front of you, arms and wrists dropped as usual, and begin to feel club face positions, a shade open, a shade closed, until right hand and club face work in harmony, linked for feel.

The thickness of the grip is important. It can make or mar club head feel. Just as professional golfers are meticulous about the alignment of grips, we are also meticulous about the thickness. The illustration shows the actual size of my hand and it also shows the size of my grip. Most club golfers seem to think there is something macho about using a thick grip on a club. There isn't. If you use a thick grip then you aren't going to get a really delicate, light hold on the club. The odds are your fingers can't get round that club satisfactorily and you probably won't position the right hand for the power and control I am going to show you. A lot of men will hold a relatively

thin grip or even a thickish ladies' grip far better than they grip the clubs they are trying to use. Unfortunately, the beginner or long-handicap player often doesn't have the opportunity to try grips of different thicknesses and has to be guided by his professional. The manufacturer will often put on a grip which is suitable for someone like myself or Seve. Most good golfers have large hands and they also have hands which are very flexible and easily form a really good hold on a club. Get a grip which feels small enough to adopt the grip I have shown, but not so very thin that the fingernails of either hand dig into the rest of the hand or that you produce excessive tension. Keep the grips in good condition and change them regularly. A slippery grip will produce tension as you try hard not to let go. A new grip every season can give your clubs a new lease of life.

A REPETITIVE GRIP

Good golf is very largely concerned with repetition. There are many players who get superb results with what don't look to be great swings. I myself was an example of a player who achieved a tremendous amount with a few faults but through sheer repetition I made them work. You need to go through a definite process to learn how to grip the club correctly and be able to repeat it. It is important that you grip the club the same way each time, getting the hands on comfortably and repetitively. Most club golfers are unable to get the hands on the club the same way each time without fiddling around and generally feeling a little uncomfortable. Golf is not like racket games and most other sports where the weapon you hold is in your hand virtually the whole time. In golf you have to take out the club afresh and take hold of it, getting the hands set correctly and feeling comfortable within the space of a few seconds. It can often take months or even years for the newer golfer to be entirely happy with his grip on the course. Often he feels rushed and hits shots before the grip feels comfortable. Indeed I see people practising where it is so obvious that their grip isn't entirely natural. They hit one shot and then instead of loosening the grip ready to play the next shot, will hold on to the club for grim death, pulling the next ball out of the pile towards them without daring to let go with either hand! What I would suggest is that you always keep a club around the house, preferably one with exactly the same grip as the rest of your set, and just practise handling it each day and taking hold of the club so that you really can take up your grip, left hand and then right hand in two simple movements, feeling comfortable without any fiddling and readjustment.

Try exactly the same on the practice ground. Take up the club with the left hand and then set on the right hand, set the club face to the ball and feel ready to hit immediately. The less fidgeting and fiddling you can do before you start the better. You will often see tournament players like myself almost playing around with a club in our hands just before addressing a ball. This is often simply a release of tension, finding relaxation. But what we also want is a grip that will not shift or move out of position before the takeaway, certainly not in the takeaway and most definitely not during the swing. You want a light, relaxed grip which is easy to adopt and which stays the same throughout.

It is well worth checking whether your grip does stay the same from start to finish of the swing. An excellent exercise is to line up a row of four or five balls and start at one end of the row, gripping the club, hitting each and then stepping forward to address the next ball, hitting one shot after the other without the hands moving on the club at all. This doesn't mean that they should be firm. By contrast they should be relatively loose and relaxed but without any slipping or moving anywhere during shots. Ben Hogan, I am told, once lined up twenty balls and, without shifting his grip, landed all on a distant green with his 2-wood. Whether or not this piece of golfing folklore has been exaggerated over

This shows the actual size of my left hand beside a golf club. It is important to get a grip the right size – many club players with hands far smaller than mine try to use excessively large grips, usually resulting in a slice

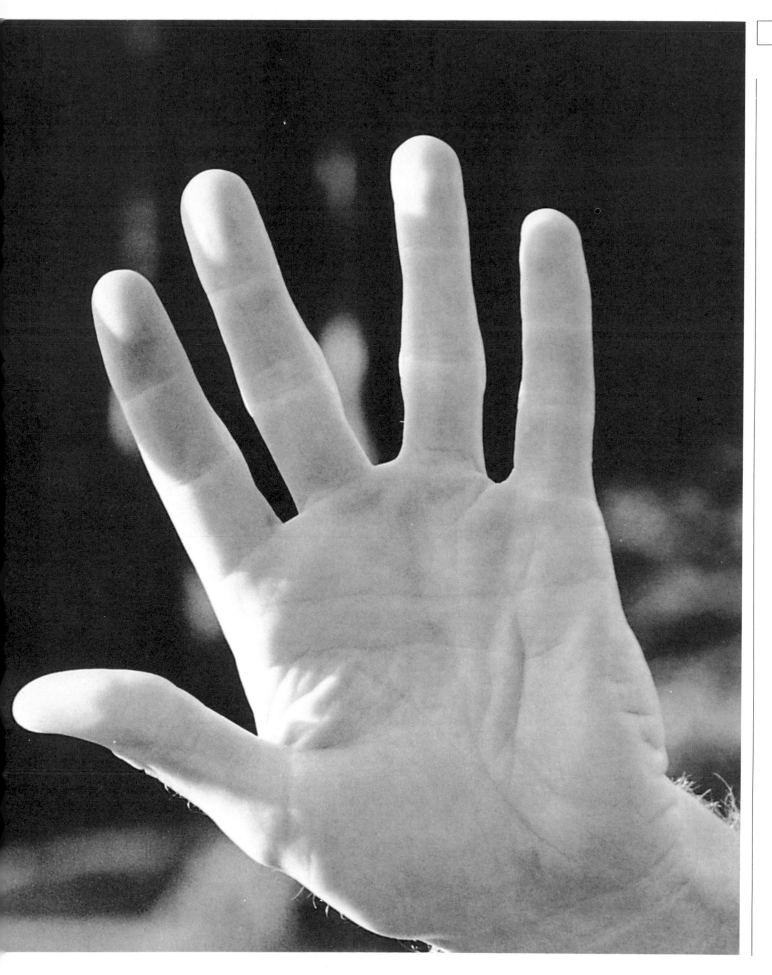

the years, it is a reminder of just how controlled the grip of the master golfer really is.

We will see later when talking about the swing that most golfers have something which triggers them into action. This may be some slight movement in one of the knees, a tiny forward press or some other little action which tells the body that it is ready to go. What you have to be very careful of, and particularly again I am addressing this advice to the very good golfer, is that the slight movement which triggers away your swing is not some unwanted fidgeting or adjustment in the grip. Particularly under pressure you can try to keep the grip fairly loose and relaxed at address and then incorrectly just tighten the left hand a shade in the takeaway. The whole positioning of the hand can easily move a fraction and can often determine why a player will have certain bad shots under pressure. The grip needs to stay constant. Often you need a professional adviser or someone who really does know your game inside out to watch closely for any slight unwanted movement which creeps in.

The feeling in the grip should always be of the right hand being behind the shaft with the left thumb fitting snugly into the pocket in the palm of the right hand. If you get unwanted movement in the grip, it is likely to be the right hand either opening up fractionally off the left thumb during the backswing or, for the longer-handicap golfer, the left hand opening off the club in the backswing and then closing again in a slightly different position. Keeping this constant grip throughout the swing is vital, again with the proviso that there must not be excessive tension.

THE INTERLOCKING GRIP

I am a strong believer in the Vardon grip. The hands are brought into position where they can work well together, the little finger of the right pulling them snugly together and keeping them working in harmony. For a tournament player the Vardon grip also gives enough freedom for tiny adjustments, perhaps where you need to produce a little draw or cut

spin on a shot. For myself I could never imagine playing golf with the interlocking grip. But it is, of course, a grip which is used successfully by Jack Nicklaus and, amongst the women, by Nancy Lopez. The interlocking grip can prove easier for the player with small hands or particularly one who finds difficulty in getting the separation I described. If you find it unnatural to separate the little finger of the right hand from the third finger, then the Vardon grip may give you difficulty. The commonest fault amongst players who find the separation hard is for the third finger of the right hand to creep up so that you get a double finger overlap. Players who do this often don't realize what is happening. In the interlocking grip the index finger of the left hand and the little finger of the right hand interlock, fingertips outwards. It is a grip which has been very widely taught since the 1970s but I am not sure how good it really is. If you do the interlocking grip correctly then it is really only the ends of the fingers which interlock and the grip should look exactly the same to somebody watching you. The only visible difference is that the little finger of the right hand shows slightly more from the front. The positioning of both hands should be the same, with the lines between thumb and index finger again pointing up to the right ear or right shoulder and with the right hand predominantly behind the club.

There are two points that worry me about the interlocking grip. First, it only gives you six fingers on the club. The index finger of your left hand which should, after all, be one of your strongest fingers is now lost from the grip. I believe this often makes players hold the club excessively tightly and perhaps lose flexibility in the wrists. Although I have gradually learned to see golf as more of a right-handed game, the left hand certainly does have its part to play in both the long game and short game. My own feeling if I take the index finger of the left hand away from the grip and put it outside in the interlocking grip is that I would lose a certain degree of control in the short game.

The second point which concerns me far more about the interlocking grip is that players who use it soon seem to slip out of the correct way of gripping the club into something which is highly unsatisfactory. Under professional guidance at first the grip may be all right. But in time what usually happens is that the player becomes lazy about the way in which the two fingers interlock and probably starts pushing the two right down so that the whole fingers interlock instead of just the ends. This often means that the left hand will slip too far under the club and the right hand in turn will also go under the club. It is almost as though the player now has insufficient hand to get a really good grip. The player then often produces a rather open-looking grip where the line between the left thumb and index finger tends to go to the left shoulder and that between the right thumb and index finger tends to point outside the right shoulder. I don't like the interlocking grip for this reason. For the club player who uses it because of the difficulty in the spread of the fingers, it may be a very good alternative to the Vardon grip. But for the junior golfer or anyone wanting to play the game at a really top level I believe the merits of the Vardon grip strongly outweigh those of the interlocking one.

The baseball grip, where you have all eight fingers on the club, is the third choice. Again I do not believe it is the grip for a top-class player. The hands can easily work in opposition and for the good golfer could easily lead to hooking under pressure. There is nothing to keep the right hand in position and all too easily the right hand can slip underneath, in turn closing the club face through impact.

Having said that, the problem of many club golfers is entirely opposite to that of the tournament player. We tend to hook the ball, you tend to slice the ball. If the Vardon or the interlocking grip produces tension and gives too much firmness in the wrists and hands, the baseball grip may help you achieve the feeling of looseness, if anything helping you square up the club face through impact. For the good player, the difficulty with this grip is that the hands can work loosely and almost in opposition to each other. For

the long-handicap player and beginner this often isn't such a bad thing. I would not, however, recommend this grip for anyone other than someone who is a natural games player. I would also as far as possible see it as a grip which is used initially, with the idea of the player going on to a Vardon grip as his skill improves. Here it has particular use for young juniors and players with relatively small hands. At least it encourages looseness and free-dom where the interlocking grip often produces stiffness and lack of speed through impact.

The grip is important. It is often impossible to get the really good golfer to look hard enough at his grip and to be prepared to alter it and tolerate initial feelings of discomfort.

If you are convinced a grip change is necessary, work patiently through the changes. Take time on the practice ground, perhaps between seasons, to perfect it. Don't expect it to work immediately with full shots; start first with 60-yard wedge shots, learning to relate hands to club face, and gradually work up to the woods – but slowly, patiently. A good grip is vital. Without it the whole game becomes difficult. Granted, you may get the occasional fine golfer who works so hard that he achieves success despite a bad grip. But, in the main, anything less than a perfect grip will produce some problems with direction or power.

Without a good grip everything else that follows in this book will lose some of its effect. And yet when I play in a pro–am on Wednesdays I can nearly always tell the standard of each of my partners from the very way in which his hands are set to that club in the first loosening-up practice swing of the day. Some players have wonderful hands which just fall into place and make the game look so easy and effortless. Others struggle with a clumsy, totally unsatisfactory grip which destroys their game from the word go. Review the grip periodically at the first sign of any trouble with the flight of the ball. Go back to basics. It isn't something that you can ever safely forget.

Setting up for success

THE ADDRESS position for the golf swing is vital. It does various things. First of all it sets your whole body in a position where it should be as easy as possible to make the correct movements in the swing. If you set your arms and legs correctly, it helps them make the right movements. Second, the address position should give you a feeling which is lively and active and ready to generate power. Third, combined with this feeling of coiling up and being ready for action it should give you a sense of relaxation and of freedom to generate speed. Fourth, it should give you balance, for golf, although a stationary ball game, needs as perfect balance as any moving ball game. Fifth, the address position is totally geared up to aiming everything in the right direction and getting you to hit the ball on target. The address position is absolutely crucial. If you are a new golfer there isn't any reason why you can't get it right. If you are an established player you will usually find that any fault which creeps in with the swing stems from some slight error at address.

If you watch the world's leading players on the practice ground you will see them continually fiddling around with the address position, while teachers and caddies view them from every angle to ensure that the aiming and ball position are spot on. An odd inch out here and there can be crucial.

I am going to start by looking at the address position with a 6-iron. It is much the same positioning for all the long clubs but I want you in particular to understand the ball position and to see the type of posture I use before we work right through the full set of clubs. I am going to begin by telling you what I do and what I feel to be important in the address position. We will then work systematically through a routine for achieving this and getting true repetition.

THE FEET AND LEGS

First, the width of the stance. I look at the width of my stance in relation to the width of my shoulders. I am 6 feet 3 inches tall and fairly broad but you can see that the width of my stance is such that the outside of my feet are slightly wider than my shoulders. If we take a line straight down from my shoulders it falls just inside the outside of my feet. You need to get this kind of width so that when you move in both backswing and throughswing the weight is never allowed to transfer out onto the outside of the feet. It mustn't get on the outside of the right foot going back, nor on the outside of the left foot going through.

The positioning of the feet is important. Club golfers often walk up to the ball and set their feet in a haphazard way. The right foot should be turned out just a little from square. The left foot should then be turned out a little more than this, perhaps about 10 degrees or so. At the same time the knees are pulled in slightly, my feeling being of squeezing from the muscles on the inside of the thighs. This sets up a little resistance to counter any lateral leg

The address position with a 6-iron shows the ball approximately three inches inside the left heel, the width of my stance just wider than my shoulders and the arms hanging loosely. The right hand is below the left on the club. It must pull the right shoulder down and not forward. The left side, from waist up, is stretched, pulling up slightly from the left hip, and with the right side relaxed and compressed

movement or any rolling of the feet in the backswing. It is a squeezing in rather than a bending forward of the knees.

Do be precise about the foot position. If you have the right foot too straight in front or even turned in a little, which was my old fault, it restricts the hip and body turn in the backswing. The right foot needs to be positioned to allow you to get a full turn in the backswing, while the left foot needs to be turned out sufficiently to allow you to turn through towards the target in the throughswing. The fault for the good player is often that he restricts the turn on the backswing by almost edging the right foot in a little. The club player, by contrast, will often get into considerable difficulty by turning the right foot out too much. If the right foot is turned out at address more than just a couple of degrees it makes the backswing seem very simple but will often restrict the player's throughswing, making it difficult for the right foot to spin through on to the end of the toes as it should by the end of a full swing. If you turn the right foot out excessively it is difficult to get the foot vertical, the sole of the shoe out behind you, by the end of the swing.

The ball is positioned maybe 3 inches or so inside my left heel. This is my starting point for the fairway shots. More about that later.

ARMS, HANDS AND SHOULDERS

As you look at the rest of the address position from the front you will see that my arms hang loosely down, with the hands pushed very slightly ahead of the ball, but with no definite feeling of trying to keep the left arm and the club shaft in a straight line. There are several points you need to look at in getting this correct address position. First, your right hand is below the left on the grip. This is going to do one of two things. It is either going to pull the right shoulder and hip forward or, as is correct, it sees the right shoulder drop below the left. This is simply done by extending the left side from hip to shoulder and by compressing the right side slightly. Combined with this is a feeling of lifting the left hip and edging

Taking the arms and club out of the way, this is how my legs feel. The weight feels slightly on the insides of the feet. I set up some resistance in my legs, squeezing in slightly with the inside muscles of the thighs. The right foot is turned out very slightly and the left a little more. If the right foot were turned in it would restrict the backswing turn; if turned out it would restrict the leg work in the throughswing.

it forward a touch. Club golfers often find this shoulder position difficult and don't naturally adopt the correct shoulder slope. Second, it is important to realize just how loose and relaxed the arms are. I feel that both upper arms hang very relaxed while in contact with my chest, the arms hanging almost vertically so that my hands are virtually under my chin. The looser I can get at this point the better I like it. I cannot emphasize enough to the club golfer how very loose and relaxed this position feels. It is true that the left arm is straight and will, it is to be hoped, stay straight in the backswing, but there is no feeling of tension whatsoever. The right arm is also relaxed with the elbow slightly bent and dropped into the side.

It is well worth noticing at this point how my arms are set to the ball. If you look at any professional golfer I think you will be aware of the inside of the arms almost facing you. In other words the left elbow is pointing slightly downwards and the right elbow too is pointing down towards the right hip. Good golfers most definitely do not have the elbow bones pointing out to the left and out to the right. The arms hang, and again let's emphasize the looseness of hanging, with the insides slightly upwards. The club golfer will often find it unnatural to turn the left wrist to get the hand slightly on top of the club without the elbow turning incorrectly to face the target.

For the club player who finds this position difficult to achieve, the best exercise is to stand with the hands together, little fingers touching so that the palms face upwards and then, without moving the arms, simply to turn the wrists so that the palms now face downwards The movement should be done from the wrists, keeping the arms virtually still, elbows diagonally down.

The head position should be simple. I just look at the back of the ball but do not in any way turn my head or try to view the ball predominantly with one eye or the other. The more natural I can keep it the easier it is to repeat. From the correct position, if I just lift my head, my eyes are horizontal and parallel to the line of the shot.

THE POSTURE

One of the major changes that I made to my swing concerned the leg work. My leg work was loose and in particular there was a feeling of shifting to the left and letting the left leg bow out in the down and throughswing. The correct movement is for the left leg to turn out of the way through impact, so that the weight is transferred back from the ball to the heel of the left foot with the left leg and left hip simply shifting round and not out to the left. This action of the left leg is absolutely crucial in producing a good and solid golf swing. What it means is that you

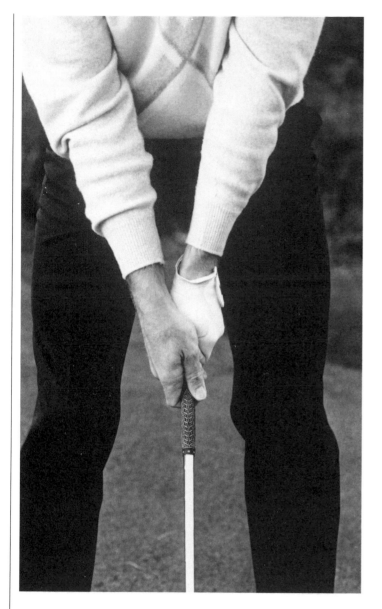

The positioning of the arms is crucial. See how the insides of my arms show, elbows down and not out to the sides. This allows the arms to fold correctly – the right in the backswing and, more importantly, the left in the throughswing

Right With the correct posture, my arms hang to put my hands roughly beneath my chin, shoulders relaxed and upper arms held against my sides. The legs feel straighter than they look, springy and active with the hips held up high and bottom out. The back feels flat with just a little tension in the lower back at this stage – an angle and feeling which remains virtually constant throughout the swing. Bending is from the hips *not* the waist

have to produce the correct posture at address and in particular you have to get the legs and hips into the right type of position. You have to give the legs room to work in this way.

The correct posture obviously requires a degree of bending over to produce a swing which makes the club head come down and catch the ball at ground level. There has to be some bending over. Where you bend from and how you bend is absolutely critical. What you need to feel is that you bend from the top of the legs by sticking your bottom out. You do not sit down. You do not bend from the waist. You do not sag at the knees. You do not droop at the shoulders.

You stand upright. You stand up at

your full height with your legs relaxed – the legs being relaxed in exactly the same way as if you were standing watching a golf tournament. You wouldn't stand with bent legs and you wouldn't stand with your legs pressed back into their sockets. You stand with your legs relaxed and with your hips at their natural height. In taking up the address position you have to bend your upper half forward so that your arms are going to hang and take hold of the club beneath your chin. To get the hands beneath your chin you have to move your hips and bottom back and literally stick your bottom out, lower back flat. As you do this, the weight should be naturally brought onto the balls of the feet so that you feel

This shows an excellent practice drill for producing the correct posture. Stand erect, feet apart, arms relaxed. Just relax at the knees until they come forward to your shoelaces. From here you need to bend at the hips, making space to bring the hands together beneath the chin. The upper arms hang beside the chest, shoulders relaxed – never with the shoulders tense and the arms pushed out in front of you. The lower back is flat, showing just the slightest hollowing and a little tension, never drooping from the waist. The legs stay naturally relaxed, weight springy and towards the balls of the feet. With the head lifted the eyes are horizontal and parallel to the line of the shot. As the head drops the same parallel position is retained

springy and lively and ready for action. The knees will stay slightly flexed, just coming forward over the shoelaces and no more, again just relaxed, without any feeling of sitting down or bending them. Remember that I am 6 feet 3 inches tall, a height that many people consider too tall to produce a really orthodox golf swing. People used to assume that I should sag at the knees and sit down and kept telling me to sit on a shooting stick.

Instead, what you need to feel is that the hips are kept up and back so that there is room for the left leg to turn

through impact without the leg bowing at all.

As you can see, my emphasis is on adopting a tall position. In particular it is this feeling of the hips being up and the bottom out which encourages good leg action. Club golfers seem to be under the impression that professional golfers sit down and indeed many of us have in the past allowed the legs to be bent and not really given room for the left leg to work through impact. If you look at instruction books from the 1950s and 1960s one of the key phrases was 'to hit against a firm left side'. There

were pictures of players with very straight left legs through and beyond impact. The emphasis was on standing up tall; the legs worked through to a stable and balanced position. Emphasis then started being put on adopting a sitting position at address; players lost sight of what was really meant, which was to stick the bottom out. Instead they began to feel that the hips should be lowered into what was a slightly squatting position. Let's make no bones about it. If you get the hips low and you start sitting down, the left leg simply has not got space to work

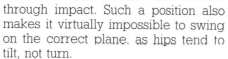

through impact. Such a position also makes it virtually impossible to swing on the correct plane, as hips tend to tilt, not turn.

So even if you are tall like me, get the feeling of standing up tall, give yourself space to use your legs and think 'bottom out' – even if it does sound rude – rather than thinking of sitting down, which may sound polite, but isn't what is meant at all!

My head is then held fairly high so that I look down my face at the ball and do not have the head over in a lowish position. You should feel that your head is up high enough that if you lift your eyes without moving your head you can still see out in front of you. Then as you turn through in the golf swing there is no need for the head to rise. You will simply find yourself following the flight of the ball naturally without the head being brought up in any way.

As you will see in a moment, posture and distance from the ball are closely linked. As a general rule, the professional golfer is able to stand closer to the ball than is the club golfer. He does this by adopting good posture, and by

This shows the comparison at address between the 9-iron and driver. The relationship and angles between the arms and back stay constant. Bending more with the short-shafted 9-iron brings my hands in closer than when standing naturally more erect with a driver. With this feeling of keeping the upper arms against the chest, distance from the ball should be easy to monitor

doing so produces a reliable club head path through impact. Broadly speaking the closer you stand to the ball, the smoother the curve through impact. Stretching to it produces a sharp curve, and with it erratic direction. The key, in many ways, is in the angle of the back and in the way the arms hang from the shoulders.

If you bend from the hips, *not* waist, the back and, in particular, the lower back should stay flat. Perhaps there is just the slightest hollow in the lower back, just a little tension and firmness. The arms then hang downwards, the upper arms staying in contact with the side of the chest. In this correct position the area around the collarbone remains relaxed, shoulders down. The whole back stays fairly flat. Once the correct posture is adopted the lower back keeps the same flatness from start to finish of the swing.

With the correct posture the distance from the ball becomes easier to monitor. The relationship of upper arm to chest remains fairly constant, the top of the arms just squeezing against the body, yet allowing sufficient freedom in the left arm to be able to draw it back across the chest in the backswing. From 9-iron through to driver this arm – chest relationship stays much the same.

As you bend over, bottom out and up – not drooping in the back, the short-shafted 9-iron brings your hands close into you. Stand naturally more erect with the driver and the same arm/chest relationship gives more clearance of hands from body.

To explain this precise position, we must draw a comparison with the incorrect one. In the wrong posture, bending tends to be from the waist and back, instead of hips. The back droops, the shoulders pull up and become tense, with the arms pushed out from the shoulders. From this bad position the looseness of shoulders, arms and wrists is lost. The player tends to stand too far from the ball, producing a poor plane of swing and erratic direction.

DISTANCE FROM THE BALL

One of the difficulties with golf is that there are so many variables. We don't play on a horizontal surface like footballers and we don't simply have one weapon to cope with like tennis players. We play up and down on sloping lies and on different surfaces and we have a whole range of clubs to learn to use. For this reason it is impossible to be precise about distance from the ball in terms of feet and inches.

I do think that the world's top players are probably able to get away with slightly more variation than other players. It is sometimes more a question of feel and hand/eye coordination than absolute precision. But on the other hand even we will stand to the ball on the practice ground on one day and feel absolutely comfortable and then on the next we may feel slightly uncomfortable, without any visible change. Such differences are often bound up with both the distance from the ball and, perhaps even to a greater extent, with the precise positioning of the ball in relation to the feet.

My first aid to consistency is this feeling of the relationship between upper arms and the sides of the body. I suppose we also use, perhaps unconsciously, our view of hands, feet and the ball as we prepare for the shot. Practise when playing well, and at this stage study the view you get, using the driver and 6-iron as yardsticks for days when the game seems more difficult. If you are a player for whom distance

from the ball is a constant problem, take precise measurements for both clubs, using a metre rule if necessary, and again during a period of success.

I think it is true to say that club golfers on the whole don't appreciate just how close good players are able to stand to the ball. Remember, too, that the taller you are the closer you need to stand. I am sure any of my pro – am partners of 6 feet 3 inches, standing with the ball in my footprints, would feel uncomfortably close. Instead of standing up tall, bottom out to give space, they would probably tend to droop in the back and sag at the knees. Second, the arms would tend to be pushed out too far in front of the player, shoulders tense, instead of hanging the upper arms to the side of the chest. For the good player, distance from the ball can change week by week, one often edges further away in the search for power. Perhaps during a period of success one becomes almost over-confident and complacent, stretching to it a touch or moving the ball forward an inch or so. Here can lie the reason for the end of a purple patch and the clue to keeping a good golf swing finely tuned.

THE BALL POSITION

I play the ball 3 to 4 inches inside my left heel for standard fairway shots. Let me explain why. First an explanation about leg action.

I was brought up like many golfers with the idea that what you did through impact was to produce tremendous leg thrust, the right knee kicking in before and through impact and the left knee bowing out to the left so that the weight got almost onto the outside of the left foot through impact and stayed there until the follow-through. Emphasis was on a real kick with the legs and what I and many players were taught was to thrust to the left with a lateral movement before turning to face the target. I have pictures of myself and indeed of many professionals in my age bracket where the left leg is horrendously bent through impact, moving out to the left in what I now realize to be an unsatisfactory and unstable position. We were taught to shift and turn and with the weight

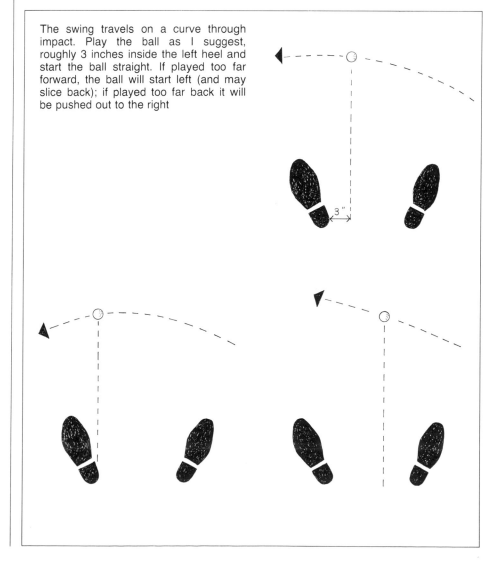

The swing travels on a curve through impact. Play the ball as I suggest, roughly 3 inches inside the left heel and start the ball straight. If played too far forward, the ball will start left (and may slice back); if played too far back it will be pushed out to the right

getting onto the outside of that left foot through impact it was an unstable position which I was unable to repeat. Indeed I didn't repeat it.

The change I made to the leg work necessarily produced a change in my thinking on the ball position. When I started working with David Leadbetter we worked at a simplified leg action where I simply turned in the backswing, the weight moving in a more circular way back onto the right heel and the ball of the left foot. In the downswing the weight turned again, now onto the left heel with the left hip and leg simply moving backwards (rather than shifting left and towards the target) before any turn took place. What we worked at meant that the left leg and left hip simply turned before and through impact, with the sliding and bowing-out of the leg to the left disappearing.

Perhaps now you will see the difference. Previously all the emphasis was on shifting the weight to the left before turning out of the way. This meant that the bottom of the swing would come down more or less opposite my left heel or even towards the left instep. Players were told to push the ball up towards the left heel and to play everything from virtually opposite the left heel. The problem of course with this was that as you moved the ball up towards the left heel it became very difficult for the shoulders to stay in a square position. I think you can see that with this stronger leg action, and the one which I will explain in far more detail, the ball position needs to be altered. Now the bottom of the swing no longer comes up towards the left heel but is going to be perhaps 3 inches inside it. This is where the bottom of my swing is going to be and this is therefore where the ball is going to be positioned. I believe that many good players, myself included, got into difficulties with playing the ball too far forward towards the left heel. For the club golfer this constant advice to play the ball forward – off the left heel – can be disastrous and one of the main reasons for the golf swing to seem so complex. Play the ball too far forward and it tends to pull the right shoulder up and forward, encouraging a steep plane of swing and the slicer's cut-across action. Edge the ball back and

the shoulders feel comfortable, encouraging a freer turn and better plane.

For the club golfer the odds are that the bottom of the swing is going to fall somewhere opposite your nose or your left eye. That is where the ball should basically be positioned. I suppose in general terms this is approximately a third of the way from the left foot to the right foot. Certainly the precise measure of 3 inches inside the left foot will vary with the width of the stance. Have a few practice swings and see where the bottom of your swing falls. That should give you a rough guideline for positioning the ball. Obviously, if the swing comes down nearly opposite the middle of the stance or too much towards the left foot you need to make adjustments to the swing until it falls in the right place. But all too often, players have a practice swing, see that practice swing come down opposite the middle of their stance and then shift the ball up towards their left heel because that is where they believe it should be played. 'Why,' they ask, 'do I hit behind the ball?' The answer is obvious.

The ball position has to vary with the lie and any slope. The better the ball is sitting, the more forward in the stance you can play it; the worse it lies, the further back you have to play it. With the driver we can, and indeed should, hit the ball slightly on the upswing; we therefore have the ball fairly well forward towards the left heel. With the ball on a down slope, in a divot hole or any lie which looks difficult, the ball is played further back towards the right foot and struck with a more descending blow. The ball position is therefore a combination of having the right starting point (3 inches or one-third of the way back or whatever) plus a feel for the lie and the contact you are trying to achieve.

The ball position also has a very definite bearing on your alignment and the way in which you meet the ball. Let's repeat the principle that the golf club travels in a slight curve as it comes through impact. Hopefully, the ball position which gives you the best kind of contact also sees the swing travelling in the right direction, the ball flies off at a tangent to that curve, heading out towards your target. If you

Direction in the setup is all important – the line across toes, knees, hips, shoulders and eyes all being parallel to the ball–target-line. The feet are the easiest to check, the hips or shoulders for many players being the most important. The right hand is below the left on the club and will easily tend to pull the right shoulder or hip forward. Both need to be edged back to ensure a perfectly parallel position and to make the takeaway and turn on the backswing as easy as possible

play the ball too far to the left, the shoulders are usually brought into an open (left-aimed) position, so that the club head meets the ball in a correspondingly left-aimed direction. This is the common problem of the club golfer who pulls the ball left with irons and slices the ball right with the woods. The ball is simply too far forward and the shoulders get out of line.

By contrast, if you play the ball well back in the stance, which you are likely to do with a bad lie or for a wedge, the ball is caught while the swing is still slightly right-aimed. Again, the exact positioning of the ball in relation to the feet, and here I am talking about adjustments of an inch or so, can have quite a bearing on the way in which your shoulders feel at address. Play the ball too far forward

and it may feel most uncomfortable; edge it back an inch and you may suddenly set up with much more comfort and a feeling that the swing is going to be easy. With the ball 3 or 4 inches inside the left heel the shoulders and hips should feel comfortable, the right shoulder should naturally drop down and back and the swing feel as though it can move on the correct path. With the ball too far forward, the right shoulder and right hip easily edge up and forwards and the feeling of comfort is lost.

DIRECTION

Now last, but by no means least, the question of lining up. I hope it goes without saying that it is no good having

a perfect setup, perfect grip and perfect golf swing if the whole thing is misaligned. It sounds obvious but many players simply do not spend enough time getting themselves on target. Let's look first at what should happen. Ideally we want what is called a square stance, square meaning parallel. Let's assume we have two parallel lines, like a railway track. The ball should travel off on the right-hand line towards the target and your body, from toes up to shoulders, and indeed eyes, should be set parallel to this. That sounds relatively easy, but in fact it isn't that simple to adopt systematically. Someone like myself is aiming to hit the ball with my driver perhaps 300 yards – about the length of three soccer pitches. My alignment has got to be absolutely spot on or on anything but a wide open golf course I am in trouble. The odds are that if you simply setup to the ball from the side you would normally stand, you won't aim perfectly. There is often some optical distortion: many players aim dramatically off to the right or the left without knowing it.

What almost all tournament professionals do, and what I suggest you do, is to approach the shot from behind. Leave your clubs on the other side of the ball, have a couple of practice swings and then very definitely go behind the line of the shot to see a straight line to the target. What I do from there is to walk round to my approximate address position and then, with that line in mind, set my club face perfectly squarely on target. I then take a cue from the positioning of the club face and set my feet in a position parallel to that line. From there I need to feel the knees, hips and lastly – but almost most important – the shoulders all following that same parallel line.

The feet are the easiest to check; you can put the club down along your toes, go round behind again, and check whether you really are square. The shoulders are possibly the most difficult to get square and in many ways the most crucial. If you get the shoulders square to the line of flight you can get away with a slight misalignment of the feet. But if you get the feet perfectly parallel and the shoulders slightly off line, the whole swing can fall apart. You can check the feet yourself; you need someone else to check your shoulders. What you *should* notice, in this alignment, is that with the feet perfectly parallel there should be a slight element of looking over the left shoulder as you turn to look at the target. You may need to have the feeling of just keeping the right elbow and the right shoulder back slightly to get that perfectly square position. Again, the further forward in your feet you play the ball, the more difficult this shoulder alignment is likely to be, and the more your shoulders may go away to the left. If you play the ball as I recommend – 3 inches or so inside the left heel – the shoulders should fall into position.

Do keep an eye on the alignment of the hips. These too need to be perfectly square, left hip kept slightly up and

forward, right slightly back. This enables the body to turn correctly and the club to move back on the inside.

If you do get into difficulties with alignment, an alternative method is to choose a spot in front of the ball directly on line with your target, and to concentrate on lining your club face over that rather than simply looking at something in the distance. You will then set your feet and shoulders parallel to this and having done that, trust it before you look up at the target once more. This can be particularly helpful on a hole where the tee is off line or where you are going across a fairway or round a dogleg and the direction feels particularly awkward.

I would also at this point emphasize the way in which you set your head. In order to line up well I always feel the line along the eyes should be as near as possible parallel to where you are going. Some players have an exaggerated idea of turning the head away to the right to view the back of the ball. If the line of your eyes gets off line then direction becomes difficult to judge and the odds are you will shift into an incorrect position. While on this subject let me mention, in particular, players who wear glasses or the club golfer who is constantly urged to 'keep your head down'. The feeling you should have in the address position is very definitely of holding the head fairly high. Golfers who wear glasses, and particularly those who wear bifocals, will almost always get the head over in too low a position in an attempt to look through the middle of the lens. This low position restricts the backswing and often makes it virtually impossible to swing through without the head lifting. The feeling should always be of looking down the cheekbones and never with the head in a horizontal position. If you are someone whose friends tell you repeatedly that you lift your head, then do make sure you hold it high enough at address to allow it to stay still.

The setup is crucial. It must feel comfortable, but on the other hand it must be correct. Look at your posture. Stick your bottom out and get out of the way of yourself and hang your arms as loosely as you can ready for the freedom and power which is going to take place in your swing.

My swing

I AM GOING to deal with the swing in two ways. In this chapter I will describe what I do and what I feel. In the next chapter I will deal with the development of the swing, taking it through from its simplest stages to advanced techniques for the tournament professional. I will work initially with the 6-iron and then explain how the same swing relates to the whole set of clubs.

A MODERN SWING FOR THE GOOD GOLFER

Most good golfers, particularly if they start really young, tend to hook the ball to the left. You are taught initially to hit the ball with your hands and wrists, to produce freedom in the hands and wrists and with this to generate club head speed and distance. Most good young golfers will at some stage find that the right hand, if they are right-handed, becomes dominant, crossing over the left hand through impact and probably tending to close the club face on the ball. The result is a tendency to hook. Most are taught, as I was taught, to develop the left hand and left arm and to see the swing as very much a left-sided action, where the left arm and hand pull the club through, with the right remaining fairly passive. That is how I learned to play the game and obviously I did so successfully. One of the main points I worked at in restructuring my swing was to be able to see the game as a right-handed one. I felt I could hit the ball as hard as possible with my right hand but without feeling any tendency towards hooking. I am going to teach you the same approach.

I was also brought up with the idea that the leg action through the ball required a definite lateral movement to the left before the hips turned through to face the target. I realize now that this movement got me, and indeed gets many players, into difficulties. I am going to teach you the natural way to use your legs, leading to a more repetitive action.

Before starting any explanation of the swing I also want to say something about the plane of the swing. Many club golfers believe quite wrongly that the club should move on a straight back-and-through path; they misguidedly think that by keeping the club on line in this way there is a greater chance of a straight shot. Indeed you frequently hear players talking about taking the club back straight for 18 inches or see them extending the club out exaggeratedly towards the target. Whatever type of swing you adopt, whether you follow my ideas or indeed follow those of some other world-class player, you *must* move the club on a curved path in both backswing and throughswing. There are no straight lines in a golf swing. In adopting the correct posture you will be set up with the weight towards the balls of the feet. Your bottom will be sticking out and your back and head, therefore, will be tipped over at an angle to the vertical. The longer the club you use (i.e. the woods) the less you will bend over and the shorter the club the more you will bend over. The body action is simply a rotation on the plane you have set.

USING THESE PICTURES

These four sequences show my swing from different angles with a 6-iron. To use them to their fullest see each frame as a stage along the way of *movement*. Don't assume each represents a static position. I have tried to explain what I feel to have happened frame by frame through the sequences, and also to give an idea of my key thoughts at

A1

C1

various moments of the swing. Flick through the pages to see movement, isolating perhaps one part of the body to examine its role throughout the swing, remembering that what I feel and think always happens earlier than it shows. The text gives my key movements stage by stage. It does of course all happen so fast that thoughts have to be limited to one or two. By no means do I think – and nor must you think – of all these various movements in one swing. Think of the swing as one whole movement. Then isolate one area of the swing or one part of the body and study and perfect it. What, for example, does the left leg do? Study and read about it frame by frame. Work at it slowly, without the ball, then with the ball for easy shots. Once perfected, put it back in the swing and to a certain extent forget it – just jogging your memory over it and giving it a once over from time to time. Then take another facet and so on. Don't think of too much at once. Work at new thoughts on the practice ground, not the course, using the medium iron or ¾ pitch shots where possible to groove the feelings.

By the time you venture on the course, everything must be switched on to automatic pilot as far as possible. The swing mustn't seem hard. Technique thoughts must be kept to one or two at the most, rehearsing feelings mentally as preparation or in a practice swing. Address, balance, tempo and the strike – those you can think about. Perhaps one swing thought, and that's it. Thinking has to be positive, forwards and very much geared to getting the ball on target. Leave the complexities of the swing to the practice ground and be patient!

ADDRESS

The address position feels very active, the whole body begins to be keyed up in anticipation of the swing – right hip raring to turn, left side setting up resistance and almost holding it back. This is a strong feeling, happening in the couple of seconds before the swing starts. The whole feeling is of right side pulling, left side resisting, so that when I decide to go it all happens smoothly but sharply. My whole swing

is a question of pull and resistance –
one side pulling and the other resisting
– for a powerful coiling effect and then
a release of power. The overall feeling
of the backswing is of right side
turning back against the resistance of
the left side and right knee. From the
top of the backswing, everything pulls
away against the resistance of the right
shoulder, hips and legs. This coiled-up
feeling is set right from this moment.

▷ **Feet.** My weight is on the balls of
   the feet and slightly on the insides
   of the feet. The outside of my stance
   is just wider than my shoulders, with
   the ball positioned about three
   inches inside the left heel. The left
   foot is turned out about 10 degrees,
   right foot turned out slightly less.
▷ **Knees.** My knees are pulled slightly
   inwards, a feeling the right knee is
   going to maintain throughout the
   backswing. The insides of the thighs
   feel strong, squeezing in and yet
   pushing out at the same time.
▷ **Hips.** The left hip feels slightly up
   and the right down and back, ensuring that the line across the hips is
   parallel to the line of the shot.
▷ **Shoulders.** The shoulders are
   relaxed, my right shoulder very
   definitely drops below the left, the
   right side of the body from hip to
   shoulder being relaxed and compressed.
▷ **Arms.** My arms hang loosely, with
   the upper arms just pressing gently
   against my chest, setting my hands
   just about below my chin.
▷ **Hands.** My hands are just ahead of
   the ball. I experience a sense of the
   right hand just having a little setting
   in the right wrist, rehearsing the
   feeling it will have at impact.
▷ **Elbows.** The insides of both arms
   are visible, elbows pointing slightly
   downwards. The right is relaxed
   and ready to fold away into the side
   on the backswing.
▷ **Head.** My head is held high enough
   at address to allow me to keep it
   level throughout the swing.

Last, direction. The line across toes,
knees, hips, shoulders and eyes are all
parallel to the line of my shot, the club
face aimed squarely on target, and my
grip set with the right hand behind the
club and so aimed at the flag.

B1

D1

A2

C2

THE TAKEAWAY

The backswing is very definitely started with a feeling of taking the club away on the inside. It starts with a turn, emphasis for me being on turning the stomach away. I don't want any lateral movement at all. I want to send the right shoulder and hip back behind myself. Back and round, not out to the side. Everything in the right side starts back as a unit, pulling against the resistance of the left side. The key is to pull the whole right side of the body back and to let the left follow. It all has to happen quite sharply, setting the whole tempo for the swing. The main points of emphasis in the takeaway are as follows.

▷ **Knees.** They very definitely resist the turn. The right one stays still. The left may move a touch, being pulled against its resistance. When it does move, its objective will be to point in behind the ball.

▷ **Legs.** These just maintain the feeling of resistance, moving but again being pulled into motion by the turning of the stomach.

▷ **Hips.** The right hip is sent back and round behind me to move round in the rest of the backswing, no lateral movement at all. This is a really key area for me. It isn't just a movement straight back or I might get a straight right leg. I send the right hip round as though I am inside a spring. The right knee stays still, and the right hip is coiled. If you move the swing away with the arms and hands you can get into all sorts of poor positions. But if you turn away with the stomach it seems physically impossible to stop the shoulders and arms following correctly. I try to turn everything away as a unit to get the club away from the ball on its inside path.

▷ **Shoulders.** The right shoulder, like the right hip turns back behind me, led into this movement by the turn of the stomach. I want to send it directly behind me, with no lateral movement. Not even a fraction to the right or it destroys the whole synchronized start to the swing.

▷ **Arms.** These are pulled into movement by the body turn, but no independent feeling of their own yet.

▷ **Elbows.** The elbows move away in harmony with everything else, the right one perhaps just tucking in and down a touch. It mustn't pop out. It feels as though it almost starts working in towards the stomach.

▷ **Hands.** These are passive for a moment.

B2

D2

A3

C3

In the split second of the takeaway the body turns. Stomach and right hip turn a couple of inches, the club head moving in harmony with this, moving considerably further.

After that split-second movement, the hands and wrists began to move; in reality the movements are almost simultaneous. The movement of the wrist is a backward hinging of the right wrist, setting it back on itself. It is the backward hinging I feel, apparent in **sequences A, B and D,** rather than the upward hinging against the thumbs.

This part of the sequence shows the movement already having been initiated. It doesn't start at this moment. It has already happened by this stage of the swing. My words of instruction to myself to start the club back are 'coil and set'. The wrists haven't rolled or cocked upwards against the thumbs, but have cocked backwards. By coiling and setting in this way, the club, at hip height, is well behind me on its inside path, preparing all the time for its inside attack on the ball.

Sequence C could be misinterpreted to suggest thoughts of width. In fact just the opposite is felt. The right upper arm stays into my side, with a definite feeling of folding, not stretching.

▷ **Knees.** The right knee is still, turning against its resistance. It holds its position all the time.

▷ **Hips.** The right hip continues to turn behind me. The hips now take over the role of the stomach and take over the coiling action for power.

▷ **Shoulders.** These are very definitely turning; the right shoulder is moving behind me.

▷ **Arms.** These are moving in harmony and staying connected with everything else.

▷ **Elbows.** The right elbow is tucking in close and folding. This action works in harmony with the wrists beginning to set.

▷ **Hands.** The backward setting of the right wrist is happening just as quickly as possible at this stage. The key action at this point is to hinge the right wrist back into its maximum set, as quickly as possible. It moves on the plane of the swing, setting it back and up against the forearm, not just cupping it up.

The 'coil and set' messages of the takeaway have by now been put into motion.

B3

D3

A4

C4

At this point we see the results of the coiling and the setting in the takeaway. **Sequences A, B and D** show again how this continues to take the club round behind me, the feeling throughout being of the backward, not upward hinging of the wrists. The body continues to turn, tightly coiling and turning against the resistance of the knees, particularly of the right knee.

▷ **Knees.** The knees still feel as if they are providing considerable resistance. The right knee stays virtually still. The left knee is by now being pulled into motion, beginning to point in towards a point somewhere behind the ball. This happens as a result of its address position, with the thighs and knees pulled in slightly narrower than the feet. Remember, they resist this movement.

▷ **Feet.** The body is still turning and coiling, and the left knee points in. This produces weight transference in the feet. Pressure begins to move forward onto the ball of the left foot (not rolling onto the inside) and backward towards the right heel as the right hip moves back and round.

▷ **Hips and shoulders.** The large muscles continue to turn the right side back behind me. The left side is obviously being pulled round, left shoulder feeling to stay up throughout this turn.

▷ **Arms.** The left arm is being pulled across the chest, the upper arms staying fairly tight to the body.

▷ **Elbows.** The right elbow continues to fold and point down.

▷ **Hands.** The right wrist is fully set back by the time the arms reach their horizontal position. The setting has now taken place on plane. The messages to produce this were given far earlier. From here the larger muscles of body and legs can take over.

B4

D4

A5

CONTINUING THE BACKSWING

Throughout the rest of the backswing the hips, shoulders and stomach continue their coiling action against the resistance of the knees. The feeling of the turn is of a very horizontal one, the shoulders just turning on the plane set at address. There is definitely no tipping or tilting; the feeling of the shoulder turn is of a more level plane than it always appears. As the turn continues the left arm, although stretched, is simply drawn across the chest without any feeling of independent lifting of the arms. The right elbow in turn stays close to the body, say 3 to 4 inches away but not actually touching; **sequence B** shows how it folds in and down. **Sequence D** shows the result of the early hinging back of the right wrist and can be seen clearly

C5

still fully set. This gradually works into a position *under* rather than *behind* the club.

Sequence B is the particularly instructional one at this stage, showing the flattish angle of the shoulder turn and the left arm drawing across the chest rather than lifting.

▷ **Feet.** The weight is now pushing round onto the right heel and ball of the left foot. Again there is resistance, this time in the left heel. The leg and foot action turns against it, but the left heel resists any tendency to pull it off the ground.

▷ **Elbows.** The right elbow continues to stay tucked in, pointing down and not out.

▷ **Hands.** The right hand is fully hinged back and now begins to adopt a position beneath the club. The left wrist has adopted a flat-backed position.

B5

D5

A6

At this point I am very nearly at the top of the backswing, continuing the feeling of coiling the stomach and shoulder turn against the legs. The shoulders have continued to turn on their flattish plane, the left arm drawing across the chest, right elbow folding in. Again let me emphasize the coiling feeling of turning against the legs, the right knee staying pinched in but the left knee pointing in far more than it feels. My feeling is of turning against the knees, but the left knee inevitably pulled in to this point.

By now the body weight is turned quite substantially backwards onto the right heel and forwards onto the ball of the left foot, the left heel still not actually lifting but pressure by now being pulled off it.

Sequences A and B show the direction of the backswing. My full turn is not yet completed and as a result the club shaft points left of the line of the shot. The club will eventually point parallel to the line of the shot as the swing is completed. (All too often players place so much emphasis on having a backswing where the club is parallel to the shot that it encourages an incorrect lifting in the backswing. It isn't parallel until the turn is completed.)

C6

At this point the messages I am giving myself are of turning the movement into reverse. My thoughts are of producing resistance in the right side and moving the left away from it. This of course won't show until later on in the sequence. The feeling now is of bringing the legs and lower half of the body into reverse, while in reality the arms and club head are still moving back and up. They are finishing the last moments of transition between up and down. There is no actual pause. Everything is solid in the wrists, but the suppleness in the body just allows the arms and club to go further while the lower half moves into reverse.

▷ **Knees.** My left knee has now been pulled in to point behind the ball. It has resisted all the way, and at this point thoughts are on turning it away again to pull the movement into reverse.
▷ **Elbows.** The right elbow stays down and forwards.
▷ **Hands.** This elbow action and the hinging of the wrists sets the right hand beneath the club (not behind it), flat back to the left wrist – particularly noticeable in **sequence A.**

B6

D6

A7

C7

By the time I reach the top of the backswing my body weight has turned round towards the right heel and ball of the left foot. I still feel considerable resistance in the knees, the right knee staying as nearly as possible in its address position without hampering the turn. This gives a feeling of the shoulders turning fully, back towards the target, but being coiled from the knees or waist up and very definitely against the resistance of the knees. My lower back still feels to have the same degree of very slight tension as at address, back still flat.

The result of the early hinging back of the right wrist can be seen. Having hinged back in the takeaway it is now predominantly beneath rather than behind the club shaft, and, most important the left wrist is in a flattish position. This in turn is going to encourage the correct attack into impact. Once everything drops into reverse the club head is going to be well behind me, right wrist hinged back, enabling me to hit the ball with the right hand. The right elbow is neatly folded into an approximate right angle, upper arm still fairly close to the side, elbow down. With the turn completed, the shaft of the club is just about horizontal and parallel to the line of the shot. You can also see that the line of the club face is parallel to the left arm and the back of the left wrist, with the wrist in a strong, square position.

▷ **Feet.** The weight has turned towards the ball of the left foot and the heel of the right foot, again resisting any tendency to pull the left heel up.

▷ **Knees.** The right knee has barely moved, the whole turn moving against it. The left knee has been pulled in to point behind the ball, but again with a real feeling of resisting this pull.

▷ **Legs.** The legs are tightly coiled and at this point the feeling is of leaving the right leg where it is and moving the left leg away from it. The movements I am thinking about won't show up until the next frame.

▷ **Hips.** I sent the right hip back and round behind me, feeling fully wound up. Having turned it fully it is now going to feel resistance while the left side moves away from it.

▷ **Shoulders.** The right one has turned away. The feeling is now of leaving it there, setting up resistance, for the arm action to swing away from it in the downswing.

▷ **Arms.** The left arm has been drawn across the chest, both upper arms still feeling quite close to the sides.

▷ **Right elbow.** Its feeling is of being kept in and down.

▷ **Hands.** The right hand is well under the club, the back of the left wrist is flat and parallel to the leading edge of the club head. This gives a strong position in readiness to pull down.

B7

D7

A8

C8

THE DOWNSWING

The change of directions into the downswing is where a good swing is made. The whole feeling of the backswing was of turning the right side against the resistance of the left side and the right knee. Now the roles are reversed. The right shoulder is in a potentially destructive, dominant position. The feeling now is of setting up resistance in the right shoulder, leg and foot and pulling against this resistance. Swinging against this resistance the club has a maximum chance of attacking the ball on the correct plane from the inside.

My object at the moment of change of directions is one of lowering the plane of the arms as they pull down from the top, so that the right wrist stays hinged back and will then be able to generate full power into the ball. There are three specific moves I make at this point.

▷ **Shoulders.** The first move is in the left shoulder. It feels to rise immediately to set the action into reverse. I suppose in reality the left shoulder has been drawn towards the right in the backswing, shoulders slightly rounding. Now the left moves away from the right, lifting, which will if anything force the arm plane down behind me.

▷ **Right elbow.** Second, the right elbow resists any feeling to push the hands and downswing out and forwards. In a split second the arms drop. The feeling then is of pulling the right elbow in and forward as though bringing the elbow in directly below the hands. This again acts to drop the hands back and lower the plane of the attack.

▷ **Legs.** Third, the most advanced of the movements, a feeling of keeping the right knee, foot and indeed the whole right side still, while the left knee is felt to separate from the right leg to start the leg action for the downswing. This action, bringing the whole swing into reverse, happens a moment the club reaches the top of the backswing – club still going back, legs moving forward. The feeling – and let me stress again it is a feeling – is for the club to be held still for a moment, apart from its slight drop in plane, while these movements start away from the resistance of the right side.

The effect of these three movements is a feeling of lowering the plane of the arms and club, the right elbow dropping in slightly, the left arm dropping slightly behind me. This results in the club shaft being lowered, and now aiming left of target. In other words, I am making what feels to be a slight downward and inside 'loop'. This is an essential movement to resist the body's natural tendency to push the club out and forward (producing an outside loop) with the right hand, arm and shoulder.

B8

D8

A9

C9

At this point we see the results of my movements from the top of the backswing. **Sequences A and B** show quite clearly how the club is dropped back behind me, ready to attack the ball from the inside. The right wrist has maintained its hinging or setting initiated in the takeaway and is ready to deliver a strike on the ball from the inside.

Most apparent at this stage is the movement of the left leg, separating from the right; the right knee is very definitely not kicking in but still very much in the position in which it started, right foot still flat on the ground. The feeling in the left leg at this stage is definitely not of it bowing out but of it pulling back behind me ready to be virtually straight through impact.

Having coiled correctly, sending the right side round behind myself, coiling the right hip up as much as possible, the resistance has now changed. Now the left side is pulling down and the right side resists for a split second. This is long enough to get the hands almost to the hitting area, while the whole right side feels to stay back and behind me. Everything feels as though the left side is pulling away. The right side is held back a moment and then the right arm itself can move from its coiled right angle, uncoiling to generate power. It all separates away from the right shoulder – the distance between right hand and right shoulder increasing all the time.

▷ **Feet.** The right foot now provides resistance and won't move until pulled through. The left foot thrusts backwards into the heel, again sending weight back and round behind me. There is no lateral weight shift.

▷ **Knees.** I have already felt the left knee separating from the right one to start the leg action into reverse. Its feeling now is of pulling back as though beneath the hip, resisting any lateral movement.

▷ **Legs.** There is very definitely this feeling of separating left leg from right leg, right leg resisting the movement through, so that the whole feeling is one of the left side opening away from it.

▷ **Hips.** The left side really is pulling and I am trying to send the left hip back behind me. Again there is no lateral movement at all. A slight lateral movement of an inch or two will happen, not consciously but as a result of the lift of the left shoulder in the change of direction.

▷ **Shoulders.** The left shoulder has continued its feeling of lifting and moving away from the right one. It has to go back to a high position, pulling it up to its original height. The right shoulder firmly resists the movement of the rest of the body. It holds back and everything moves away from it, left arm dropping and pulling away from it.

▷ **Arms.** The club and arms have dropped a fraction to lower the plane. Now the crucial feeling still is of the left arm opening away from the right shoulder and indeed of the right elbow and right arm also stretching away from it. This is a question of leaving the right shoulder where it is and feeling this rapid opening up away from it, left arm pulling and separating from right shoulder.

▷ **Hands.** The hands are still holding on to their wrist setting, ready for delivering power into the shot.

▷ **Elbows.** The right elbow feels as though it moves under and forward, allowing everything else to move away from the right shoulder.

B9

D9

A10

At this stage I am now a split second away from impact. Let's think what it feels like rather than what it looks like. Feel and look can be quite different, for what I feel happens at this point in reality shows up a split second later in the next frames.

Everything so far in the downswing has been a pull away from the right side, which provides the resistance. The left side has pulled down so well into the hitting position that the right side is still behind in the hitting area. Now the right side can hit as hard as it likes. It all moves in as though it is in one unit. I don't try and make anything go faster. Right hip, knee, shoulder and hand can literally come round and squeeze the ball out. The only parts of the body to feel any release are the forearms which will rotate into impact, maintaining the right wrist position. At this point the emphasis is on hitting hard with the right hand, not releasing right through and allowing the right wrist to straighten, but releasing some of its backward hinging into the position it held at address. It releases but I try to resist this release all the way. So that is really what is in my mind at that point. Let's see what has actually happened in preparation for impact.

▷ **Feet.** The right foot is just being pulled into action, but note again that it is pulled by the left side rather than doing any thrusting of its own. The right side has to give at last. Weight is very definitely being pushed back into the left heel with the left knee and hip moving back behind me.
▷ **Knees.** The left knee is feeling as though I am sending it back and underneath me, a far more backward movement than is apparent at this stage. The right knee and leg are resisting, but by now are being pulled into motion.

C10

▷ **Hips.** Again the feeling in the left hip is of sending it back and round behind me, no lateral movement at all. The right hip is still in a resisting role.

▷ **Shoulders.** By now these are virtually horizontal, the left shoulder having pulled up and backwards in the downswing without the right shoulder dropping at all. It is just going to come round into the ball as a unit.

▷ **Arms.** Both arms have definitely worked away from the right shoulder, seeing the space between left arm and right shoulder continually widening from the top of the backswing through to impact. The message I will now be sending to my left arm is going to be to get it out of the way beyond impact. The moment the ball is hit the arms will be turning and folding, the thought being initiated, I suppose, before impact.

▷ **Elbows and wrists.** My right elbow has dropped into the side, but not excessively close, the right wrist still being set back on itself in just the position it adopted early in the takeaway. In other words it is in a late hit position. This does *not* mean the angle you see in **sequence C.** It means the direction of attack we see in **sequences A and B**, the club being brought into the ball from the inside – from behind me. From here I can use the right hand all I like and really generate power with it.

B10

D10

A11

C11

IMPACT

And now for impact itself. I have attacked the ball from the inside, hitting hard with the right hand from behind myself, the right wrist releasing slightly into impact in the same wrist position adopted at address. The feeling, however, is as though trying not to release. I resist releasing all the time. Centrifugal force just makes it happen. In other words at address there was a slight setting in the back of the right wrist. This setting then increased dramatically in the back swing. The wrist then released this hinging but only back to the same position as at address. The right wrist never releases back into a perfectly flat position but will (from now through to the end of the swing) hold that very slightly set angle, a movement you can follow in these pictures right into the follow-through. The feeling I would describe in my hands now is of holding the club face square, almost holding it off so that the hands don't cross, just nipping the ball away with a small divot.

My left leg really does feel by now to be pulling backwards, thrusting weight back into the left heel and eventually beginning to pull the right knee on through and to ease the right heel off the ground. But the right knee at no stage kicks or thrusts. It still resists the action and is simply pulled through by the rest of the movement.

The arm action is deceptive. The right elbow has been kept fairly close in to my side, in the main a result of its tucked-in position at the top of the backswing. The left arm is straight *but* I haven't locked it or tightened it. It doesn't feel rigid nor do I in any way stress firmness. It is simply the natural extension that has resulted from moving at speed. My feeling at this stage with the arms is going to be to fold the left one in and tuck it away just as soon and freely as possible from this moment on. The arms are going to rotate to continue the action. The feeling is as though I am going to hinge the movement through from the left elbow to allow the wrists to stay firm through and beyond impact.

▷ **Feet.** The left foot is pushing firmly back onto the heel and the right is just being pulled through.

▷ **Knees and hips.** The left leg really does pull back behind me, still with a feeling of sending the left hip backwards and not out to the side.

▷ **Arms.** The upper arms are still fairly close in; the feeling here is that the arms will rotate on through, wrists staying set. There feels to be a hinging from the elbows so that the wrists can stay solid, not a feeling of the arms staying straight and the wrists rolling or flipping independently on the end of them.

▷ **Hands.** The feeling here is of the right hand really controlling the club face through impact, holding it square to the line of flight without the right wrist straightening or rolling over on the end of the arm. The right hand just resumes its slightly set position from address and then will hang on to that position right the way through to the end of the swing. Again it totally resists any release. It is the holding of this right wrist angle into and through impact that produces massive leverage.

▷ **Elbows.** The right elbow is the one you will see bent. At this point my thinking is very definitely in keeping the left upper arm and left elbow into the side beyond impact, getting the arm out of the way and almost hinging the movement through from a left elbow pivot.

B11

D11

A12

C12

THE THROUGHSWING

And now just beyond impact come some of the most important parts of the swing. It isn't simply the result of striking the ball well. Aim for the correct movements beyond impact and these help to achieve the delivery you want.

Let's look first at the left leg. It is by now clearly pulling back into a straightish position, weight pulling backwards into the left heel. Look through **sequence D** in the next few pages to see this pulling-back action, the left leg eventually straightening, weight firmly concentrated on the heel as opposed to the ball of the left foot. The right foot is being pulled through onto the toes only at the very end of the swing and from this stage on is still almost resisting the action.

Now for the arms and in particular the left arm. The appearance may be that the arm stays rigid. People talk so often of width and extension. My *feeling*, in fact, is that I keep the upper left arm just as close to me as possible with the arm folding inwards, elbow in, not, of course, breaking outwards. When done well, swinging at speed, the folding away is nothing like as apparent as it feels and will only show up much much later than it seems to happen. It feels narrow, but looks wide. Obviously the speed of the swing forces the arms out but I try to keep the left arm in.

By this stage the arms have rotated to mirror almost exactly their positions in the takeaway – pictures 3 and 4 of each sequence. **Sequences C and D** in particular show the way the arms have turned, very clearly bringing the club from a toe-up position in the backswing to the corresponding one in the throughswing. I don't feel this happens from any form of hand action, but from the folding and leverage from the elbows – right in the backswing, left in the throughswing. The main visual departure from a true mirroring back and through looks, no doubt, to be the far greater folding of the right elbow in the backswing than of the left elbow going through. Let me stress again the definite feel of folding in the left elbow at this stage, disguised I suppose by the tremendous speed of the whole swing.

The feeling at this stage is that I continue to hold the club face square but by now the whole body is being allowed to turn as a unit. The left side turns away, pulling with the left as fast as possible and yet now just allowing the right side to turn into the ball as a unit. The feeling really is of keeping the upper arms against the body and allowing the whole body to begin its turn through to face the target.

▷ **Hips.** I am really sending the left hip back and out behind me to allow the turn on through of the body.

▷ **Arms.** The feeling here is of the upper arms staying in tight and particularly the upper left arm really staying in firmly to my side.

▷ **Elbows.** This is the key feeling here: the whole movement through of the arms feels that it now hinges from the left elbow. The feeling is of the unit of lower arms, wrists and club remaining firm as a unit, arms rotating, rather than the wrists flapping and flicking on the end of straight arms.

▷ **Hands.** The right hand still feels really in control. The right wrist tries to hold its fully set position and feels that it will maintain this right the way through to the end of the swing.

B12

D12

A13

C13

This is where the results of a good swing can be seen. **Sequence A** shows the arm rotation which has taken place, the turning of the arms matching the backswing. The left arm is continuing its feeling of turning and folding into the body. This allows me to swing the club through into this high position, not by any feeling of stretching or width – far from it – but through a feeling of getting the left arm out of the way for the right to swing through in the correct, inside but high path. Again don't in any way interpret the pictures as being of extension. The left elbow is very definitely feeling as though it folds in, as opposed to breaking out: my thoughts at this stage are of really pulling the left upper arm into the side while allowing the body to turn on through to face the target.

The pull backwards of the left leg can be seen, simply a turning through of the legs and hips with no bowing outwards of the leg. The right knee and right foot are beginning to be pulled through, definitely not thrusting or kicking and having resisted this movement as long as possible. I feel the left side really turning and pulling everything through, trying to lead the arms and hands through as a unit.

Sequences A and B show how the throughswing should correctly mirror the plane of the backswing as much as possible, arms having the feeling of rotation just as they did in the backswing

▷ **Feet.** Weight really has been thrust back onto the left heel.

▷ **Knees and hips.** Again the feeling is of sending the left knee, leg and hip behind and round and not out to the side.

▷ **Shoulders.** The shoulder plane now matches the plane of the backswing. The right shoulder resisted being moved all the way during the downswing into the hitting position. Having held it back for long enough it is now allowed to turn through quite freely, right shoulder beginning to cover the chin and not being forced underneath it.

▷ **Arms.** Here I am trying to keep contact with the left upper arm to the top half of the body as much as possible.

▷ **Elbows.** The feeling is of the left elbow really hugging in close to me as though the arm rotation and powerful leverage through and beyond impact take place from a left elbow pivot. Again let me emphasize that the elbow feels as if it is working in much closer to me than will ever be apparent from photos.

▷ **Hands.** The right hand is firmly set in its address position through to the end of the swing; if anything the angle in the back of the wrist actually increases at this stage.

B13

D13

A14

C14

As the swing approaches its finish, the rotation and folding away of the left elbow can be seen quite clearly. **Sequences A and B** show just how close the elbows stay in the correct action, the left arm folding away and inwards. Let me stress again that this both feels to have happened earlier than it shows and feels more pronounced than it looks. Again the action mirrors very closely the corresponding position in the backswing, arms having turned and rotated as though from the left elbow, matching the plane, hand and club face position. The wrists still feel firm with this turning through being from elbow and arm movements, not hand action as such.

At this point the movement back of the left leg and left hip can be seen quite clearly; the whole leg and hip action is contained within the width of the stance, weight pushed back onto the left heel or flat on the foot, rather than on the outside of the foot.

Let's summarize the feelings from top of backswing to here. At the top of the backswing I hold back with the right side just long enough for the left side to move everything into reverse. Left shoulder was brought round towards the right, left arm across to the right, left knee in towards the right. I then felt the right side to hold back a moment for the left side to open away from it. Having waited this moment, the whole right side can commit itself to the shot and can release.

The feeling in the right hand is of definitely resisting straightening it. I hold the club face square – 'holding it off' – with the right hand. The angle in the right wrist never straightens, being held in a slightly set position through impact, the setting actually increasing again through to the finish. I don't feel any hand action through impact. All the way I am trying to hold the maximum right wrist set I can, but inevitably the right hand returns to its address-type position. I feel the body pull it all round with a whiplash effect. You are trying to make the body and shoulders move fast beyond impact – or even a moment before – to pull the hands and arms through, upper arms and elbows feeling to stay in tight. Much tighter than it looks in the pictures. If the body and shoulders were to stop then the hands would take over. I want to feel the left shoulder and left side moving as fast as the hands. Obviously that's physically impossible. But the feeling is of everything turning through as a unit from impact, right wrist staying in position. The left side has to turn as fast as it can to stop the hands taking over.

B14

D14

Here, just a moment before the end of the swing, the plane of the whole swing becomes very apparent, matching closely the plane of the backswing. Hips and shoulders have turned through with a feeling of a fairly level, horizontal plane. The shoulders have turned back and on through on a constant plane – no tipping or tilting – bringing the right shoulder naturally round to cover the chin and in no way forcing it down and under it. The hips, too, have continued their natural turn, left leg pulling backwards – not sideways – onto the left heel, hips now facing the target and pulling the right knee and right foot through to this

A15

C15

position where the knees touch. The folding away of the left arm and closeness of the elbows really are apparent, and begin to bring the club round in the same plane as the backswing.

One word about the back. I emphasized at address that it feels straight, just with the slightest feeling of a little hollow in the lower back. With the back correctly set in this way at address it retains this angle and slight tension throughout the swing. It simply turns in the backswing and turns in the throughswing. It does not move from a drooped position to an arched one. It is constant throughout – one less moving piece to worry about.

B15

D15

A16

C16

THE FINISH

And now for the finish of the swing. In part this is the result of everything that has gone before. But in many ways it is understanding and aiming for this position that keeps the throughswing on the correct path and with speed. The shoulders have continued to turn through and are now horizontal, more truly horizontal in fact than the shoulder turn in the backswing, but feeling to be a perfect mirroring. I suppose in reality the follow-through is just slightly longer than the backswing, hence this slight difference in shoulder position. The left arm has folded and turned into its final position, upper arm horizontal and elbow forming a neat right angle – not an acute angle. That would signal a collapse. No, this is a firmly held right angle, powerfully still in control. **Sequences C and D** show that the elbow has folded inwards, enabling the elbows to stay close together to the end. The rotation through the ball kept them together, bringing the club head through to its toe-up position at chest height in the throughswing. Elbows then stay together. (This is very different from the arm action of letting the left elbow buckle and break outwards, which would result in elbow spread at the end of the swing and the left elbow flying out behind me.) So tight-together-feeling elbows at this stage.

Notice, too, the length of the finish, the
club shaft settling in neatly behind me
– and perfectly safely, giving freedom
to generate speed in the swing.

And as for the leg work, well that
keeps me perfectly balanced throughout the swing. At this point the left leg
has been pulled backwards, knee not
locked, but the leg otherwise feeling
straight. The weight is very definitely
pulled round and back into the left
heel, as opposed to the ball of the foot,
and certainly not with any feeling of
approaching a potentially unstable
position on the outside of the left foot.
Sequences A and B should show just
how, from this angle, the weight is
balanced over the left heel, the left leg
straight but the hips naturally shifting
slightly left for balance, far more on the
heel than flat on the foot. Because of this,
and the pull back into the heel, the toes
of my left foot can just be seen to be
easing off the ground in **sequence A.**

In reality, the swing doesn't quite
finish here. There is a moment's pause
– it feels like a second or two – before
the arms are lowered in front of me,
legs motionless and perfectly
balanced, while I stand and watch the
result of the shot. And for this 5 to 10
seconds the leg work still has the
feeling of perfect balance. I want to
control the ball for its whole flight,
landing and run; I make sure I am on
balance and able to control myself the
entire same period.

B16

D16

To groove the swing I move through it stage by stage in set positions. These photos (see right) are taken of those set positions. They are still, posed pictures – not action ones – as the previous sequences. They show what I feel happens at the various points of the swing. As an exercise they are a strengthening and stretching exercise, in which one feels the resistance where necessary in the swing and works against that resistance. Let's look first at the front view.

Address. Nothing different here. A set position, of course, anyway.

The takeaway. Here again I am feeling the whole movement being initiated with a turning of the stomach. By producing this small body turn it brings the arms back, the club head, of course, moving a couple of feet while the stomach simply seems to turn a matter of inches. Immediately there is this feeling of turning against the resistance of the knees. This is the feeling of coiling.

Halfway back I add the wrist setting. Coil and set. The feeling, let me repeat, is more of a backward hinging than an upward one and so more apparent in the next sequence. But here again I continue to turn against the resistance of the knees. The right knee stays motionless. The left knee starts pointing in behind the imaginary ball, but I am resisting that breaking in of the knee, squeezing both in again from the muscles on the inside of the thighs. I really coil against them.

At the top of the backswing the shoulders are fully turned, back to the target. The shoulder turn feels really horizontal, left shoulder up and covering the chin, only just giving me a view of the imaginary ball. It feels as though the knees don't move – they do, of course, but I really turn the stomach and shoulders against their resistance. I feel coiled up – like an archer drawing back the bow. Hold it back, tightly wound, and then RELEASE. Let the thing go. So here we feel real power. The good exercise here is to turn and really stretch against the knees, pushing yourself just as far as you can go.

And now for the crucial change of directions. The other angle shows the arm action; this shows the legs. Here the feeling – an advanced one – is of

1

2.

5

6

3

4

7

8

holding back the right side and right leg and starting down with the left knee separating away from it. A movement seen in a fairly small number of top golfers. A wonderful sensation once you get it, but not an easy thought for Mr Average. In harmony with this, the arms have pulled down, ready for a rounded attack into impact.

Impact. Here the feeling of the leg and footwork is seen. Forget about lateral shift. The feeling now is of really turning the left leg and left hip and pulling the left knee back under me, thrusting back into the left heel. The left hip really shifts on back, never getting beyond the outside of the left foot. The arms and hands return to their starting point, the right wrist being forced to release almost entirely its set, but never releasing further and actually straightening.

And here beyond impact the arms have rotated: left arm folding away, upper arm staying in, just as the right one did in the backswing. The back of the right hand faces the camera as the left did going back. The club face in turn mirrors the takeaway. The wrists still feel firm, the rotation and folding done from the arms and left elbow and not the wrists.

And so to the finish. The shoulders and hips have turned through with their same nearly horizontal turn of backswing. The left leg has pulled back and round towards the heel, left toes just easing up. The right knee and foot are eventually pulled through, onto the tips of the right toes, knees touching.

That is the first and simpler dimension of the golf swing. More people look to swing a club well from this direction than in our second dimension.

Now for the second dimension of the golf swing – the far more critical one. Here we really do see the plane and direction of a swing (see photos overleaf).

First, a reminder about address. The feeling is of standing tall, bending from the hips not from the waist, and flattening very slightly the lower back. This back angle is going to be maintained throughout. The legs are relaxed, not feeling bent. They only bend to counterbalance the upper body tipping forward. The hips are held up, bottom out, giving room for the legs to turn through. In particular, the left leg must have space to turn through. The arms are hanging loose, upper arms in. The angle between arms and club shaft here is the angle you see in **frame 2** of the sequence from the other angle. The left arm is just visible through the break of the right, everything parallel.

In the takeaway, the stomach and shoulders start their turn against the resistance of the knees. The club is pulled back on the inside, initiating it all with a hinging backwards of the right wrist, setting the wrists early for the rest of the swing.

And now as the backswing continues, the right wrist can be clearly seen hinged back on itself, the back of the left wrist flat, the right elbow folding in and pointing down. This will bring the right hand predominantly beneath the club at the top of the backswing, keep the left wrist flat and encourage an inside attack through impact. The shoulder turn simply follows the plane set by the angle of the back at address, left shoulder neither dropping nor lifting off this plane.

At the top of the backswing the shoulders have turned fully on this same plane, left shoulder almost covering the chin. The right elbow forms a neat right angle, pointing down and in, right palm almost beneath rather than behind the club. The left arm is drawn across the chest, not lifted up and noticeably leaving the plane of the shoulders. The club shaft is now perfectly horizontal, left wrist flat, and with the leading edge of the club face square to the angle of the left wrist and arm.

Now for the feel of the change of directions. The whole plane of the left arm and club drops to bring the club down behind me. The feeling, shown here, is far more pronounced than what shows in the action pictures. The angle in the right wrist is still fully maintained back on itself, the right elbow drops into the side of the body and is kept well behind me. This gives the classic space seen between left arm and right elbow in almost every good player. This demonstrates the feeling of a true 'late hit position' – from which the club head is going to attack the ball very much from behind me and not down the line. From here I can really throw it out and deliver power with the right hand.

And here is the feeling just beyond impact. Most important the right wrist is still slightly set back – the same position it assumed at address. It won't ever fully release and straighten, but will hold the club face on target just beyond impact and will still be in this same position by the end of the swing. It resists releasing all the way. The left leg can be seen pulling under me through impact.

Beyond impact the turn on through of hips and shoulders can be seen, following the plane set at address and developed in the backswing.

And here, at the end, I am turned on through to face the target, weight centred more or less over the left heel, not ball of the foot, shoulder plane mirroring the backswing. The left elbow has folded into the side through impact, and although now folded into a right angle, is kept almost in front of me – never splayed out behind me – elbows quite close together.

1

5

2

3

4

6

7

8

Developing the swing

– a lesson for Mr Average

I AM GOING to start my look at the development of the golf swing with a chapter for the beginner and long-handicap golfer. The average club golfer – and certainly the beginner – needs a swing which is simple. It will then become more complex when you look for a higher degree of precision. The reason I am starting with a section for the beginner is that your needs, as a rule, are quite different from those of the tournament player. The problem of the tournament player is generally that he hits the ball vast distances, but may have slight directional errors, the over-riding fault and most common problem usually being a tendency to hook. The average club golfer, by contrast, usually needs to work at obtaining much greater distance to his shots and is far more likely to be hampered by shots which slice away to the right. I therefore want to give you this initial advice to get you to the point from which my thoughts and methods can really bear fruit. Don't see complexities before you are ready for them, and even then be selective in recognizing which advice applies to you and which does not. This is one of the drawbacks as a rule of instructional books. It is easy enough for a world-class player to tell you what he does and how he thinks he does it, but the club golfer can't always relate to those thoughts and know how to sift profitably through the advice.

LOOSEN UP FOR LENGTH

By no stretch of the imagination do I believe that the average golfer is going to be able to learn a really good swing straight off. We have to take the swing through stages, first of all enabling the beginner to get freedom and club head speed, and to produce a fairly acceptable contact on the ball.

What the long-handicap player or beginner needs to do is to get that club head moving freely with the beginnings of being able to produce the right sort of plane of swing and attack on the ball. The odds are that he can't immediately use the plane and swing I am advocating and will have to start with something more workable. For the beginner the address position and grip are identical to those I have already explained, with the ball slightly further back and only just ahead of the centre of the stance. There must be no sitting and drooping at address but much more a feeling of standing up tall, sticking the bottom out and hanging the arms beneath the chin. There must be a definite angle between the arms and the shaft of the club, with a feeling of the wrists being dropped and as loose and free as possible. I cannot emphasize enough the question of relaxation. The club golfer usually wants to hang on to the club for grim death and when you talk

about loosening up will say things like 'I feel out of control'. Believe me, if you want to hit the ball 220 yards you are going to feel out of control. You aren't going to prod or steer the ball that distance. You are going to have to acquire freedom and the confidence to let fly at it. Give it a go and don't be afraid of bad shots. You have to risk bad shots in golf to make the good shots happen. So loosen up and relax. But relax doesn't mean bending those knees. Stand up, stand tall and feel as though you've got space to get the club moving. Let's make the swing feel simple. Like in other games, the technique only gets difficult when you become a good player. Swinging a tennis racket to me is the simplest thing in the world because I don't pretend to be a great player. To Ivan Lendl no doubt it is complicated and technical. Same with the golf swing. For the long-handicap player it has got to be simple. For me as a champion it becomes technical and precise.

Right, here we go. The first thing you are going to do is to waggle the club back and through with your hands, simply hinging the club back so that the right hand flips back on itself towards the elbow and the left wrist arches and moves forward a couple of inches; make it free and easy. After a couple of preparatory waggles which should loosen you up, simply have the feeling of turning your back to the target and lifting your arms up, emphasizing the left arm so that the club sits up on your left thumb. Feel the left thumb really supporting that club ready to give it a whoosh in the downswing. Probably at this stage you are best to let the left heel just ease off the ground so that you can get your back to the target. As you do this keep your head up and have the feeling of the left shoulder turning, as your back turns, to cover your chin. From there, push the left heel back down to the ground, transferring the weight from the ball of the left foot back onto the heel of the left foot while turning yourself through towards the target. At the same time and perfectly co-ordinated with this, swish the club down and up the other side so that you support it once more on your left thumb, club dangling on your left shoulder.

In simple terms what we are going

to do is to get the club up on the left thumb and through onto the left shoulder. Left thumb, left shoulder. Give yourself freedom and just get the feeling of swinging and swishing the club with your hands and wrists so that it feels loose and easy. Loosen up and just get the club in your fingertips and don't strangle the wretched thing. You aren't going to let go. The club head on the end of that shaft is a very heavy chunk of metal and a club head on its own will probably feel much heavier than the whole club. Swing it – the club head – and become aware of its weight. If you hold too tightly the feeling of the club head will disappear and the whole thing is going to feel stiff. Think of club head speed and don't try for a feeling of power in your body or your hands.

Right, now let's try that over and over again, simply swinging the club up to the top, supporting it on the left thumb and then swishing it through so that it dangles on your left shoulder. Don't at this stage be more precise than that. Turn your back to the target and support the club on your left thumb and then turn on through to face the target so that it dangles on your shoulder. Let's start at the wrong end first and see what happens at the end of the swing. In the finish you need to feel that you are turned to face your target and your weight should be perfectly balanced on your left heel with the left leg straight though not awkwardly locked and rigid. The right foot will have spun through onto the tip of the big toe. You should feel that your body is turned through to face the target, with the hips in particular fully turned through. There will have to be quite a twisting in the left leg to leave the left foot in the position it started but to have turned you through. This is an important move for developing the swing further. Although the left leg is straight you should feel kind of sunk down on the straight left leg so that the left heel is directly under the middle of the hips. In other words, you don't feel stretched up on the left leg and balanced on the ball of the foot, but should feel balanced on the heel and should look balanced on the heel to someone viewing you from the direction of the target.

Now for the arms. At this stage we

want to get real freedom in the arms and to teach you to get the left arm out of the way for the day when the right hand can really swing that club head through and generate power. Most people don't know what to do with their left arm and it gets in the way. I am going to teach you right from the beginner stage what to do with that left arm. The moment the club head swishes through the bottom of your swing you are going to let your left arm turn and fold away so that by the time you finish your swing your feeling is of the elbows being fairly close, relaxed into approximately a right angle and with both wrists relaxed back on themselves, club dangling on the shoulder. If you look at your club shaft the odds are that about 4 inches below the bottom of the grip is a label. Feel that the shaft at approximately the point of that label rests on your shoulder. Your hands will be up somewhere in front of your left ear, wrists really loose and flopped back on themselves and the elbows bent. Now do this a few more times, again up on the left thumb in the backswing and then through onto the shoulder in the throughswing and feel that the wrists really are relaxed back on themselves at the end.

At first, you may find it difficult to get the club shaft landing on the shoulder. It looks comparatively simple but for many players it isn't. If you keep the left arm too stiff your club won't settle on the shoulder but may catch you on

1

Stand tall, bottom out and up – and relax. Legs feel loose, *not* bent

2

Turn, letting the left shoulder stay fairly high to cover the chin. Don't worry if the view of the ball feels close to being restricted by the left shoulder. This is correct; you only see it with the left eye

the top of the head. Nor should you let the elbows collapse completely into an acute angle or you finish up virtually strangling yourself. Nor must the wrists be stiff. Don't think you are getting the right position when you aren't, if all you are doing is breaking both elbows excessively and keeping the wrists firm. When you get up to the top of the backswing you have created potential hit in the wrists. By the time you get to the end of the swing you have to have released the swish into the ball. You shouldn't feel the wrists being stiff and firm or in reality you have still got hit left. Get rid of it and get it into the golf ball. Loosen up, let fly and get the club settling on the back of your shoulder.

Now let's take this a stage further and try the swing with a ball. The contact for the beginner is absurdly difficult unless you have a really well trained eye for a ball. To develop the swing easily, I suggest you start by teeing the ball up on a lowish peg and get confident at being able to strike it properly. If you aren't a natural athlete, you might do better by trying to hit a tennis ball into a net. It will give you a larger object to aim at. If the contact feels easy you can forget about that and concentrate on the swing. If you sit the ball down on the ground, particularly if there isn't much grass, the contact will feel difficult; all you will do is start picking the club up and chopping it down. So tee it up well or use a plastic ball or a larger ball to give

3

4

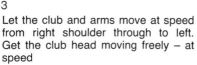

Let the club and arms move at speed from right shoulder through to left. Get the club head moving freely – at speed

Learn how to finish the swing, how to put the brakes on. Settle it neatly on the left shoulder or neck. The better and smoother this braking system the more clun head speed you can generate. Then hold it and check the balance. Either stand and admire the shot *or* stand and concentrate on where it is going – but finish the swing!

you confidence. Try exactly the same swing with the ball, up on the left thumb and through onto the shoulder. Let that left arm get out of the way and really get the feeling of swishing on through so that the club lands safely at the end of the swing. Most club golfers never learn where the end of the swing goes and for that reason they can't generate power. Start straight away by knowing where the end of the swing is going to land. Rather like driving a fast car or taking off in an aeroplane, the first thing you want to know is how to stop or land the wretched thing. Same thing with the golf swing. Learn where it finishes and that will teach you to get club head speed.

Don't let the club get round the back of your head. Land it on your shoulder or neck. If you aren't making contact with your shoulder then it probably means that you aren't folding the left arm away quickly enough. Remember that the arm doesn't break outwards but must fold inwards. The right arm naturally tucks itself in on the backswing. Do the same with the left in the throughswing. The moment the club head gets to the ball let the left arm almost fold and flick up from the elbow to form a neat right angle at the end of the swing. The club shaft may at first give you a hefty whack on the shoulder instead of settling there smoothly. If so, just time it better to get rid of the hit into the ball.

Now let's look at the swing in a little more detail, remembering again that I am aiming this advice at the long-handicap player.

THE BACKSWING

Good golf requires a perfect blending of left side and right side. If you are right-handed the odds are that your left arm and hand are fairly weak. I am going to teach the good golfer how to make the swing feel to be a right-handed action. But remember that we are already probably fairly ambidextrous. You need to build up the left side. Have a feeling in the backswing of really turning the left shoulder and almost lifting the left arm so that you know the left side is working in harmony with the right. Practise swinging the club from address up to the top of the backswing with your left hand only. Make it work correctly at this stage so that the right hand can eventually generate some speed.

Learn also to turn the shoulders in the correct way. Most club golfers want to tip their shoulders. You either lift it with the arms (preferably the left rather than the right arm) or you dip the left shoulder down to force it up. The first is right and the second is wrong. Feel that you turn the shoulders almost horizontally, almost with a feeling of lifting the left shoulder to cover your chin and at the same time lifting the left arm.

I want to explain what it looks like *to you* when you get to the top of the backswing. If you move the left shoulder round correctly it will cover your chin. Your view is almost as though the left shoulder is going to hide the ball. It doesn't and you should quite clearly see the ball over the shoulder with your left eye. But the two look close. The view from your right eye is probably blocked by your nose and left shoulder. Now if you do the wrong thing and dip the left shoulder down you are going to see a big space between the left shoulder and the ball at the top of the backswing, and may, in a really bad action, see your own feet. You will probably feel far more

secure with this kind of view but it is wrong. It means that the left shoulder is going down and you have the beginnings of an up-and-down swing which will later cause so much trouble. So let the left shoulder turn and just see the ball over it. Again bear in mind that if the ball is fairly central this good turn will seem much easier than if you try to play the ball opposite the left heel.

In the backswing get freedom and have the feeling of turning the body. The weight transference for the good player is not a side-to-side kind of movement but is a turning. Initially you may need to feel that you turn and almost shift very slightly to the right. At the top of the backswing the weight should probably feel as though you are almost on the right heel, the left heel probably pulling up an inch or so. Now the club is supported on your left thumb and ideally what we hope for, if the shoulder turn is sufficient, is for the shaft of the club to point roughly parallel to the ground and roughly parallel to the direction in which you are hitting. Don't be too precise. But have a feeling of turning and beginning to swing the club round behind you rather than picking it up in the air. Have a feeling of the left shoulder staying up rather than dropping and you are well on your way to a good plane of swing.

Building the swing

My THOUGHTS on the golf swing are based on seven key concepts, several involving swinging the golf club on the correct plane. This is particularly important for a player like myself who is tall. But even for the player of average or below average height it is all too easy to swing the club in an incorrect plane. The plane of the swing is crucial to my thoughts on the game. You will, no doubt, read much in this book, and in this section in particular, which is different from advice you have previously heard or read. I will also try to dispel many of the myths about the straight left arm, width and extension. And then, for the really good golfer in particular, I am going to teach you how the game can be a right-handed one – yes, right-handed, without any fear of hooking or becoming excessively right-side dominant. Some of my ideas may seem revolutionary; others are perhaps new or very precise ways of looking at so-called old-fashioned teaching ideas. Work through them patiently with a 6-iron. See how they intertwine, by all means, but look at them stage by stage, trying to perfect each as you go.

KEY 1 – THE PLANE OF THE SWING

TURN NOT TILT. THE TRUTH IS IN THE LIE!

Many golfers wrongly think of the golf swing as an up-and-down movement, producing a straight back and throughswing. They seem to think that if the club head is swung back and through in a straight line it will hit the ball straight at the target. Sadly it won't. The club cannot be swung back and through on a perfectly straight line with good results, any more than you would dream of swinging a tennis racket back and through on a straight path. If you swing a golf club back and through on a straight line you are moving off the correct and natural plane and will neither produce good direction nor generate power to your shot.

The centre of your swing, in very simple terms, is your neck. You swing your arms and turn your shoulders around that point and that point isn't directly above the ball. If we draw a line from the ball to the centre of the shoulders that in itself tells us that the club must move round in a circular path and through again in a circular path. The odds are that it won't feel natural. Indeed, for perhaps ten to fifteen years there has been a move away from this concept of turning in the backswing, with leading players themselves falling for this fallacy of seeing the swing as too much of a straight back, straight through path. For some this was produced by a tilting of the shoulders. More commonly by a definite feeling of lifting the arms in both backswing and throughswing to get the arms working freely away from the shoulders. With a good player this doesn't need to happen; we want a swing where the arms, club and body turn and move on the same plane, without any pronounced extension or lifting in either backswing or throughswing.

Players like Ben Hogan and Sam Snead, with truly classic swings, simply followed the turn of the body on

both backswing and throughswing. The plane of the swing was then gradually seen as a more upright movement, swinging the club straighter back and straighter through with the emphasis on lateral movement to the left through impact, with width and extension both back and through and the emphasis on the height of the hands and arms. Many of us followed the example of Jack Nicklaus with his comparatively high and wide swing until we found ourselves getting into difficulties. Gradually many of the world's top players have looked again for a flatter plane of swing, realizing the wisdom of taking the club away in harmony with the body turn and then letting it produce the same roundness in the throughswing.

My whole idea of the plane of the golf swing is very much like that of Hogan's. His concept, in one of the most famous illustrations of all golf instructional books, was to have a large sheet of glass inclined to the vertical, the player's head above the glass, with the rest of the body plus the club head and ball beneath it. The whole feeling of the swing was to move the club on such a plane that the arms and club swung and stayed beneath the sheet of glass, both back and through, everything naturally following the turn of the body.

My concept of the swing is related to the lie of every club in my set. If I take the long-shafted driver, with its comparatively flat lie, the plane of my whole swing is going to follow that angle. When I move up to the short-shafted 9-iron, with its much more upright lie, my swing is going to follow that plane.

Not only do players often have the wrong concept of the swing, believing it to be straight back and through, high and wide, but the very nature of the strike needed on the ball tends to encourage the *wrong* movements right from the time a player first picks up a golf club. His introduction to the game and his very first lesson or experiment will often determine how his overall concept and shape of swing develop.

Developing the plane
Even with the correct concept of swinging a club on a circular path, for many people it isn't that easy. The major difficulty for the novice is that it is hard to make a good contact with the ball. There are three reasons. First of all he is faced with a club which has a long shaft and a comparatively small head, giving him a difficult weapon to use. Second, he has a ball which is very small and which seems difficult to hit.

But third, and most difficult, is that the ball sits on the ground and the ground literally gets in the way of his swing. Most games players turning to golf think the game is difficult because the ball is stationary. It isn't the stationary ball that makes it hard; it is the fact that it sits on the ground. Most people can pick up a putter and quite naturally move the club back and through without any real difficulties. They are simply trying to hit the ball along the ground. But as soon as the beginner picks up a golf club with some idea of getting the ball airborne his instinct is probably to lift the club up in the air with the idea of getting it down into the ball. The ground seems in the way and he is unlikely instinctively to want to swing the club round in a circle behind him and round again in a circle as he swings through.

Look at it this way. If I had no golf training and picked up a golf club and was told to hit an exact spot on the ground in front of me, the easiest thing to do would be to pick the club straight up and chop it straight down. In this way I would feel I could naturally strike the exact point. If I swung the club low along the ground or round in a curve the odds of making contact with the exact spot would be fairly remote. That, in broad terms, is what the beginner and long-handicap player will want to do in his golf swing He will want to pick the club up, chop it down into the ground and then lift it up again so that he produces a very up-and-down swing. That is not the way the golf club should be moved, but for most people it is all too easy and simple to do it that way. Unfortunately, this up-and-down action is also aggravated if the player falls into the trap of playing the ball opposite his left heel. From there he is never likely to turn; play the ball several inches further back and he might.

If you attack the ball in an up-and-down manner you cannot generate any speed in the club head by using the right hand. When you come to Key 3 on setting the right hand and Key 7 on hitting with the right hand, you will find that a good plane of swing is essential for both of these. If you swing the club up and off the plane you will always have the feeling of having to hold back on the shot to steer it straight and will almost certainly never develop your maximum club head speed and distance. Not only will the wrong action often feel natural, but you may even be unlucky enough to have a club professional who himself believes that golf is played in this way. The person who swings with a straight back and through, up-and-down swing but does not develop it to his maximum potential will almost certainly be prone to pulling the ball left as he attacks the ball with his hands or slicing the ball away to the right if his hands are at all slow and lazy. To complete my explanation of why the plane has to be a circular path, let's draw an analogy to the way you would throw a football. If you hold a ball in both hands and stand sideways to the target, the natural way of throwing the ball and generating power is to turn your back to the target and to turn through, the arms moving round behind you and through and out towards the target. If you pick the ball up high and try to throw it, you will find you can't generate power. All that happens is that you virtually drop it to the ground in a fairly powerless way. Similarly, imagine yourself holding a squash racket and banging a ball as hard as possible with a right-handed forehand towards the front wall. Even picking the ball up from a fairly low bounce you would swing the racket round behind you, drive it through the ball and continue on round again. There would certainly be no inclination in either of these actions to pick up and lift the football or to pick up and lift the squash racket. But in golf, it is so easy to fall into this trap of a lift because you are collecting a ball which sits on the ground.

Learning the plane

Let's look first at a series of pictures with my driver and my 9-iron. The angle of the shaft of the club in each dictates the plane of my swing. With

1

2

5

6

1

2

3

4

7

8

These shots of 9-iron and driver show how the plane of swing is dictated by the lie of the club. Halfway back the setting of the wrists puts the club on this plane. By the top of the backswing the left arm is on plane; in the throughswing and finish the same plane is evident. Change club or lie and the same rule applies

Check the swing plane in the takeaway. The setting of the wrists should take the club away into a plane of swing that follows the lie of the club

the correct address position the angle of the club determines my posture and the degree of bending from the hips. With the upper arms slightly squeezed against my sides I am simply going to turn the shoulders on their natural plane and let the arms move to follow that same plane. Halfway back, having turned and set the wrists correctly (see below), the shaft of my club is going to follow its own plane. By the time I get to the top of the backswing the left arm again follows this same overall pattern. If I attack the ball correctly, we see the same plane before impact and the same pattern being completed again after it. A comparison between the 9-iron and the driver shows the full range of clubs

and yet how this same overall shape of swing applies.

You can check this feeling by setting a club shaft or cane diagonally in the ground as shown, checking the halfway-back position for angle and checking the left-arm plane against it in a mirror. If you move off this plane in this hip height position, it should be obvious, either setting it back on too low a plane, or far more commonly, picking it up too steeply and off the plane.

As I move through the backswing my feeling is of the left arm being drawn across the chest and therefore moving on the same plane and being fairly tightly connected to the shoulder turn. In a perfect plane I believe shoulders and arms will turn in harmony. But if anything, it is definitely preferable for the left arm to be on a slightly *higher* plane at the top of the backswing than the plane of the shoulders. In reality the swing does contain an element of arm lift in both backswing and throughswing, producing this slightly higher plane to the arms. The swing is 'round and up; down, round and up.' As a rule the lift just happens. The roundness of the backswing and timing of 'down before round' in the attack is the thought. Under no circumstances do you want a shoulder plane where there is a tip and tilt and the left arm allows itself to drop below the plane of the shoulders. The top-class player should certainly feel left arm and shoulder plane perfectly together; for the club golfer the shoulder turn may, if anything, be flatter than the arm plane.

The first stage to a good plane, having assumed the correct concept, is to adopt the right posture. Refer back to the chapter on the address position. The feeling is of standing tall, bending from the hips not waist, bottom out and up, lower back flat. The angle of the back now determines the plane of the swing, back and through, the shoulders and hips turning on this natural plane.

Here are several exercises to give you the feeling of turning on the correct plane. In the first, hold a club in front of your hips, turning back and turning through, ensuring that the club and in turn the hips move on a constant plane. Second, hold a club behind

1

2

Turn the hips back and through on a constant plane

your neck on your shoulders, having adopted the correct posture. Turn back and turn through, ensuring that the end of the club comes through at the same level in front of you on the backswing as it does on the throughswing. It won't point down to the ball. If it does, you are tipping and lifting. It will point out to a spot in front of you and if the plane is symmetrical, it does the same on both halves of the swing.

A third exercise for developing a good plane is to practise swinging to an imaginary ball, say, 12 to 15 inches off the ground. From there simply swing the club round behind you and through again, imagining you collect the ball at this height. What you will be feeling now is a fairly horizontal plane. Obviously the club does rise and fall, but the feeling of roundness is probably far more simple than with a ball on the ground. You can take the experiment a stage further by hitting balls from a side slope, preferably with your feet on a fairly flat ground but the ball positioned slightly above you. This

also encourages the feeling of roundness.

I now have to convince you that you can then put a ball on flat ground in front of you and feel much the same kind of plane of swing. Once you learn to do this correctly you can use your right hand in the throughswing, generating as much power as possible with the right hand and really producing club head speed. Your thoughts must be of swinging the club around in a circular path and the ball flying off at a tangent to the circle towards your target. The swing is round then up, down, round and up. The turn must come before any upward movement. Set a club shaft along your toes and practise turning until the club head moves behind that club before any feel of a lift. Almost feel it move behind your legs while resisting any upward arm lift. The club head will of course come off the ground as you turn but *feel* it stays just as low as possible. Then, and only then, allow any arm lift to happen.

1

2

Develop the correct plane to the shoulder turn, club pointing out to the same spot, back and through

As you are doing this, let me repeat my views on the ball position in relation to the feet. Many golfers are taught to play the ball excessively far forward towards the left foot as though off the left heel. This encourages a bad tilt and tip of both hips and shoulders. In my own game I play the ball a good 3 inches inside the left heel. This encourages me to turn away from the ball. Obviously the precise distance inside the heel varies with the width of your stance. But if working at correcting the plane, it will do no harm to play the ball almost back to the middle of the stance, if only as a temporary measure. From here the shoulders will adopt a position conducive to turning. This view of the ball will encourage a feeling of turning away from it, allowing you to turn your back to the target. It will encourage you to take the club away in its correct path while clearly seeing the ball.

If the ball is played too far forward to the left a good shoulder plane will give a far less comfortable view of the ball, the left shoulder almost feeling it will hide it. Play with the ball forward and you are likely to tilt and with it to pull and slice; play the ball in the correct position – well back of the left heel – and feel freedom to adopt the correct plane.

And, last, as proof of just how flat the swing can be, try kneeling down and hitting the ball with a 3-wood or driver, ball teed up reasonably high. The odds are that in the first few attempts the club head will strike the ground several feet behind the ball. Only by swinging on the pre-set plane of the club can you strike the ball cleanly. Once you do, the flight of the ball – preferably with a slight draw – will convince you just how a club can be swung.

Always think of swinging the club on the angle it adopts at address. Whether on a flat lie, standing below or above the ball or with this experiment of kneeling down, the same rule applies. Let the club dictate your plane.

KEY 2 – THE POWER COIL

GENERATE POWER THROUGH PULL
AND RESISTANCE.

My whole concept of generating power in the golf swing is one of pull and resistance. One part of the body always seems to be resisting another part for a feeling of strength. Try this simple exercise. Press your right fingertips against the left ones just as hard as possible. The hands, and indeed, the whole arms and shoulders, push and resist at the same time. The feeling is one of power.

In the golf swing the feeling of the backswing is of turning the right side away, not with a loose turn, but resisting this turn with the left side of the body and with the right knee. The feeling is of the knees and feet staying still; in reality they don't. But I really pull and turn against them. At the top of the backswing the position is tightly coiled, like an archery bow drawn back and held. Release it and generate power. The feeling then is a change of roles. Now the right side holds back and the left pulls away against its resistance.

But for the moment let's concentrate on the power coil.

The first stage is to learn to turn correctly. Hold the club more or less halfway down, at arm's length, the end of the club into your stomach. Now

1

turn, concentrating on your stomach, just feeling the slight pull in of the knees. The club starts in a square position. As you turn your stomach the club stays in this square position in relation to you. Body, arms and club move as a unit. This is the feeling of the start to the body turn – the first movement of the takeaway.

Now with the idea of the initial turn, let's have the feeling of power – coiling to create energy for the downswing.

2

An exercise for checking the plane of the hip turn – turning back and turning through on the same plane throughout

1

2

3

3

This exercise shows the feeling of turning the stomach to start the power coil. At each swing of the turn the club face is square to me – club face and leading edge just following my body turn

4

The backswing requires a turn, getting the back to the target, and bringing the club round on the correct plane until it points roughly parallel to the line of the shot. If you turn insufficiently the back won't face the target and the odds are the attack won't be sufficiently from the inside. Initially in learning to turn, the left heel may have to rise and the legs and hips may have to turn very freely and rather too loosely.

Only at the point at which you turn sufficiently can you begin to add the resistance I am now going to explain. Let me remind you of the feeling in the legs at address. There is a definite feeling of slight tension and considerable strength in the muscles on the insides of my thighs. They have this strange pull-and-push feeling – pulling in and yet pushing out. As I turn, my feeling is of sending the right hip back and round behind me and sending the right shoulder back and round and yet really feeling the knees resisting all the time. The right one really does stay still. The left will in fact move in towards a point somewhere behind the ball, but it doesn't point in freely. It resists all the way.

As this power coil continues, my weight turns. It doesn't shift to the side. My weight turns away, weight being pulled round onto the right heel, right knee still motionless. There seems, in fact, considerable weight into and through the right knee itself, almost as though the swing pivots from the resistance of that knee. Again there is a resistance in the left side to counter this. As the body turns, weight is pulled forward onto the ball of the left foot, *but* – for the good, supple golfer – without the left heel being pulled off the ground. Pressure comes off the left heel but it doesn't lift. (If you can't at first get a good turn without some foot movement, let the left heel rise a touch – *never* let it roll onto the inside.)

4

5

6

To achieve a good power coil, hold the club behind your neck, normal address posture, knees pulled in from the inside of the thighs. Practise turning the shoulders fully, back to the target, without the knees moving at all. The exercise is difficult and only the very advanced player is likely to achieve the perfect position in this practice routine. But the feeling from doing the exercise, even if less than perfect, is going to teach you the feeling of setting up resistance and a tight turn in the backswing.

Develop a good power coil – weight sixty/forty right foot to left – and you are in position to move left side away from right for maximum energy in the throughswing.

KEY 3 – SETTING THE WRISTS

Most of the key concepts we are looking at involve the plane of the swing, achieving roundness and attacking the ball in the correct circular path. Looking at the golf swing from the front, straight on at the player, shows very little. In terms of hand action we are led to believe that the wrists hinge and cock upwards in the backswing and then hinge and cock upwards again in the throughswing. Indeed, in the simple, beginner's swing that is what happens. The wrists hinge the club up onto the thumbs both back and through. But when we look at the swing from behind the line of the shot the second dimension to the wrist cock shows. This is where the truth about the wrist break can be found. Let's see how the two dimensions are related.

The first is the wrist break which you see when you look straight at a player. To understand this, address the ball with your normal grip and look at the angle which you have created between the arms and the club shaft. Now simply hinge the wrists up and down so that you bring the club shaft up towards you. What you are doing is hinging the wrists up in the way I described to the beginner. I explained to him that the backswing is a turn of the body combined with a kind of lifting of the arms and a hinging upwards of the wrists onto the left thumb. If you look at a player from

This shows just how everything coils in the backswing – really winding up against the legs. Remember that the left leg is resisting all the way. It is pulled into this position, feeling really strong to start the movement into reverse

The wrists can hinge in two ways in the backswing. The right wrist can be hinged or cupped upwards against the thumb. This in itself does not create power. The movement is fairly limited and weak. It can also be set backwards to a right angle – the wrist set used to create power and leverage

This exercise requires strength and suppleness – deceptively so. My feeling is of trying to turn the shoulders fully without the knees moving at all. The right does stay still; the left gets pulled in to point behind the ball. You try not to let it move. It is then so fully coiled with resistance that when you let it go it pulls the whole thing into reverse. There is also tremendous pressure in the right knee and lower leg, the coiling almost centering around it

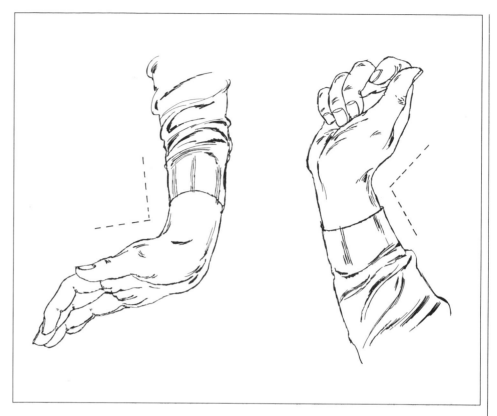

straight on that is what you see and what most people mean by 'cocking the wrists'. Most club golfers do this, and it is usually all they understand by cocking the wrists. This is the upward hinging. I refer to it as 'cupping' the wrists – an action which has its place for the good golfer in certain areas of the short game.

I am now going to explain the second dimension to the wrist cock and explain what late hitting means and how the two are related. In the first dimension you hinge the wrists up and are simply preparing to whip them down again. That would be great if you wanted to pick the club up and to smash it down on the ground in front of you. But we want to generate power and to generate power in a kind of sideways, virtually horizontal direction. Right, now let's look at the other kind of wrist cock. Take hold of the club with your ordinary grip and you will see that your right hand is behind the shaft. At this point simply hinge the right hand *backwards* so that it flips back on itself, forming more or less a right angle. It comes directly back against the forearm, with no rolling of the wrist. This is a movement you may not have done before in the golf swing.

To develop the feeling of the correct movement, hinge the right wrist backwards so that the club shaft is set parallel to the ground and parallel to the direction you are going to hit the ball. Simply hinge it backwards, easing the right elbow into your stomach and right hip. In doing this, the left wrist arches forward a couple of inches, left arm in turn moving out in front of the right. The feeling from here should be that you can generate power, swinging the club out again at the ball, simply by releasing this backward wrist break and returning the right hand to its original position. This is the correct powerful wrist break you want to develop. I refer to this throughout the book as 'setting the wrists'.

This backward wrist set is the one you use in other sports. Learn to use it in golf. If you pick up a tennis racket or squash racket you swing it back with your right hand and simply cock the wrists back into this kind of position. Similarly, if you pick up a tennis ball or a cricket ball and you want to throw the thing, you are going to get your hand behind your head and cock the wrist back in the same way. It is this that is the powerful kind of wrist action and the one you are going to

Hinge the right wrist back on itself — backward against the forearm, club parallel to the shot, parallel to the ground. Then coil to the top of the backswing. The right wrist remains set, the back of the left wrist flattens

With the wrists set in the correct way, bouncing down from the top brings the hands into a 'late hit' position, hitting from behind me. This posed picture shows the feeling of a late hit. The club is behind my hands and the right hand can hit. Late hitting has noting to do with timing or delay. Think of it as hitting from behind your hands (visually) at this stage

Cupping the wrists instead of setting them brings the hands into a hitting position with the club head level or in front of them. Now the right hand is in a weak position. Its only leverage is downwards and in effect it has to hold back for fear of dragging every shot left

learn to use. For the good player it is no longer an upward movement against the thumbs; that is already taken care of in the address position. It has to be a backward, power hinge.

Feel again the backward setting of the wrists, taking the club back to its horizontal, parallel-to-the-shot position. From here, and gradually learning to do it simultaneously, turn the right shoulder directly behind you and move to the top of the swing. The right arm will then turn and fold so that at the top of the backswing the right arm forms what is virtually a right angle with the right hand more or less underneath the club. The old teaching idea of this is to feel like a waiter carrying a tray. It isn't a bad example at all, and I would suggest that you actually get hold of a tray and sit it up there out to the right of your head to feel the right hand and arm position. Keep repeating the movement, setting the right wrist back and completing the backswing. As you do this the left wrist should now start producing a flat position at the top of the backswing. You now have the second dimension of the wrist break.

What happens from here in starting the downswing is that your arms pull down a few inches. It is smooth, not exaggerated; they have simply gone up to the top of the backswing and will then pull down a little. As they move down, you should now feel that the right hand is going to stay in its cocked position but will now be behind the shaft of the club, having a feeling of being able to throw the club out and round at the ball through impact. This is what we mean by late hitting. Most people are confused by the idea of late hitting and think it means a delay in the downward uncocking of the wrists. That isn't late hitting. What we mean by late hitting is the cocking back of the right wrist and the way in which the hand and wrist then release the club back through the ball. What this means, if you use the right hand correctly, is that your club will go much more around your body in the backswing and will then attack the ball from behind you during the downswing. Let's say that late hitting means hitting from behind yourself. There is a very marked difference in the position from which you will attack the ball, first if you use an upward wrist cock – cupping the wrists – and second if you use the correct kind of wrist cock – setting the wrists.

To see the difference, I suggest that you stand with a hedge behind you and try to swing the club up to the top of the backswing. If you do the wrong thing you could virtually stand with your back touching the hedge and swing the club quite easily up to the top of the backswing. You would simply be hinging the wrists upwards. If you do the correct thing and hinge the wrists backwards you will probably feel that you have to be some 2 to 3 feet from the hedge or the club will swing back at it and round in quite a dramatic way, probably catching the hedge at a much lower point than you would imagine. If you stand behind a good tournament professional golfer, you will be aware of where the club head goes and how dangerous, in fact, the good player's swing could be to anyone standing behind him. This, then, is what late hitting is all about. It is the setting back of the right wrist on itself, a position which is quite naturally held until you feel ready to generate power with your right hand through impact. Once you can get this position and can hinge the wrist backwards, you should have the feeling of then being able to hit hard with the right hand through impact in a round, out and round way.

I hope by now that you will see that if you have an up-and-down swing, all you have is the first dimension of our wrist cock and that the downward movement which it then produces in the attack is a weak one. If your concept of the golf swing is to swing the club straight back and up you will lack this power hinge unless you compensate in some other way. If the swing comes up and down the line, you cannot use the right hand.

I would add here that many golfers are led to believe that the club is hinged upwards, rather than backwards, by an obsession with pointing the club parallel to the target line at the top of the backswing. It is true to say that if you hinge the wrists upwards the club shaft will point in what they would describe as 'the right direction' however long the backswing. When you swing on the correct plane, combining it with a powerful wrist set, the club shaft is still moving in a rounded way as it approaches the top of the backswing. Only when the swing reaches a certain length will it point truly parallel to the shot. Swing slightly short and it points left and swing slightly longer and it points to the right. This is not a question of having the club laid off in one position nor across the line in the next position. But pay too much attention to trying to point the club parallel to the line of the shot and you can fall into the trap of this weak upward cupping of the wrists.

The backward hinging of the wrists is so crucial that it is a movement I always rehearse before the takeaway. Sometimes I feel a very definite hinging, ensuring that the club is moved back into its position, parallel to the ground and parallel to the shot. At other times the rehearsal is more of a gentle waggle in the wrists to ensure that they are loosened up in the correct direction.

Sometimes the setting of the wrists is a very conscious movement; sometimes it isn't. The power coil and wrist set must work together. Usually my thoughts are first to coil, meaning my hips and stomach, and then set, meaning the right wrist. If the coil happens first – and I literally say it to myself – the right hip just moves a couple of inches and the club head has gone perhaps 2 feet. So as the stomach (and right hip) moves, the club head has to go. In that split second I think 'set'. If for some reason the wrist action doesn't feel comfortable I might have to stress that first.

The key thought varies from player to player, and may vary for one player almost from week to week. If you tend to pick the club up, then the feeling is of turning the stomach, then setting the wrists back. If slow in the hands, emphasize the wrist setting to trigger it away.

In changing my swing I had to work away from an upward cupping of the wrist into this backward setting. At that time the feeling of setting had to take priority – setting the right wrist back a split second before the coiling feeling. The player changing this part of the swing may well have to think 'set, coil' until the two really can take place in harmony.

Don't think of setting the wrists as being iron shots only. With the longer shots – fairway woods and driving – you need almost more wrist set. It keeps everything tight and compact for power. When shots seem lifeless, practise setting fully, then coiling to the top. Power will follow.

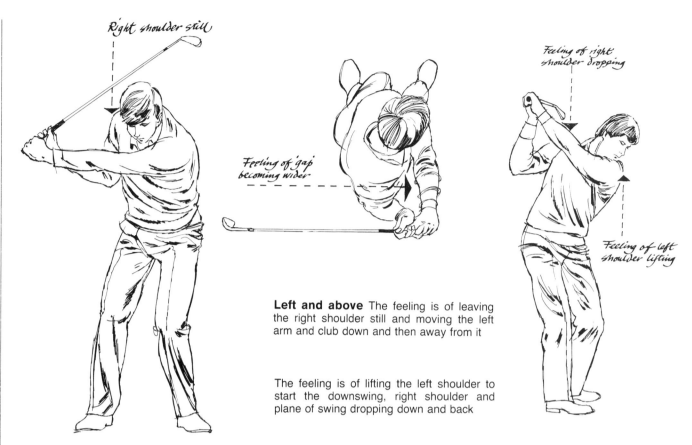

Left and above The feeling is of leaving the right shoulder still and moving the left arm and club down and then away from it

The feeling is of lifting the left shoulder to start the downswing, right shoulder and plane of swing dropping down and back

KEY 4 – REVERSING THE SWING

The change of directions in the golf swing is in many ways the most difficult and most crucial part of it. Much of the good work is done in creating the right plane to the backswing and in setting the right wrist back on itself for an inside attack – the late-hit position. But we also have to create an even greater safeguard, ensuring that the right shoulder and right side of the body stay passive for a moment while the swing is reversed.

Let's remind ourselves that the backswing is a question of drawing and turning the right side back against the resistance of the knees and the left side. Having got to the top of the backswing the roles are reversed. The right side is in a potentially very destructive position and particularly for the right-handed player can do all sorts of damage. What we have to do is to ensure that it now stays in position (or feels as though it stays in position) while the left side pulls against its resistance. The overall feeling is of leaving the right hip and shoulder

turned away while the left side moves away from it. In reality, at the top of the backswing the left arm has been drawn across the chest with the left shoulder now slightly rounding inwards towards the right side. We have to resist any feeling of the right shoulder, right hip and right knee pushing power into the shot at this time. Our overall feeling is to leave the right side where it is and draw the left side away from it to change directions.

Let's see the precise feelings we need to have. There are several ways in which you can feel this change of directions. One person may need to emphasize one movement; another person will find more benefit from another thought. One month one thought may feel to be important, the next month another may take its place.

As a first thought, the whole arm action must move away from the right shoulder. From the top of the backswing the space between the left arm and the right shoulder must rapidly increase. So, too, must the space between the hands and the right shoulder increase immediately from the top of the backswing. The right shoulder is left where it is, the club and arms

move down and away from it, through impact and to-wards the left shoulder. This is per-haps the simplest way of getting the concept of the passive right side. The arms and club in turn should feel as though they eventually pull the right side through, the right knee and foot moving in response to the arms rather than thrusting in power them-selves.

More advanced, but giving an even greater safeguard against a dominant right side, is to try to lower the plane of the downswing in relation to the backswing. Left to its own devices, the downswing will almost always come outside the backswing. To ensure this doesn't happen and to allow me to generate power with the right hand, my feeling is of dropping the plane of the attack. The feeling is of doing three specific things from the top of the backswing, all again with the same object of producing an inside, shallow attack. The first feeling is one of starting the downswing with an upward turn back of the left shoulder. This has the result, if anything, of dropping the right shoulder and keeping it back rather than letting it come up and forward.

1

2

The right elbow drops down and tucks in a touch, bringing the hands back behind me for an inside, shallow attack

The second feeling is of turning the right elbow under and in, again with the result that the right hand will drop down and back rather than coming up and forwards. Once again the result is of dropping the plane, if anything, slightly lower and behind the plane of the backswing. The feeling is of a very definite downward and inside loop – a feeling which is dramatically greater than will ever show in the swing. Having felt the elbow drop in, as though the elbow itself points forward, the feeling can then be of letting the elbow be moved away from the body with a feeling of rapidly widening the space between the right hand and right shoulder.

The whole of this, whichever way you think of it, is a means of making the right shoulder and right side of the

1

body passive for a moment while everything else moves away from it.

The most advanced of the techniques, and one which really is only for the world-class player, is to have the feeling of a knee separation in the change of directions. I explained how we turn against the knees in the backswing, pulling against their resistance. In the throughswing the overall movement is one of turning the legs on through, not bowing the left leg out to the left, but simply pulling the left hip and left knee back behind me. For the very advanced player, it is an added bonus to the swing if you can feel the right leg really does stay still in the change down, the left knee separating away from it. Once again, in reality this is the right side having moved back and the left side now pulling against its resistance. In the backswing, despite the resistance in the knees, the left knee is pulled towards the right knee. It is closer to the right knee than it was at address. Now the feeling is of leaving the right leg still for a moment and drawing the left knee away from it.

The knee separation pulls the swing into reverse. It happens a split second before the club reaches the top of the backswing and in effect brings it to a momentary halt before pulling it into reverse. In that last 2 or 3 inches of the backswing, the left knee is felt to separate. For those who can make this slight movement, it again acts to leave the right side still, ensuring that it is

passive, and to move left side from right side. For the advanced player who can achieve this the exercise should be one of hitting shots with the right foot staying flat on the ground almost to the point of impact, feeling that it is pulled through only at the very last moment. For the club player this could dangerously throw emphasis on to the shoulders, so it really only is an exercise for the very good golfer.

If knee separation can be achieved, it too will help keep the right side back and combined with the other thoughts will, if anything, help to drop the plane of the attack for a shallow, inside delivery into the ball.

KEY 5 – ARM ROTATION AND THE POWER WHIP

Let's look at the way in which the arms move and turn in a golf swing. Go back again to the idea of throwing a football. As you turn to the right your arms will naturally rotate, with the right elbow, back of the right wrist and palm of the left hand all turning down.

Now as you swing through, exactly the opposite thing happens. The left arm will fold away, and the left elbow, back of the left wrist and the palm of the right hand will turn over – let's say 45 degrees to vertical or horizontal. In other words we get a very natural turning of the arms as the body moves. Exactly the same thing should happen

The feeling of knee separation for the top-class golfer. Left knee moves away from right. Right resists. The left then pulls firmly back behind me

2

3

4

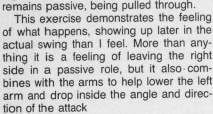

FOR THE ADVANCED PLAYER

Combined with this feeling of lowering the plane of the swing, we have the most advanced of swing techniques – knee separation in the change of directions. I explained how we turn against the knees and then simply turn the legs on through. For the very advanced player it is an added bonus to the swing if you can feel the right leg really does stay still in the change down. The left knee then separates away from the right, pulling the downswing into action, and again ensuring that the right never thrusts but remains passive, being pulled through.

This exercise demonstrates the feeling of what happens, showing up later in the actual swing than I feel. More than anything it is a feeling of leaving the right side in a passive role, but it also combines with the arms to help lower the left arm and drop inside the angle and direction of the attack

1

2

3

4

5

6

7

in a golf swing. The arms have to turn quite naturally in the backswing, right elbow and left palm diagonally down as you go back and then left elbow and right palm diagonally down as you go through. The two halves of the swing must mirror each other, arms turning and folding in an identical manner both back and through. This should keep the club swinging on plane throughout the swing and make it just as easy as possible to produce a square club face through impact.

The left-arm fold

I am now going to teach you to forget everything you have heard or read about extension, width, a straight left arm beyond impact and the high finish. I am going to explain to you how the majority of golfers get into trouble through a left arm that won't get out of the way – too straight a left arm, if you like.

Golfers throughout the world struggle to get a straight left arm on the backswing. In reality, what happens in a good golf swing is that the left arm swings across the chest in the backswing and stays fairly straight and extended. Whether or not you do this easily depends how free your left arm moves from your shoulder. To feel this backswing movement hold the left arm out in front of you, palm of the hand downwards, and practise swinging the left arm across in front of you so that it virtually touches the right shoulder. This in effect is what happens in the backswing. If you find it easy to draw the arm across your chest, the odds are it will stay straight. If you find this difficult, then you may need to turn the shoulders more in the backswing to get your arm in the right position, or just assume your left arm will bend. I don't think it is the end of the world if the left arm does bend; even if it does stay straight it should be relaxed with little tension in it. What tends to happen is that players are so indoctrinated with thoughts that the left arm must be straight in the backswing that it becomes stiff and rigid. Far more players then get into difficulty *not* because they have a bent left arm in the backswing but because they don't know what to do with it in the throughswing. If we look at the concept of arm rotation we see that the left arm must

be allowed to bend and fold out of the way in the throughswing in order to match the movement of the right arm in the backswing. We have to learn to get the left arm out of the way so that the right hand can hit.

I am going to explain what has to happen to the left arm and why it has to happen. Let's take you back to holding some sort of racket and trying to hit a ball. It wouldn't be difficult for most of us. If you look at the movement involved, the swing through will take your right hand across your body and fairly close to the right shoulder. Now hold the racket with two hands in much the same way you would hold a golf club, left hand above and right hand below. Now try and swing the racket and you will immediately be aware that the real difficulty is to get that left arm out of the way. It blocks what you want to do with the right. This is exactly what most people encounter in the golf swing. Their left arm gets in the way through impact and they don't know how to generate speed. Forget everything you have read about extension and trying to keep the left arm straight beyond impact. It cannot happen. For those of you who don't believe me, hold the club out in your left hand with the arm straight, stretched out towards the target. Right, now with the club held out like that, how on earth can you get your right hand onto the club beyond the left? The only way you can do it is if you bring your shoulders right round or if you drop your right shoulder right underneath. If you are aiming at doing this beyond impact for a full swing, you are totally misguided.

The left arm has to fold away in much the same way as the right one did in the backswing. In fact, if you think about it, it almost has to fold away more. In the backswing the right arm folds but the right hand is out further from you than the left. In the throughswing the left is closer to you and the right one has to extend out. The left arm has to be got out of the way to let you hit.

Again we have to take the thing in stages. The movement I make is specific and precise and we are going to look at how it happens. First of all, learn to let the left arm fold. See how the right one does it in the backswing, well let the left arm do it on the throughswing. If you keep your left arm straight at the top of the backswing, the odds are that by the time you reach impact the bone of your left elbow is facing out towards your target and your left arm isn't in a position to turn and fold. It jams. All it really wants to do from there is break outwards. If it breaks outwards, you finish up with a flying left elbow at the end of the follow-through and your elbow is going to be round and way behind your

In this exercise I have a towel firmly trapped between the chest and upper arms. To keep it there the arms must fold correctly, the right one as one would expect in the backswing but the left as well in the throughswing. The whole of the upper arms are kept close to the side throughout, keeping the arms not only folding but also correctly following the plane of the shoulders

head. What we are going to do first is to work at folding the arm in and if anything folding it up in front of you.

The first exercise to try is to hold the club in the left hand and grasp your left arm just above the elbow with your right hand. Now swing your club with your left arm and feel the arm being very definitely restricted and folded into the body as the club goes through. The upper arm stays into the side. If you then try it without the right hand assisting, you should feel the left arm

very definitely folding away just like the right one does in the backswing. Start in this simple way and then feel the same type of action when you put both hands on the club. By the end of the swing the left arm should really move into a right angle, with the elbow more or less in front of you and pointing downwards. It definitely doesn't stay straight and break outwards. If you look at a lot of the world's great players with this thought in mind, you will see this very definite fold-up,

1

2

5

6

7

much later than it feels, but without any extension out towards the target.

By contrast, the club golfer often tries to hold the left arm firm beyond impact, believing this is what the professional does. Often golfers believe a major fault is for the left arm to bend beyond impact. What they are seeing in photos or videos of themselves is invariably the arm folding the wrong way, buckling out instead of folding in. Upper arm should stay in, elbow downwards to correct this fold-away.

There are several exercises you can use to develop this feeling. One I use as a definite drill to pull in the elbow is to use a loop of surgical rubber, round my waist and left arm at the elbow. The elastic has just sufficient give to allow me to make a good backswing, but I then feel the resistance pulling the upper arm and elbow in through and beyond impact.

Try as another routine trapping a head-cover or small towel between the left upper arm and the chest, trying to hold it there in the throughswing. Once you can do this, extend the exercise further to trap a towel across your chest and under both upper arms. Swing with this trapped-in position to feel the arms folding and being pulled in, particularly again stressing the left one folding while working at speed beyond impact. The backswing may feel slightly restricted, but the feeling in the left arm is gradually developed.

Last, an exercise to ensure that you do get freedom beyond impact. If you look at any club you should see a label 4 or 5 inches down the shaft from the grip. Practise swinging the club and landing the label on that shaft on your left shoulder. Try staying looking down at the ground as you swing through and really ensure that the shaft of the club gets right round behind your neck until you see it in the finish almost pointing down at the imaginary ball. If

3

8

4

9

10

you keep the left arm too straight you will find the shaft of the club misses the shoulder. The fold-away isn't sufficient.

Once you learn to fold the arm away properly, the right hand and arm can hit through without the right shoulder being pulled down or round.

Perfecting the power whip

Our next stage is to look more specifically at the way in which the arms work so that you can really see how the club face squares up through impact. When done correctly, through arm rotation, the feeling of squaring up the club face begins to happen quite naturally.

There are two ways in which we can generate power and leverage through impact. We have two points from which a powerful hinge can take place. The first is from the wrists and the second is from the elbows. If you feel that you play golf with the left arm staying straight and extending through impact, the hinge and hit has to come from the hands and wrists. The feeling will then be of the wrists and hands having to work fast and furiously to square up the club face, on the end of fairly straight arms. This feeling can move the club face rapidly from open to closed with potentially erratic results. To test this, hold the club in your left hand and while keeping the arm straight and fairly still swish the club through with the wrist. Players who have an idea of hitting against a firm left arm through impact, hitting and stopping beyond impact, are in danger of the wrists flicking through, often closing the club face in a search for power.

The second way of producing a power whip is to use arm rotation, bringing the club through with firmish wrists, worked from a hinging and rotation from the elbows – almost a whipping through, with the left elbow in particular feeling as though it stays close into the waist. Now the radius of the whip does not just come from the wrists, but from the left elbow. The radius is longer, with the club face moving in a far more predictable manner, staying square more easily. Again let's emphasize that feel and appearance on the high-speed camera don't always match. Thoughts move

1

2

6

7

Working at arm rotation, mirroring the movements exactly in backswing and throughswing and allowing the arms to turn over, left going back and right coming through

3

4

5

8

9

10

ahead of what shows up as happening.

Crucial in getting this feeling of a power whip from the left elbow is to allow the arms to rotate, backswing and throughswing matching. To see the rotation, swing your arms back into a golfing position without a club in your hands. You can either do this with your hands simply 6 inches apart, or try it by holding a small football in your hands. The aim is to get the arms mirroring that position exactly in the throughswing. Now as you swing through the left arm is going to fold and turn downwards while the right arm comes over, again into angles roughly 45 degrees to horizontal. Look at the series of illustrations and you will see how the pictures match. The left hand is almost in a tray-carrying position, palm of the hand virtually upwards while the right arm follows this. It is this position which the club player very rarely achieves, but which has to go with the correct feeling in the back-swing. What I want you to do is practise this over and over again, keeping the palms separated by about

An excellent exercise without the club for feeling the correct plane and arm rotation of the swing. With the backs of the hands together in this way, the arms are almost forced to turn and fold. Frames 4 and 5 also show the feeling in key 4, lowering the plane of the left arm and in turn the swing through the change of directions

1

2

3

5

6

7

4

6 inches but just getting the feeling of the arms turning. As you do this, relate it to your golf swing by simply turning your body and following with your eyes the way your hands work. Let yourself turn and move freely, feeling your weight turn onto your right heel and through onto the left heel. But get the arms working, seeing how the two halves of the swing must mirror each other to keep the swing moving on plane. You can see how close the left elbow has to stay to your body and your hip as you turn on through. There is no question at all of the arm staying straight or breaking out. It literally does turn and fold away. Try the movements with a small tray to produce the correct feeling. First of all hold the tray supported with your right hand, up by your right ear, the elbow a right angle and the wrist a right angle. Now hold the tray on the left hand in exactly the same way and feel those two similar right angles. If you are somebody who plays golf bending the ball away to the right, the odds are that you will never have experienced this kind of feeling at the end of your golf swing. But that is what we are going to learn.

Let's try and get the same feeling with a golf club in your hands. You are going to feel a precise mirroring of

backswing and throughswing. You have learnt to set the right wrist on the backswing and to fold away the right elbow. Now you are going to do precisely the same with the left arm as it goes through. Start with the club head 10 or 12 inches off the ground, which should give you the feeling of a fairly flattish turn. Swing back and allow the right arm to fold away; swing through and allow the left arm to fold and turn away. Now gradually lower the club head to the ground and keep on doing the same thing until you can begin to feel the club brush the ground. In many ways the longer the club you use, the easier it is going to be, so perhaps experiment first with a 4-wood and then take it down a stage to a 6-iron. Although we are going to look at the delivery into the ball as a right-handed action, we still have to do a lot of work on the left arm. By the time you have tried to generate speed with this action you should be feeling that you actually whip the left arm through, almost pivoting it from the left elbow. The elbow feels as though it stays tucked in as the lower arm and wrist whips through.

To feel this, imagine yourself holding a table-tennis bat with your left hand and trying to whip a little left-handed backhand shot over the net.

8

9

10

You can see how the elbow would virtually stay motionless while the forearm would whip the bat over. That is just the same sort of sensation you are going to get at the bottom of the swing. The left upper arm stays pretty close to the body as you go on through, with the elbows staying in and the forearm and wrist beginning to whip. Whenever you hear a good player saying that there is no conscious hand action through impact, or that the hands are fairly passive, you can be sure that the length to his shots is generated from this power whip from the elbow.

Now as you try this with the golf ball, just keep experimenting with it until you begin to feel that the club face starts squaring up through impact, and the throughswing matches backswing.

Now a couple of words of warning. We have talked all the time about turning well in the backswing and making sure that the club head comes behind you with a backward setting of the wrists. You must attack the ball from the inside in what feels to be the same kind of curve as you took the club back on. It won't be identical but it needs to feel it is. Your feeling should then be of getting the club head through with the arms turning and never with any feeling of the right shoulder forcing the club through. It is an arm rotation that we are working at. You also need to understand that the feet have to work and that your legs should turn through, so that by the time you finish the swing your hips are going to be facing the target. Don't let it become a flat-footed kind of action where emphasis is put on arms and shoulders alone.

KEY 6 – POWERFUL LEGWORK

TURN THE LEGS – DON'T SLIDE THEM.
CONTAIN THE TURN.

The leg action I am going to advocate may well be very different from your usual movements. Players have been doing two things which I don't believe are truly compatible. They have tried to play the ball too far forward in the feet, opposite the left heel, while at the same time trying to attack the ball from the inside. This has required a distinct

slide to the left through impact, a tipping of the hips off their natural plane and a bowing out of the left leg into impact. My feeling of the correct leg action is that it is certainly powerful, but that it is a circular turn – with no sideways movement either back or through – the turn being fully contained within the width of my stance.

The odds are you may have thought of the leg action as some kind of powerful kicking or thrusting, possibly actually bowing the left leg out through impact, moving onto the outside of the left foot in the throughswing and kicking in sharply with the right knee to generate power. All of this probably gave you the feeling of a lateral movement to the left, to bring the bottom of the swing down somewhere opposite your left foot and give you the impression of the legs driving through to create power. In doing this, it is likely that your left leg has been bent at the end of the swing in a position which is probably far from stable or powerful. This type of leg action tends to go with a high, straight back-and-through backswing which I believe most of the world's top players now see causes problems.

Completed footwork and balance, through onto the left heel and the big toe of the right foot. The left leg twists, and the toes of the left foot are free

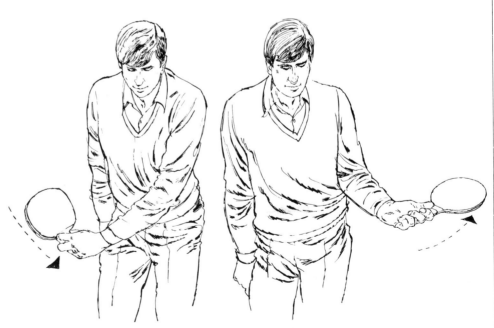

With a correct power whip from the left elbow, independent wrist action is kept to a minimum. The feeling is like a little left hand backhand top spin shot with a table tennis bat

Developing the leg action

The leg action should be seen as one of a natural turn, keeping your head, neck and spine as the centre of the whole rotation whilst simply feeling your hips turn both back and through.

At the address position your weight should be on the balls of both feet. The position feels springy and lively and ready for action. It should also feel powerful and balanced. We have dealt with the leg work in the backswing in Key 2. As you take the club back your body turns. The weight is transferred as though you are standing on a circle. Weight is simply transferred slightly round into the right heel and into the ball of the left foot. Now we feel the resistance of the right knee and the creation of the power coil against the knees. There is a feeling of weight being down and through the right knee, as though the turn pivots from it rather than from the foot itself.

We have then seen how the downswing is started by a movement of the left side away from the right side. Feel now that the left knee and left hip are pulled back behind you, the weight now transferring backwards from the ball of the left foot towards the heel. The right leg is gradually pulled through – with emphasis on pulling and not thrusting – so that the right foot spins through onto the big toe by the end of the swing. There is very definitely no lateral movement to the left and very definitely no movement out onto the outside of the foot. By the end of the swing the weight should be balanced on two points, namely the heel of the left foot and the big toe of the right foot. The left leg should be straight though not locked, and the feeling should be one of balance and stability.

The right knee does not kick in through impact; it gets pulled on through. The left knee does not bow out but pulls straight back.

In the finish of the swing we have to find perfect balance. As you look straight on at the player the balance should be pretty obvious. The weight is going to be balanced somewhere between the left foot and the toes of the right foot, my feeling being of the weight almost entirely on the left.

But if we view the player from the direction of his target, we should see that there are two very definite points of balance, the left heel and the right toes. The left leg should be straight but not extended upwards. The feeling should be of sinking onto a straight left leg so that the heel is definitely the point of balance. The toes of the left foot should almost ease slightly off the ground, but with no feeling of the weight going onto the outside of the foot.

If you work the legs correctly in this way, the head should be able to stay absolutely still and your impact position from a flat lie with a medium iron should be roughly 3 inches or so inside the left heel, not out towards the left foot.

Vital in getting this natural leg turn is to hold the hips high enough at address. The posture, even for a player of my height, has to feel one of standing tall. The legs feel relaxed, knees flexed a touch, but hips high with no sitting. Bent legs aren't relaxed legs; they soon become very tense and, most important here, if predominantly bent will lower the hips and fail to give the left leg the space it needs to turn on through. If the legs are too bent at address, particularly if this is combined with having the ball too far forward in the stance, they will bend through impact with the hips failing to clear on through. Feel the legs straightish but relaxed, bottom out. Stick it out. Much better than sagging and losing the necessary space for good leg action.

As an exercise, hold a club behind your neck and turn to the familiar power coil, setting up resistance in the knees. Now simply turn and pull the left knee and left hip back behind you, keeping the leg action contained within the width of the feet throughout, lower back straight. Try the same exercise with your hands in your pockets rather than above your shoulders. Stand with the side of your left foot against a wall and feel that you can turn back and then turn through, having space to move the left hip freely past the wall without your knee or hip moving out into it. The feeling back and through is just of the right side moving back; then the left side moves back. There is no feeling of any sideways movement other than the initial leg separation for the advanced player.

Often the club golfer will need, in addition, to exercise the left leg so that it can do the correct thing. At address, the left foot is turned out just a little – perhaps 10 degrees. By the time you finish the swing the left foot is going to be in the same position, but you are going to turn your hips through to face the target. Very often players find it difficult to get this kind of twisting in the leg. Practise the movement by holding the side of a table or something at waist height and just feeling your twist in the left leg, letting the right foot move freely onto the toes. If you don't get the twist in the leg, at impact and beyond you may well leave the weight on the ball of the left foot instead of transferring it back to the heel, wrongly finishing with the left leg bowing out. The hips, in turn, are likely to face out to the right, often causing shots which push to the right or are possibly dragged away to the left. The left leg may need some exercising to give it freedom to work properly.

This good leg action is linked to the plane of the swing, giving you an ideal contact with a medium iron well inside your left heel. Particularly when you move on to the fairway wood and driver, you should find you can get a much better squeezing kind of attack without any tendency to shift to the left and chop down on the ball.

The leg action was developed further, looking at leg separation, as one of the most advanced moves in Key 4. Suffice at this time to say that the feeling from the top of the backswing is of almost leaving the right leg where it is, while beginning to shift the left leg and left knee a touch before the right. It really amounts to the leg action becoming a left-sided turning away rather than a right-sided pushing and thrusting.

Legwork and balance

Right from the setup we aimed at getting the weight on the balls of the feet for a feeling of springiness and liveliness. But we also want to generate power and we want to keep perfect balance throughout. Most golfers who think they swing too fast are usually guilty of losing balance. They let the weight fall forwards towards the ball. They don't so much sway from

1

This shows the exercise for powerful legwork. From the power coil position, shoulders and hips turned against the resistance of the knees, the legs simply turn on through on the same plane. The left leg pulls back behind me, no bowing out of the leg, and all fully contained within the width of the stance. The leg action is circular ; in the backswing round onto the right heel and the ball of the left foot. In the through-swing the transference is back into the left heel, forward onto the ball and then the toes of the right. The knee action 'criss-crosses', left knee pulled to the point behind the imaginary ball, right pulled on through ahead of it

2

3

4

side to side, as come forwards onto it. Remember that from the top of the backswing the weight is pushed back from the ball of the left foot into the heel and in turn the left knee and the left hip turn out of the way. By the time you reach the end of the swing you should be balanced on the left heel and the big toe of the right foot. If anything the toes of the left foot will feel free and when viewed from the direction of the target the body should be centred over the left heel. The club player tends to turn in the backswing and get the weight coming forward onto the ball of the left foot, but then never get it back onto the heel. As he comes into the shot the right knee probably kicks in so that somewhere through impact the weight gets too much on the balls of both feet, to the point where the player is almost falling onto the ball. Frequently he finishes in what looks like a relatively balanced position but where the weight remains on the ball of the left foot, left knee bent, hips facing out to the right. He doesn't realize he is off balance, but usually only holds the follow-through for a split second before taking a step forward with the right foot to steady himself.

I want you to learn this really good leg work and to learn perfect balance. When you look at most tournament professionals you will see that we swing the club with tremendous speed

and it finishes somewhere through towards our neck or left shoulder. Very often under pressure or in bad weather conditions we then strive as hard as possible to hold the balance at the end of the swing, even to the point where the shaft of the club stays in position at the finish. More commonly however, because of the speed of the club, there is a kind of recoil where the arms and club are brought back down in front of the body almost immediately the swing has finished. The club player shouldn't do this. Hold the end of the finish, with the club stationary on your shoulder, or virtually on your shoulder for a good three seconds. Count it through – one ... two ... three. If you can't hold the balance, ask yourself why. Are you on your left heel and is your left leg round with the hip out of the way?

For the really good player you may well need a recoil. You may need the club shaft to be brought back off your shoulder, but what you must do, and I cannot emphasize this enough, is to recoil correctly. As you recoil you must watch the ball to the end of its flight with the legs turned through facing the target and the weight really pulled back onto the left heel and perfectly balanced. Keep the legs motionless to the end of the shot. Remember that if the professional does spring away from a shot early, it is usually because he is so excited at its result that he wants to get after it. If you see the club player move away from the end of the swing it is usually because he hasn't completed the throughswing and isn't balanced.

KEY 7 – HITTING WITH THE RIGHT HAND

Once the club golfer has learned to turn powerfully, bringing the club behind himself and setting the wrists, he is in a position to hit hard with the right hand. He can achieve whatever release he needs to throw the club head into the ball to square up the club face. For him this counteracts a slice. The rest of this section is advanced and for the good golfer with the opposite problem of a tendency to hook.

Most good golfers are prone, if anything, to hooking. Very often this occurs not so much because the right hand is dominant but because the right hand doesn't work in the correct way. Again, I think there is often too much emphasis placed on the left arm being kept straight through impact. This tends to produce an action where the arms stay fairly firm and the wrists release with a kind of throwing action through impact, which closes the club face. The exercise of hitting and stopping on a straight left arm often aggravates this problem of the wrists flicking and rolling. Instead, the arms should turn, left arm folding in, with no independent rolling or throwing from the wrists. Often the advice is to weaken the grip, which in other words turns the left hand unsatisfactorily far round to the left, combined with the feeling of a dominant left arm which guides and pulls the club through impact. Although this is what happens, the *feeling*, particularly for the advanced player, is of resisting the release of the right wrist set all the way. It will release, but feel you're hanging on to it from the top of the backswing right through impact. Feel you hit with the right forearm leading the hands through, rather than the hands catching up. Move everything faster than the hands. Inevitably some release does happen by impact, but resist it. Then feel you increase the wrist set again through to the finish. It gives the impression that the right hand has to

be relatively passive. Indeed if the left hand grip is too weak, the right hand does have to be passive. The left hand offers no resistance for the right hand to work against. Weakening the left hand can aggravate a hook, not cure it. If the right hand can be made to work correctly it can give you extra length and probably produce a better feeling for squaring the club face up through impact, while giving the necessary finesse for the short game.

To be able to use the right hand correctly the arms need to work properly, combining arm rotation with a power whip from the left elbow. There has to be a definite turning and folding of the left arm. By all means, practise with the left arm to strengthen it, but never with the idea of keeping the left arm straight through impact. Nor should the feeling be of flicking the club head through with the wrists. What it should be for the advanced player is far more a feeling of turning from the left elbow rather than from the hands and wrists. If you whip the club through from the wrists the radius of the swing is, in effect, the length of the club shaft. If you whip through from the left elbow, then the radius of the swing is the left forearm and club shaft. The feeling at first may be of the throughswing being narrow, but in fact it is just the reverse. The wrists can stay relatively passive through impact and now need no hinging because it all comes from the left elbow.

With that under control, you need to be able to use the right hand. Many good golfers are naturally left-handed. Many others work at strengthening the left hand. There is no doubt that the world's top players have well developed left arms, hands and wrists and, I suppose, in terms of strength are probably far more ambidextrous than most people. But having said that, it is the right hand I am going to teach you to use.

The first stage for this was learning to set the right wrist back fairly early from address. At address there is a very slight cupping in the back of the right wrist. The wrist then hinges back as we have seen; by the time the back swing is completed the right wrist is fully set and fairly well under the club.

As you change directions in the downswing, the right wrist stays set

This is all part of the tournament players' swing, recoiling from a powerful follow-through with the arms, but keeping the legs motionless to the end of the shot

back on itself while the arm action drops down, bringing the hand into a position at roughly hip height, where it is behind the shaft of the club. From here the right hand can deliver a ferocious blow out at the golf ball, never straightening and flicking through, but simply returning to its very slightly set position set at address. Indeed, at address both hands showed a very slight angle in the back of the wrist. The action is of returning the hands into this position,

never allowing the left wrist to bend back on itself through impact, but instead ensuring that the left elbow stays against the side, the body turns through and the whole unit of forearms and wrists now moves through together. Beyond impact the action is of the wrists staying in this pre-set position, if anything, of the right hand bending back on itself again in the movement beyond impact.

Let's look at the illustrations to see exactly how the right hand works stage by stage in the swing.

It starts with a slight setting at address. It then hinges backwards almost simultaneously with the turn of the body in the takeaway. It is now fully hinged back. As the turn and movement of the arms continue, it stays hinged backwards to the top of the backswing. The arms then pull down and it stays hinged backwards in virtually a right angle. It then returns to its slightly set position, repeating address almost exactly in the impact position. As it moves through it stays set, elbows feeling as though they stay in contact with the body. By the end of the swing the wrist increases the slight setting it had at impact. In reality, the left wrist does move back on itself at the very end of the swing, but never to

The right hand is slightly set at address, wrist not entirely flat. It then hinges directly back against the forearm quite rapidly, holding this to the top of the backswing, right hand now feeling to be under the club. With the hand coming into the hitting area the wrist is still set back, the club head well

behind the hand. From here it can hit hard, releasing back into its address position, but resisting any release all the way. It resists straightening out, holding the club face square, from there moving through the ball and up, the wrist holding its set and then setting more by the finish

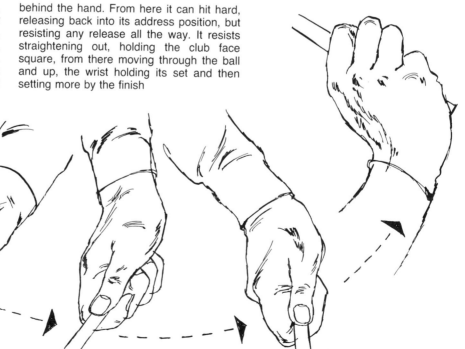

the point where the right wrist will fully straighten.

The feeling for the good player in using the right hand is one I would describe as 'holding the club off through impact'. In other words, there is a concentrated feeling of holding it square to the target for a few inches beyond impact. From there it is as though the body turns away behind me to the left and by doing this the club is brought into a toe-up position in the throughswing. The toe-up position is not produced by a rolling over of the wrists, but by this feeling of working the whole of the forearms and club through as a unit, as though from the left elbow. The feeling is as though the club face is brought back with the right hand into its address position and then held square and almost worked upwards for a moment beyond the ball.

To be able to use the power of the right hand you have to use it correctly. Again it is a question of pull and resistance. This time you pull fast and furiously with the left side of the body. The right hand works hard to resist the club head pulling it through and straightening out in the impact zone. For the good golfer, the left side must pull on through. If the left side stops, the hands take over. You set the right wrist in the backswing. You then release it into the slightly set position it had at address by impact. From there you don't feel any more hand action. You try to make the left side move fast beyond impact to pull the arms and hands through. It *feels* as though the upper arms and elbows stay in tight, with the left shoulder and whole left side trying to move as fast as hands and club head. They can't, but everything feels as though it turns through as a unit, right wrist staying in position. Having felt this turn through as a unit, arms rotating, toe of the club upwards, the feeling is of the club head then working on upwards, the setting of the right wrist increasing, and both wrists showing some cupping by the finish. This in effect mirrors the round and up feeling of the backswing, to give a round and up feeling to the throughswing.

Right from address my very strong feeling is of the palm of the hand and the club face being perfectly aligned.

I feel that the right hand really does hold the club face square through impact. Whatever I feel with the palm of the right hand is also happening to the club face. If I feel I want the club face held a touch open, the hand simply makes the movement I want the club face to do. If it feels as though it stays a fraction open; the club face will stay a fraction open.

Drawing the ball

What I also want to be able to do is to draw the ball, moving it just a touch from right to left, without feeling there is any danger of it becoming a hook. Let me explain for the good golfer how to draw the ball. In reality, you have to set the direction of the swing and club face very slightly at odds with each other, the direction of swing and club face converging. In other words, we have a slightly closed relationship. The dangerous way of drawing a ball, but the way in which most people try to draw, is by feeling the club face

The advanced way of drawing a ball (top), attacking it from the inside, club face on target before impact, wrists passive. The easier but less accurate way of drawing the ball (bottom), club face turning through impact, requiring more independent hand and wrist action through impact

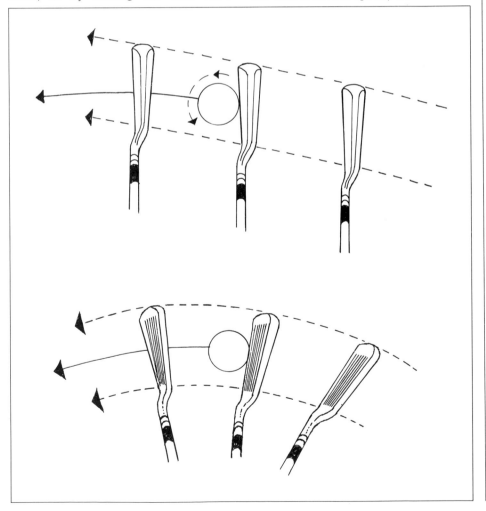

closing through impact, by allowing the hands and wrists to roll slightly through impact. The advice is often to attack the ball slightly from the inside, which means, in other words, that you are going to start the ball slightly right of target, allowing the right hand to roll over and close the club face. This, in effect, is dangerous because the club face comes possibly from a slightly open position into a very closed position beyond impact. The wrists move independently on the ends of the arms, instead of arms and wrists turning and rotating as a unit. This is the action for a pronounced hook, but unsuitable for a controlled draw.

The other way of drawing the ball, and the one which is a true draw and a correct action for a good player, is to produce a slightly closed relationship through impact without any independent wrist roll. The feeling should be simply of putting sidespin on the ball by feeling as though the club face looks on target fractionally before impact, moving that square club face from in to out across the back of the ball, so that sidespin is delivered while the club face actually looks on target throughout. Top-class players who draw the ball as a rule do this. In effect, they aim the club face where they want the ball to finish, i.e. at the target, and move the swing on a slightly in-to-out path, in other words, in the direction in which they want the ball to start. This is the way the advanced player should be able to draw the ball, taking all independent wrist movement out of the action, producing this slight sidespin without any wrist roll, wrist flick or feeling of closing the club face. It is certainly the better and safer action of the two, moving the ball just a few feet from right to left, perhaps where extra run is wanted or the contour of the green invites this approach.

Once you have used the right hand correctly, you should be able to feel the ball held perfectly straight, the club face held slightly open or a slight draw-spin put on the ball without any change of grip and without any feeling of wrist action through impact other than the right wrist returning to its address position.

But do remember that in order to use the right hand properly the action beyond impact must be correct. The arms must rotate. The left arm must fold away for a power whip from it rather than the wrists. The legs must turn through, left side leading and right side following, trying to feel as though the left side tugs and turns away as fast if not faster than the arms are moving. Remember, too, that the right side of the body is potentially destructive at the top of the backswing. You must learn to hold it back. Resist for a moment while the left side moves away from it, giving time for the right arm and right hand to be dropped into the position from which the right hand can be used to its fullest.

Through the bag

THE SAME SWING will stand you in good stead from the driver to full pitching wedge. The basics stay the same, but the clubs will feel and react differently, mainly because of the range of lengths of shaft and lies to the clubs. Your pitching wedge sits completely differently from your driver and this dictates the kind of swing you make. Here are some key thoughts to take you through the full set of clubs.

THE BALL POSITION

At this point I want to talk more about the ball position. Good golfers will vary the ball position quite considerably, not just for the different clubs but far more based on the kind of contact needed. The 6-iron from a good lie should have given you confidence and helped bring out the best in your swing. I suggested adopting a ball position roughly 3 or 4 inches inside your left heel. I also explained why tournament professionals have in the past advocated playing everything up towards the left heel. They have used a kind of lateral leg work with a pronounced movement to the left, bringing the bottom of the swing opposite the left heel or the left instep. If you have followed my explanation of a simple turning leg work you will see that the bottom of the swing is going to fall further back to the point I suggest. With the ball sitting reasonably well for a medium iron this is the point where you are going to strike the ball. The ideal contact for a medium iron is to strike the ball with a very small divot, nipping out a piece of grass starting directly under the ball and going through a couple of inches beyond it. The divot should be shallow with no feeling of chopping down and digging out great clods of earth.

Hopefully this ball position will give

1

2

6

7

The short iron still has to be an aggressive shot. I want to pitch the ball all the way to the flag, getting it to stop quickly. My approach is to fade the ball a touch. I want a shot which to the spectator will look straight and yet feels to have cutspin, moving at the most 5 feet in the air. I don't open up with the shorter irons. In fact I stand squarer to the target than with a longer shot; the degree of cut from left to right is less. I obviously allow less for it.

I still want a full turn and an aggressive swing. Bad shots with short irons come from dollying the thing instead of being positive. If you mis-hit it the loss of distance is substantial. The contact needs to be really crisp. The good golfer always needs a full turn with short irons. The arms and club may move back slightly shorter, but the body must coil. A short shot doesn't mean a short turn. If the turn is incomplete the tendency is to drag the ball left. My

feeling is of turning well, attacking the ball from the inside – in relation to the direction I want to start it on – being comparatively slow off the right foot through impact, and just holding the club face off a touch to cut the ball in for an aggressive, biting shot

3

4

5

8

9

10

you the feeling of a perfect strike – a very slightly downward attack with the ball and divot. The ball position giving you a good contact should also be the one helping you to hit the ball on line. Sometimes you find a player who will get a really good strike from one particular ball position and yet get superb direction to the swing in a slightly different position. It is then a question of marrying the two together. For example, playing the ball a little further back can help you attack the ball well from the inside but may give you too much of a downward attack. Playing the ball a little further forward may be the point at which you strike the ball well but may see the swing going a little left of target. The two have to be brought together to find the ideal ball position.

There are various thoughts and ideas on teaching the ball position. Let's first get away from this idea of playing everything off the left heel. Even when top players say this is what they do, they don't. They have to vary the ball position if the lie is poor and vary it too when they move up to the shorter irons. Other professionals will talk in terms of playing, for example, the 2-iron opposite the left heel and then graduating everything back by, say, ¾ inch to finish up with the 9-iron played opposite the middle of the stance. This again is too precise. Getting the right ball position is fairly subjective and is a combination of the club you are using and the lie.

For the club golfer, an explanation about lie and contact. Let's take four lies of progressive difficulty. The first is where the ball sits up on a tuft of grass. The contact is easy and judgement need not be particularly precise. Clip the ball away with grass but no earth. Reduce the cushion of grass to ¼ inch and the contact remains fairly easy, taking the grass and just grazing the ground beyond the ball. The third type of lie is the really tight one, the whole ball above the ground but with no grass at all. Judgement has to be very exact, with a slightly more downward strike, and more definite divot beyond the ball. Last is the most difficult lie, with the ball in a slight depression. Some of the ball is lost below ground level. Once more the contact needs to be more downward,

1

2

6

7

With the 9-iron the ball is again positioned 3 to 4 inches inside the left heel. My only change in technique from the medium irons is a very slight shortening of the backswing, still swinging through to a full finish. I still make the same fully coiled turn with the body, the length of arm swing reduced a touch

3

4

5

8

9

10

increasing again the size of divot. Progressively as the lie gets worse you need a more downward attack and may need the ball further back to encourage this.

With a standard 6-iron shot from a reasonably good lie I suggested playing the ball about 3 inches inside the left heel. The better the lie the further forward you can play the ball, to the point where with a driver you meet the ball on the upswing and so beyond the natural bottom of your swing. As the lie gets worse you move the ball back in the stance to ensure a slightly downward attack. With a really difficult lie, such as a down slope or a bare lie, you move the ball back even further. You move it forward and you move it back, whether you have a 6-iron in your hand or a 9-iron. Much the same follows with a 3-wood. If the ball sits well you can play it forward and if the ball sits badly you can play it back.

Not only must we relate ball position to contact, but also to direction. If you play the ball further forward towards your left foot, the swing may have started travelling a little left of target by the moment of impact, as a rule causing a slice or pull. When you play the ball forward with a driver you have to ensure that the attack is still on line. Conversely if you move the ball back in the feet for a downward attack the club may be travelling out to the right of target at the point of impact. For this reason when you play short irons or recovery shots from a point back in the feet you may have to offset this and aim the line of the feet slightly left of target.

Understand this principle of the ball position and realize that we cannot make hard-and-fast rules about it. Tournament professionals and low-handicap players usually vary the ball position quite instinctively. Club players often address the ball in one set place and don't understand why changes need to be made.

THE SHORT IRONS

Most of what I have said about the golf swing holds true for the short irons. For most players short irons are the easiest clubs to hit well. You will probably be able to get a really good attack with an 8- or 9-iron. The club face has lots of loft which means that it doesn't impart as much sidespin as a longer club. On the whole you can probably hit the short irons straight even if you notice a bending to right or left when you get on to the longer clubs.

There are three main points I want to make, however, about the short irons. The shafts of the clubs are obviously shorter and the lie of the club is more upright. This means that you are going to stand closer to the ball and swing the club on a more upright plane than with a 6-iron or the longer clubs. If you are trying to flatten the plane of your swing as I have advocated, these clubs will bring out the very worst in your swing. If you are someone who swings the club very much up and down then these certainly aren't the clubs to practise with.

Second, a word of warning for the tall player. The short irons may seem difficult because the shafts simply feel too short. The player is often brought too much over the ball, again with the

This sequence with the 9-iron shows just how close to the ball a tall golfer is going to stand, bottom out, arms hanging vertically and still with a definite feeling of standing tall. Frame 2 also shows quite clearly the same inside takeaway and curved nature of the swing to encourage the same feeling to the plane of the swing as with the longer clubs. There is still no feeling of swinging the club up and down on a straight path

1

2

6

7

consequence of producing too steep a swing and too much tip and tilt in the shoulder action. It is essential to stand sufficiently close to the ball and yet keep bottom and hips out and up to give space to turn away on the inside. Don't stand out and away from the ball, bending the knees and drooping in the back. Your feeling should still be one of standing up tall but now having the feet in close to the ball. Keep the feeling of an inside takeaway and an inside attack on the ball, never letting it become a straight up-and-down swing. Keep the right hip and thigh back to give space. Don't let hands and right thigh have to fight with each other for position. Obviously the plane is different from a long iron but try and relate the two as closely as you can and don't fall into the trap of excessive crouching. On the question of equipment the tall player should look carefully at the length of his irons, with ¼ inch between adjacent clubs from 7-iron to sand wedge rather than the ½ inch gap often advocated.

3

4

5

8

9

10

FOR THE
ADVANCED
PLAYER

The Long Irons

With the 3-iron my swing thoughts are identical to the 6-iron, but with emphasis on tempo, ensuring that the backswing is completed, squeezing the ball away and then driving on through to a full finish.

Good tempo is the key, particularly for the aspiring tournament player using a 2-iron or 1-iron. Players tend to press for distance, often trying to use a 1-iron when they should be using a wood. They are afraid of it and rush it. You want smoothness and tempo, completing the swing. To develop good long irons trick yourself into good timing. Hit some practice shots with a 9-iron and then, having felt the divot and timing, pick up the 2-iron and hit two or three without changing anything. Not too many, and then revert to the shorter club.

I also think you have to be realistic about length – again I am addressing the tournament player. My best distances for carrying the ball in good, thin-air conditions are 180 yards with a 5-iron, 190 the 4-iron, 200 the 3-iron and 210 yards the 2-iron. Even for a world-class golfer it is hard to get this 10-yard difference right through. My 1-iron will carry 215 yards; 220 would be really pushing it. As with most tournament professionals I very rarely carry a 4-wood; almost always the 3-wood, and that I hope to hit 230 yards. The danger can be this gap between the carry of the 1-iron and the 3-wood. You have to learn to fill the gap with wood shots – landing them softly, cutting down length. Possibly horrid feeling shots, but cover the gap with the wood and *not* by trying to force the 2- or 1-iron to play an unrealistic shot.

You have to know the precise lengths of the long irons as you would the medium irons. Don't assume this 10-yard gap right through when it doesn't happen. You need to experiment with the kind of divot you want. Feel the contact. Work for example

1

My thoughts with this 3-iron are on tempo and a good contact. This sequence demonstrates my thoughts on the plane and on reversing the swing. Look first at the angle of the club in frame 1. This angle and plane shows again in the angle of the club in frames 4, 5, 9 and 15. Everything moves on plane. See too the angle of the left arm in frame 7, parallel to the club shaft at address. Frame 8 shows the tournament player my feelings in the change of directions, a definite lowering of the plane and left arm, and the tucking in and forward of the right elbow

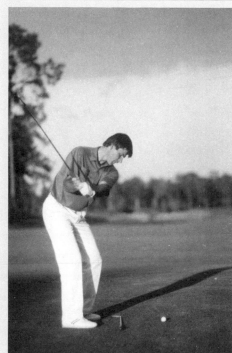

2

3

4

5

6

7

with a 2-iron from a tee peg. See how far it goes (through the air) and then try one with a medium divot and a slightly deeper one. See how the ball flies and measure it with new golf balls. My longest is when I squeeze it away with a little divot from tightish

lies. It isn't deep, but shallow and pear-shaped. It starts thin and then widens out 2 to 3 inches beyond the ball to about the thickness of the blade. Work at it deeper or shallower and compare the results.

The 1-iron has to be a utility club for

the tournament professional, just as any other iron. You need different contacts and different flights. My 1-iron generally lands and stops quite quickly. Sometimes you need to run one in, chasing it up the length of a long, narrow green. Another time, you

8

9

10

12

13

14

want it flying in high and, as Lee Trevino terms it, 'landing like a butterfly with sore feet'! It is all in the contact. Practise with a 1-iron and just keep hitting it from every conceivable lie and position on the practice ground. Get familiar with it. I developed my long-iron game by playing and using it in practice from every tee – teeing it up or playing it down, making it land softly or letting it run. Try to experiment with the grip. At all costs guard against weakening the left hand. If anything, strengthen it a fraction, to help you to hold the club face square while attacking the ball even harder.

The tournament golfer who can master the 1-iron may not necessarily use it a great deal. But it does breed tremendous confidence with the 3- and 4-irons.

11

15

The short irons: Mr Average

Third, for the beginner and long-handicap player, the short irons can cause problems. You may not strike the ball well. You probably thin the ball by catching it around its middle instead of taking the ball and a divot. If you thin the ball slightly with a medium or long iron the ball goes off slightly low and probably loses length. If you make the same mistake with a short iron and thin the ball, it goes off too low and too far. It is easy then to become tentative and instead of attacking the ball, to swing at it in a half-hearted way, never really finding the bottom of the ball. It is essential for the beginner to understand that you cannot get under a golf ball. You cannot scoop it up and loft it into the air. You have to strike the ball at the bottom of the swing or very slightly on the downswing with an iron shot to get it rising. Hit down and the ball comes up. For the longer-handicap player you need to be very conscious of looking at the back of the ball, possibly playing the ball almost opposite the middle of the stance, ensuring that you get your weight through onto the left foot to produce a downward strike.

In many ways this feeling for the long-handicap player is almost contrary to what I am preaching in the rest of the book. I am trying to get the good golfer away from any feeling of an up-and-down, straight back and through-swing. I want to convince people that the leg action should be a simple turn through without any lateral movement to the left at impact. But for the high handicapper and beginner, there has to be this initial stage of a very definite down-and-through attack on the ball to ensure it really does climb.

THE LONG IRONS

Developing the long irons

All our basic work has been done with a 6-iron. When you move on to the 2-, 3- and 4-irons, you really have to do just the same thing. Ideally the contact will still be with a feeling of striking the ball and taking a little divot beyond it. Most golfers are nervous of the long irons. The heads often seem small, the loft of the club doesn't look very inviting and where you may get away with things with the medium and short irons, you won't with the long irons.

The main advice with the long irons is to try to swing them exactly the same as a 5- or 6-iron. The temptation is to try to force the thing, knowing that the ball has to go another 20 or 30 yards. Let the extra length of shaft and the different trajectory of the shot give you that extra distance. Swing exactly the same and make sure you keep really good tempo. Don't rush the shot in an attempt to hit it harder.

One of the problems with long irons is that most players don't strike them as well as the 6-iron. As a result they may not hit the 3-iron any further than the 4-, and the 4- only marginally further than a 5-; often the trajectory on the shots is too low and therefore doesn't carry the ball well enough. In some cases the set of irons is unsuitable. The manufacturer may produce a fairly strong 5- or 6-iron which gives the player the impression that he hits the ball a long way, but this may in turn mean that the 3- and 4-iron aren't really lofted enough for the average golfer. The professional usually gets plenty of height and needs a club to keep the ball driving forward. His choice will often be for a set of irons with the weight distributed in the middle-back of the club – and with 'tournament' loft. The club golfer is as a rule better with irons with a weight pattern towards the bottom of the club to encourage height with the weight beneath the ball.

I do think you need to be realistic about your own capabilities with the long irons. You may find that you hit your 5-iron 150 yards through the air, can't quite carry 160 yards with a 4-iron, and certainly won't get 170 yards and 180 yards carry out of a 3-iron and 2-iron respectively. You probably get more run on a 4-iron and more run again on a 3-iron. This isn't really what you want for playing good iron shots onto the green. You want carry. It may be a question of having the irons set up slightly differently by your professional to produce a 10-yard difference in carry between shots. Slightly more loft may give you more carry and in fact more length; so too may a more sympathetic weight distribution.

A really good long-iron player will always have tremendous tempo. You have to ensure that you swing the club

With the 3-iron my thoughts are identical to the 6-iron but with emphasis on tempo, ensuring that the backswing is completed and driving on through to a full finish

1

2

6

7

8

all the way back and you have to give yourself time to get the club head right through. There must never be any question of rushing the shot in an attempt to make it go further. Almost have the feeling of swinging slightly more easily if anything and this should give you the timing necessary for really good club head speed.

For the long-handicap player I would suggest leaving the 3- and 4-irons alone until you feel you can use a 5- or 6-iron well. You may get little extra out of the long irons and will probably simply lose confidence and start swinging badly. Gradually learn to use them, first of all perhaps from a

tee on a par 3 and secondly when the ball is sitting up well or particularly when you are playing preferred lies. Keep the ball in the same position as you do with your 6-iron and simply concentrate on nipping the ball away with perfect balance at the end of the swing. The swing is identical but the contact is a little more difficult.

THE FAIRWAY WOODS

Once again we basically use the same swing as with the medium irons. This time we are faced with a longer shaft of club which should if anything help

3

4

5

9

10

sits, squeezing the ball away into the air. The ball is slightly further forward in the feet so that the hands no longer appear ahead of the ball. The swing again must be perfectly timed, ensuring a full turn on the backswing, making sure the swing really is completed and then again going on to a full and balanced follow-through. My thoughts are 'Turn, turn', emphasizing the larger muscles of the shoulders and back with these longer shots.

I also look for a really full setting of the wrists. Players often think wrist action is reduced with woods. I don't. If anything I make a more determined and even earlier set. It keeps everything tighter and more compact. I frequently practise fairway woods with a definite feeling of set and then coil. This seems to pick up power and crispness to the shots. Most tournament professionals only carry a 3- or 4-wood, not both. In my case it is the 3-. I have to make it produce a range of shots from 215 yards to 230 in carry. I feel the swing stays the same but work the club face through as I want it, drilling the ball forward or floating it in. When playing a slightly less than full shot, I hold the club off a touch – a shade more open – to add height and an element of cutspin. It is crucial to keep the wrists firm, without letting them break down and over-release. The last thing you want is the club head passing the hands. You need strong wrists to hold the club back.

to keep the plane of swing going around rather than up and down. Certainly, this is where any player with a very high, straight back and through-swing tends to get into difficulties. He may get by with the short and medium irons, but not with the longer clubs.

You need the feeling of swinging the club round behind you and then mirroring the same plane in the through-swing. With the standard 3-wood shot from a good lie, I play the ball marginally further forward than with the 6-iron, still using a slightly descending blow. The club head is set behind the ball at address and through impact just brushes the grass on which the ball

1

2

3

6

7

8

In this 3-wood sequence we see again the early setting of the wrists (frame 2) leading to a perfect top of the backswing position in frame 4, club now perfectly horizontal and parallel to the line of the shot – note my practice checkpoint with the club set along my feet. Frame 9 shows the left arm folding away – the feeling is of much more fold, earlier than it always appears. As with all long shots the finish is then full, the club settling right behind my neck, balance concentrated on the left heel and toes of the right foot

4

5

As with long irons, the good player needs to develop feel with the fairway woods. We may only hit two or three in a round, even on a championship course. If playing on shorter courses it is all too easy to play round after round, rarely hitting the shot. Again, they need practice – and practice into tight greens. In friendly games drop a ball down on the tee and use a 3-wood, or hit a medium iron from the tee to leave a wood to the green. Don't ignore them. Championship courses often demand good wood shots.

THE CONTACT

The contact on the ball needs understanding; look at two kinds of lie. With a little cushion of grass between the ball and ground I still like a horizontal or even slightly descending blow, just grazing the grass on which it sits. That

9

10

1

2

3

7

8

9

This 3-wood sequence shows my emphasis on a full turn with the large muscles of the shoulders. At the top of the backswing I give myself time to lower the plane of the arms and attack – while the shoulders still appear fully turned. I then squeeze the ball away *en route* to a full, balanced finish

for most people is fairly easy. The second kind of lie is where the ball is tight down to the ground – the sort of lie you get on a seaside course or heathland course in the summer. From a tight lie with an iron shot, the ball should be caught slightly on the down-swing; most low- and medium-handicap golfers have no difficulty with this. With a wood you should still

4

5

6

10

11

12

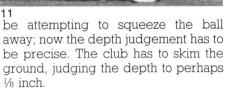

be attempting to squeeze the ball away; now the depth judgement has to be precise. The club has to skim the ground, judging the depth to perhaps ⅛ inch.

For the club golfer this depth judgement isn't always that easy. It is not so much that you brush the ground as that you bounce the club down at the ball. At the point of impact the sole of the club bounces lightly on the ground as its face makes contact with the ball.

From a tight, hard lie always have at least two practice swings with a fairway wood, making quite certain that the club head really does bounce on the ground. All too often I see pro–am partners having a practice swing which isn't correct but they then go ahead and hit the ball. Without becoming slow on the course at least get the practice swing right; think depth. Rather than thinking of the face of the club you may find it helpful to think of its sole. Pick up your fairway wood, turn it upside down and have a look at the sole plate. Visualize this and have a couple of practice swings, getting the sole plate to bounce down and up again. This is a slightly different feeling from hitting an iron shot. With an iron you very definitely pull the face of the club in behind the ball, taking the ball and divot beyond. With the fairway wood you may have to have the feeling of bouncing the club down and almost lifting it off the ground again. You want to get the sole of the club skimming the ground but you don't want to leave it in contact with the ground too long. It's a sharper strike: in and out, rather like striking a match. Do, however, keep the overall concept of the swing as a rounded path and don't let it become an up-and-down action. It is with these shots that the high, steep type of swing can produce difficulties. If the contact is excessively steep you dig into the ground and have difficulty in squeezing the ball away. The more rounded the swing, the shallower the contact, and the easier these shots gradually become.

TEMPO

The same swing thoughts apply as with the long irons. Let the club do the work and don't feel you have to press to get length. The length of the shaft will do it for you if you just trust it and maintain your normal tempo. If anything, almost swing *more* slowly than you might with a medium iron. Give yourself time to get the club head all the way to the top of the backswing and all the way through again. If you rush the swing you are likely to find your body and arms reaching the impact position while the club head trails behind. Time it really well and almost have the feeling of 'waiting for it' for a moment in the change of directions at the top of the backswing. Balance as always is of paramount importance, with emphasis on holding the end of the swing until the ball touches down or even stops rolling. Make a full finish, club on the left shoulder.

Here again let me make mention of 'width' and 'extension'. I have explained how players get into difficulties by trying to keep the club moving away wide on the backswing and by trying to stretch it towards the target on the throughswing. This has led players to delay the wrist cock too long in the backswing and to this dreadful pushing out of the left arm beyond impact. In the fairway woods just as with the irons set the wrists from the moment you take the club back. As long as you make a full turn and keep the left arm swinging back on the inside, reasonably straight but *not* stiff, you will get all the width you need. And in the throughswing again do not try and force the club out towards the target. If the club is swinging on the correct path then all you need do is to turn the arms. Let the left arm fold away and your right arm will naturally give you all the extension you need. Players who swing the club too straight back and too straight through do need a feeling of width back and width through. This is the only way they can keep the club travelling on target; trajectory tends to be high and lack power. With the correct rounded plane of swing this feeling of width is not necessary. Coil to get the club head back on the inside and then set the wrists fully. Think 'low and inside, coil and set'.

DRIVING

People say 'drive for show and putt for dough'. To win a major championship the difference is usually the odd holed putt. But to play good golf, sound driving is absolutely essential. It should in some ways be the easiest part of the game. After all you can tee the ball up the height you like to give maximum chance of a good contact. You can choose a flat piece of ground, can tread down behind the ball and choose whichever side of the tee and view of the hole you prefer. But for many, driving is the most difficult part of the game. One reason is simply that the loft on the driver is less than on any other club. If you impart sidespin to the golf ball with the more lofted clubs, the sidespin isn't as noticeable. The straighter the face of the club the nearer you strike to the equator of the ball and the more readily it takes up sidespin. You may get away with faults with the shorter clubs but can't ignore the sidespin with the driver or possibly even a 2-wood. Don't assume you do something different with a driver; the fault may just show up more. With a driver, you are tackling a difficult club and have to get perfection in the swing and strike for a successful shot. There are, of course, several world-class professionals who very rarely take out a driver and prefer the extra accuracy of the 3-wood and 4-wood or even a 1-iron. But all are able to use the driver when the need arises, unleashing the extra power and length a well-hit drive produces. Club golfers as a rule do better to forget about the driver until their method stands up to its demands. Aspiring tournament golfers need to master it, producing length, ball control and developing a routine for driving to stand up to pressure.

My swing thoughts are basically the same for every club. Remember that the swing plane follows the angle of the club shaft at address. In other words, it becomes even more rounded than with any other club. Simply turn, and turn really fully, setting the right wrist smartly back into its fully cocked position, getting the club round behind you. From there allow yourself to turn on through, releasing the wrist cock back to its address position by impact, arms rotating and folding by the finish.

Forget all those things about taking the club straight back for 18 inches, keeping the backswing wide, looking for a high backswing and high finish. If you think along those lines you are destined to have difficulty with the driver, almost certainly pulling what feel your best shots to the left and cutting the rest of the shots away to the right. We are going to work at the same simple approach of generating power in a circular path.

Let me talk you through my swing thoughts with the driver (see photos overleaf). I tee the ball roughly the thickness of my fingers, getting the height just right and dabbing the club head down a couple of times behind it to check it looks inviting. The ball is positioned roughly opposite my left heel, encouraging a shallow, upward strike. I take real care to keep the line

of hips and shoulders square, right hip and shoulder down and back.

The address position feels very active and ready to go. Particularly if looking for maximum length, everything must stay moving, usually having a free waggle to rehearse the wrist set. I also feel the impact position at address. The right wrist is slightly set already and everything is going to return at speed to this same position – everything identical except hips and legs turning through well past their address position. Just before the take-away I often lift the club head a couple of inches. From this I get the feeling of moving it down as the body coil takes place, encouraging an upward feeling into impact.

The backswing is then a powerful coil of the large back and shoulder muscles, making sure the turn is complete, with the right knee absolutely still. I turn against and almost on the right knee, keeping behind the ball with weight down and through the lower leg. Almost simultaneously with the start of the coil, the wrists are fully set, the right wrist really getting back into its right angle.

The right knee is so important. It stays still on the backswing then on the downswing I pull with the left shoulder and left side against and away from it, freewheeling right on through to the end. As this happens the right wrist releases back to its address position, holding this angle as usual through and beyond impact. Again it releases, but I try to resist the release.

Balance has to be good and solid, leg work as always from a left-side pull, not a right-side thrust. The whole thing must turn through at speed to this really full finish.

All set with the driver

1

2

3

7

8

9

13

14

15

4

5

6

10

11

12

16

17

18

Working the ball

For the good player, picturing the shot is essential. Know precisely where you are aiming and how you want to shape the shot. On tree-lined courses like Wentworth and Sunningdale pinpointing a target is far easier than on seaside championship courses. You have to conjure up a target out of nothing. But it is just as crucial if not more so. Preferably look for something on line *and* length, not on too distant a horizon in case it encourages you to press. Learn to work the ball, not just being content with going for the centre of the fairway but positioning the drive for the best possible second shot.

Practise this ball control when playing for fun. Nominate the shot to your partner, trying to move the ball both right to left and left to right with the same confidence. A tournament golfer who can't do one or the other is never going to get anywhere. There will always be a weakness; have a clear picture of what you are trying to do. If you don't play and practise on championship courses imagine specific obstacles to prepare for tight driving courses. Nominate an imaginary lake down the left, out of bounds down the right or whatever and play accordingly. Scare yourself into good driving!

Do the same on the practice ground. When I feel I am playing well I fade one, draw the next and so on, never hitting them all the same. I don't imagine specific driving holes like some players do but am constantly working to imaginary targets and situations – rehearsal for the pressure of major tournaments. Attempt it. At first it doesn't work, but you have to be prepared for some failures, lost balls, bad scores, on the way to becoming a good driver.

A positive attitude is essential, seeing the shot you want and never the one you want to avoid. If you get a bad picture, walk away and start again.

Learn, also, to position yourself correctly on the tee. Use the whole width of it. In theory, tee up left to aim away from trouble on the left; tee up right to aim away from trouble on the right. But experiment and take care. Experiment with the height of the tee. Teeing it up high should encourage you to stay behind the ball and if anything keep the ball down the left. Tee it lower and

Going for power

At the top of the backswing the left leg pulls to bring the club into reverse. The head stays still, well behind the ball, clearing the whole body through to face the target, right leg being pulled, not pushing, until you free-wheel through to a full, perfectly balanced finish

you may produce a semi-squeezing contact and a ball hanging away to the right.

In particular the tournament golfer needs to learn to cope with trouble down the left, not just by aiming away from it but rather by confidently starting the ball towards it and moving it back again in the air. If you aim right to hit away from it you can finish up standing shut, misaligning stance and club face and hooking it. Experiment with setting off down the left, keeping the left side turning fast and furiously towards the trouble, always feeling it stays ahead of arms and club head. It takes courage at first to aim towards the trouble and then to turn towards it, but it pays off.

1

5

9

The search for power

Everyone wants to hit the ball hard. Firstly, to do this you want a steady head, staying behind the ball and coiling fully against the right knee. But you must forget about hitting on the backswing. Take it back smoothly, without rushing the turn or underturning. Where you should be quicker for a really long drive is in the preparation. Don't spend as long at address. Just keep everything loose and keep everything moving; you won't hit the ball hard from being perfectly stationary. Watch players like Nicklaus, Seve, Tom Watson trying to hit it really hard; they stand up and have one quick, free waggle and they go. Then everything flows. Never try and hit hard on the backswing. Coil up and be even more solid at the top. Then make a full finish, pulling as hard as you can from the right knee with the left shoulder and upper left chest. Then keep going.

The good player who doesn't achieve as much as he should with driving usually doesn't finish well. You have to continue right through to the target at full speed. You must finish facing the target with hips and shoulders. Good players, even professionals and scratch amateurs, often stop through impact with hips and shoulders. The ball may be blocked right or more commonly hooked left as the arms are forced to cross over. Think 'Turn, turn'. Nobody is physically strong enough – even Palmer probably wasn't – to stop the club head going over in this kind of action. The left side must come right through.

Having finished the swing, balance. Get the club right through and hold it there for a couple of seconds. If you do recoil with the arms keep the legs still and facing the target. You should never lose balance. Practise hitting in street shoes or trainers. The better your balance the more speed you can dare generate through impact.

I also feel a key to added power is this slight lift of the club head at address. It helps to keep smoothness away from the ball and to encourage the correct upward strike. Lift it a touch. It gives you a trigger for starting everything back. Just take the club head up to the height where the centre of the face is level with the ball, then make it go down in the takeaway. It encourages an upward attack and finds the bottom of the swing. It also stops any tendency to tip forward with the right shoulder; it keeps it back and down.

Developing your driving

This section is aimed at the handicap golfer, with ideas for developing a good method. Use the right equipment. Avoid anything with too stiff a shaft and don't fall for the ego trip of trying to use a club with too little loft. Remember, the less loft the more sidespin and the more pronounced any fault. Experiment first with a 2-wood, 1½ or driver with at least 12 degrees of loft, but enough depth to allow you to tee the ball up well.

Let's look at the contact you want with the driver. The ball is teed up, I would suggest, about the thickness of your fingers. Aim at striking it on the upswing and never on the downswing. You want to tee the ball high enough for the top of the club head to be just above the middle of the ball. In many ways the higher you can make yourself tee the ball, the more likely you are to hit it well. We want to hit the ball on the upswing and therefore need to position the ball slightly ahead of the natural bottom of the swing, to a point roughly opposite the left heel. The bottom of the swing should still fall in roughly the same place as with a medium iron, in other words several inches behind the ball. Sweep it away on the upswing to give every chance of accelerating to maximum club head speed and of producing the right sort of trajectory. In the backswing you need to turn fully, setting the right wrist smartly back into its cocked position, meeting the ball on a circular path and then going through to the end of the swing in an identical manner to the rest of the shots.

Having the ball teed up correctly should help you produce the right plane. It is far easier, for example, than a 6-iron from a tight or poor lie. The depth of contact is easy; there should be no feeling of hitting down into the ball. Instead it should encourage a rounded plane and shallow attack. So in some ways if you are trying to change from the typical club player's up-and-down action, this shot will help you get the feeling.

1

5

2

3

4

6

Another view of the driver, showing the turn of back and shoulders, attacking the ball from the inside and then continuing through to a full, balanced finish

7

Second, I want to look more at the setup. The ball is played forward in the stance. Guard against pulling the hips and shoulders open and/or the right shoulder up. Keep the same square shoulder line as before, right shoulder down and right elbow relaxed. Club golfers as a whole find this difficult to achieve. Typically the club golfer plays the ball further to the left because he knows he should, but achieves nothing. Instead of setting himself up to contact the ball on the

8

upswing, he shifts his weight to the left, bringing the bottom of the swing directly at the ball. This produces sliced or skied shots.

Follow a definite routine to set up correctly with the driver. Tee the ball up and stand with it opposite your left heel. Instead of placing the club directly behind the ball, position it a good 5 or 6 inches behind the ball and get yourself into a comfortable position based on that club head position. Simply form a 'Y' shape with your arms and the club shaft, not pushing the hands to the left. Try to feel comfortable here with the right shoulder nicely dropped; imagine that this point is going to be the bottom of your swing. Now edge the club head forward so that you bring it behind the ball, making absolutely certain that if anything your right shoulder seems to drop under a fraction, compressing the right side from hip to shoulder a little more. *Never* have a feeling of the shoulders turning or the right shoulder lifting as you move the club head to the final address position. This should encourage the feeling of an upward strike on the ball, staying behind it and sweeping the ball away.

Players who don't drive well usually bring the bottom of the swing too close to the ball, with a tendency to hit down and either chop it upwards or almost smother it slightly. The bottom of the swing must be several inches behind the ball. If you have any difficulty with driving, always have a couple of practice swings, making sure that the bottom of the swing really is going to come several inches behind the imaginary ball. The contact should be as shallow and light as possible, perhaps just grazing the ground in the practice swing, but certainly with no feeling of crashing down into it. The feeling should be of a smooth, shallow attack. The length and lie of the club should encourage the right plane of swing. You should also have the feeling of hitting the ball from a point slightly ahead of you. In other words your feeling is of being rather behind the ball as you make contact with it, which for many people gives the feeling of a slight arching of the back through impact, and of having a little more weight left on the toes of the right foot at the end of the swing than with an iron. Instead of feeling that you get onto the very tips of the toes in the follow-through you may feel that weight is left flat on the toes though never, of course, actually back on the ball of the foot itself.

Third, let's look at timing with the driver. The driver is the longest of the clubs in the set; it is also the lightest. Club golfers often wrongly assume it to be the heaviest. The sand iron is the heaviest. In many ways the heavier head of an iron, and even the 4-wood or 5-wood, may seem to swing itself, where you may get far less feeling of the club head with the driver. This will often make players rush the swing in the search for added power. The longer the club, the better it needs to be timed and it is crucial that the change of directions at the top of the swing takes place smoothly. Having reached the top of the backswing with your driver, try to appreciate just how far the club head has to travel in returning to the ball while your body, and in particular the right shoulder, has a relatively short distance to move. This is aggravated if you don't turn fully and complete the backswing. Don't try to force the ball. If you do, it is all too easy for the right shoulder to become dominant, leaving the club head trailing behind in an open position. This again is why so many people have difficulty with the driver and will constantly cut the ball away to the right. They mistime the shot and don't get the club head back to the ball soon enough, relative to the legs and body.

So particularly for anyone who does slice the ball with a driver, let's look at it this way. We have a kind of three-horse race with the driver – the three participants being your body, your hands and your club head. Now in relative terms your club head has got an awful long way to go, the hands have much less and the body less still. You have to make sure that you time the three things correctly so that if anything, the winner of the race should always be the club head. At the moment of impact, your hands should be fractionally behind the club head, just as at address, body held back.

For this reason you may have to have the feeling, not of a pause as such, but certainly of being very smooth in the change of directions from the top. You have to ensure that the turn of the shoulders has been really full, to give yourself time to get the club head through. All too often players are in a search for power with the driver. The club player often tries to do this with the right shoulder (which is a disaster) and the good player often with a thrusting from the legs. Both will tend to get the body action way ahead of the club head and never give it time to get through. At the top of the backswing, turn and have the feeling that you are almost sitting back on the right heel. Make sure that the start of the downswing is done with the arms so that the arms start moving away from the right shoulder to start the forward movement. Have the feeling of swinging the club head through impact so that the club head and arms very definitely *pull* your right leg and right foot through rather than there being any pushing from the right side. You will then find yourself coming much more slowly off the right foot through impact, the right foot certainly still getting onto the toes by the end of the swing but very definitely not being there prematurely through impact.

Learn how the hands and wrists need to work. Again, let me emphasize that this is aimed at the club golfer and not a potential champion (who is going to have a different feeling). It is aimed at the club player, who will if anything leave the club face open, and not the potential champion, who probably closes it. The feeling for the club player probably has to be one of throwing the club head back to the ball in the downswing, setting the right hand back on itself in the backswing but then very definitely releasing it to get the club head square in striking the ball. Most people's natural timing of this throw is wrong. They do it wrong in the practice swing and certainly wrong with the ball. They wait until the arms and hands are level with the ball and at that point feel the release take place. They feel a sense of release *at* the ball instead of correctly *before* the ball. You have turned away in the backswing and set the right wrist back on itself. You have to start releasing the right wrist set somewhere during the downswing. At impact you return the club, hands and arms to their address position. Provided you get the right turn and plane of the swing, setting the wrist backwards and not upwards, you should be able to release the club head back virtually as early and fast as you like.

Jack Nicklaus once said that it was impossible to hit too early. What he meant and what I mean is that if you set the right wrist back properly to generate power, you can let fly with that hand well before your hands reach the ball. So think about the timing of your release and have a very definite feeling of throwing the club down, out and round at the ball in the downswing. The precise action is to set the right wrist very slightly at address, to set it fully in the backswing, to release it back to repeat the address position and then as near as possible to hold it there through to the finish.

Common faults

THE BEST WAY of learning to play golf is to have a positive idea of what you want to do, not a negative one of what you are trying to avoid. The club golfer, however, often has a lot of misconceptions about the golf swing and some radical faults which need ironing out before the really good work can start. I am therefore, somewhat against my better judgement, going to look at the various bad shots of golf. I will try to explain to the club player how to correct those and to relate what he does to what I am advocating.

THE SLICE

Without doubt the majority of club golfers tend to slice the ball, sending it cutting away to the right. Many players do this right through the whole set of clubs, but almost kid themselves that it isn't happening until they actually see the ball bending from left to right with the fairway woods or a driver. Do remember that if you put cutspin on a ball it loses distance, but the sidespin you notice becomes progressively greater the less the loft of the club. What you may think is a perfectly straight shot with a 6-iron may in fact have cut on it which loses distance.

Let's understand what a slice is. If you have played tennis then probably you can understand the difference between a cut shot with a tennis racket and a topspin forehand drive. You play a cut shot when you want the ball to land softly over the net so that it dies there and gives your opponent one hell of a job running from the back of the court to meet it. Let's think how you would play that. In simple terms you probably take the racket almost straight back and up, and as you hit the ball hold your right hand back, just slicing across the ball with the head of the racket. The right hand is held back and the ball plops down softly. This is exactly what happens when you slice a golf ball. If anything you start swinging too straight back or even outside the line of the shot, coming into the ball with the body almost facing your target and the hands held back, probably in a stiffish position, keeping the club face open. Now let's look at what you would do with a tennis racket trying to get a topspin forehand drive. You would swing the racket well back behind you and as you bring the racket through would actually turn the arm over so that at the end of the shot the racket head would face virtually downwards. If you look at the illustration you can see the difference in the racket head position and my right hand and arm position. The two feelings are exactly what we are trying to look at in the golf swing. In the cut shot, whether golf or tennis, the head of the weapon is held back with a stiffish action and sidespin is imparted to the ball. In the topspin, drawing type of shot, the right arm and in turn the head of the weapon come through in a different kind of path.

If you are somebody who slices the ball then basically what you need to do is to experiment with a feeling of hookspin, learning first of all to get the ball really bending from right to left, even if in a very uncontrolled fashion. Once you can feel the ball spinning both ways you should be able to correct one or other and keep the swing finely tuned so that the ball flies relatively straight. If you can only feel cutspin then it is difficult to correct.

Now why do most club golfers slice?

First, they tend to be much too stiff. My own feeling in the swing is of considerable looseness and relaxation. In fact the feeling is of being far tighter and more in control with the shorter shots and looser and freer the longer the shot. For the club golfer it tends to be exactly the opposite. He tenses up and feels tight with the long game, in a search for power, and then usually loosens up too much in the short game. By tightening up he loses the freedom in his arms and hands and simply cannot get the club head swishing through. Added to this he will probably swing the club back in far too much of a straight path which means that he is in effect almost setting up a cut-across action. Third, he probably uses a grip which is unsatisfactory and doesn't let him return the club face squarely, or even slightly closed, at impact. What generally happens with most beginners is that their hands and wrists are far too stiff, while the left arm becomes straight and rigid through impact and won't get out of the way. The player then probably decelerates into impact, holding the club face open instead of letting the left arm turn and fold and get out of the way. The club face is held open and whatever the path of the swing, the ball will trail away to the right. The golfer then becomes afraid of the right side of the golf course and constantly tries to steer the ball to the left, meaning that he probably stands facing the left of target and swings to the left of target, setting up even more of a cut-across action. Let me at this point explain what we mean when we talk about an open stance. If the good player looks at a target and wants to aim left, what he will first of all do is to aim the club face left to the point he wants to hit and then line up parallel to that club face. But in an open stance the player sets the club face to the flag and then lines the feet and shoulders up left. Now he is setting the direction of the swing and club face at odds with each other and encouraging an open face through impact.

The club golfer also aggravates this tendency to leave the club face open by several things he does. First, he is tight in the left arm and the wrists and therefore doesn't easily square up the club face. He probably also grips the club much too tightly, often with a grip that is too thick, and probably doesn't have the left hand sufficiently on top of the club. Second, he probably aims his feet and shoulders off to the left and this makes it extremely difficult to get a full turn in the backswing. As soon as he starts the downswing he gets his body and legs ahead of the club head and again cannot square it up in time. Third, what he also probably does is to play the ball far too far forward in his feet, in other words towards the left foot. Not only does this tend to turn the shoulders to the left but it also encourages an up-and-down, out-to-in action and probably restricts the shoulder turn on the backswing. He should experiment with playing the ball well back in the stance so that the shoulders easily fall into a square position at address, with a feeling of turning away quite easily in the backswing.

The slice is just like a cut shot with a tennis racket (see left), face open, wrist stiff. A draw or hook is similar to the top spin action, far freer with racket head imparting the opposite spin

What in theory the slicer has to do is to move the ball back in the stance so that the shoulders sit square and the turn seems easy. He needs to loosen up his wrists to get the club face square and he needs to turn well in the backswing to be able to attack the ball from the inside rather than with an out-to-in, cutting action. That in theory sounds fine.

In practice the problem is that the club golfer is usually terrified of the right-hand side of the golf course and nothing one can say is going to make him square up his stance, turn the shoulders more and have the feeling of aiming the swing more out to the right. It feels so unnatural and if he does do it on the practice ground he certainly isn't going to do it on the golf course. The slicer first needs to get the feeling of squaring the club face up or even closing it so that instead of worrying about the right side of the golf course he starts getting into trouble down the left. As a rule the player who does slice has an out-to-in swing, in other words left-aimed through impact. If you can get him to square up the club face or even close it, he is going to finish up with shots which fly straight left. Once he can play a few rounds of golf getting into difficulty on the left, it becomes much more logical for him to start squaring up his stance, bringing the ball further back to the right in the stance and beginning to swing the club away on the inside with the correct plane of swing.

The first stage is to loosen up the hands and wrists considerably and to make sure the left hand is brought well onto the top of the club, possibly even in the first stage with the right hand being allowed to go underneath. This should encourage the player to produce a slightly closed club face through impact. But what he also needs to do at this stage is to ensure that the ball is at least 3 or 4 inches inside the left heel with all the fairway shots and, most important of all, he must start allowing the left arm to turn and fold away through impact rather than keeping it stiff and rigid. He needs to have a real feeling of looseness in the left arm right from address, letting it be quite soft in the backswing, though it should not actually bend, and then having a real feeling of

the arm folding inwards immediately beyond impact. Again let me stress that the arm folds inwards and doesn't break outwards. Once the player can get the feeling of the left arm getting out of the way he should be able to feel both arms turning and folding in much the way I have explained earlier in the book.

For the longer-handicap player who slices, one of the difficulties is that you want him to get the feeling of folding the left arm away in the throughswing, and also if anything to let the arms rotate to a slightly more round-the-body finish. The real danger here is that instead of doing it with the arms, hands and wrists, he wants to start dragging the swing round with the right shoulder. The emphasis in making this correction must therefore be in looseness, the club being held almost as loosely as possible and the wrists staying quite floppy through the ball. Once a player can square up the club

1

2

How not to do it! A typical slicing action, turning insufficiently in the backswing and then cutting steeply across the ball in an out-to-in direction, leaving the club face open. The more you try to steer the ball left, the greater the slice spin on the ball

face through impact and even feel a hookspin, he can then make progress towards the swing I have described earlier on.

THE HOOK

On the whole hooking the ball is the fault of the good player rather than the club golfer. Quite simply in hooking the ball the club face comes in in a slightly closed position, imparting sidespin that takes the ball away to the left. The great advantage of a ball which hooks, particularly for the club player and any older golfer, is that the ball runs a long way on touching down. Ideally, if the club golfer can bend the ball slightly from right to left he is likely to get the maximum possible out of his game. By contrast, the hook is the most dangerous shot for the really good player who hits the ball vast distances. The hook can get out of control, where a slightly cut ball at least lands and stops before running into trouble. The hook shot can head off towards the rough and then bounce forward with an alarming amount of run. Players who hook tend to do exactly the opposite to those who slice. They see the ball starting to bend to the left and start aiming right with the feet and indeed with the whole swing to try to offset this. What in reality happens is that the club face probably is aimed at the target, the feet and shoulders and whole swing go off to the right and once more the direction of swing and club face are set at odds with each other, compounding the tendency to hook.

There are three basic ways in which the player is likely to hook the ball and I am going to deal with each in turn. The most common cause for a club player's hook is a faulty grip. The left hand is probably far too much on the top of the club and the right hand

By contrast, the correct attack – body turning and then waiting for the club head

1

2

much too much beneath. Through impact, all that happens is that the right hand comes in palm facing the target and by now has simply turned the club face into a closed position. The ball flies away with a bend to the left and probably loses height. In this case the player needs to check the grip, ensuring that the line between the thumb and index finger of the left hand points up to the right ear and not outside it and that the right hand is brought up into a position where it is behind the shaft at address and not beneath it. Frequently the player also has problems in getting the ball high enough – the closed club face losing loft. He therefore puts the right hand more underneath in a feeling of being able to scoop the ball into the air. Almost certainly he does so with the shorter shots and with pitching. He needs to resist this feeling and learn one of having the club resting in the fingers of the right hand with the hand feeling in a powerful position aiming straight out towards the target. Combined with this change to the grip, the player may also need to exercise the left arm and hand to ensure that both play their part in the golf swing. He may be excessively right-handed with the left hand and arm contributing nothing at all. Although for the good golfer I am going to explain how the right arm can work well and not hook, for the club golfer there does need to be this constant watch on the balance between the left side and right side. Don't feel that the left side has to be dominant or the game is going to become a left-sided one. But you do need to do something with the left hand and at least feel it is providing support at the top of the backswing.

Timing and the hook

The second kind of hook concerns the relative timing of body and leg action with arm and hand speed. I explained in the section on driving how players get the body action way ahead of the arms and hands, the club head trailing behind into impact. It is possible for the low-handicap player to start hooking the ball because the body and leg action really is too slow by comparison with the arms and hands. It is certainly far more the fault of the good player who works the arms and hands freely

This is how a player can hook with a good grip. The legs block, arms stop and the wrists are forced to turn over. In this instance I am playing an intentional hook. Compare it with the next shot (**below**) of a fading action, legs and hips turning out of the way, arms working more freely from the body. This is the feeling needed to correct a hook

and probably has a good degree of relaxation. What can happen in this situation is that the player turns, leaves himself sitting on the right heel almost too long and then whips the club head through with the arms and hands, the club head being ahead of everything else timing-wise at impact. The player who produces this kind of action will often be seen with the legs and hips facing right of target in the follow-through, the arms almost being forced to do a kind of scissor action around the body. For this reason this type of hook is very much associated with a push to the right. Much of what I am going to say now therefore also applies to a person who pushes a ball right. If the turn through of the legs – again it is a turn not a thrust –is at all slow, the hips and body are facing off to the right of target through impact. Now have a look at what this does to the arms. The arms, as it were, are now not the same length. The left arm comes from one point and the right arm comes from a point well behind it. The arms therefore do not want to swing towards the target and round naturally. They either want to be pulled excessively round to the left, with the left elbow breaking very much outward, or they want to push the ball out to the right. The fault here is that the legs and body do not unwind sufficiently quickly. The player needs to practise speeding up the left leg and left side so that he can transfer weight back onto the left heel through impact, and pull the left knee and hip round and out of the way as I advocate. The right foot too needs to be given freedom to get onto the end of the toes, and I would certainly check that the right foot is fairly straight in front at address and not turned out too much. If turned more than a degree or two this may hold the leg action back and inhibit the turn through. This player may need to have the feeling of a faster hip turn through and initially almost make the arms go through a little straighter towards the target, separating hip turn and arm swing a touch, rather than the arms being pulled too much to the left. This is the one player who if anything may almost fold the left arm away too much beyond impact in the kind of turn-and-fold manner the majority of players need to work at.

THE ADVANCED PLAYER'S HOOK

At this stage I am going to give advice aimed at the top-class player and potential champion. For us the hook can be almost as disastrous as the slice for the club golfer. If you hook the ball you will know that fear of the ball almost escaping from the club face and instantly giving the feeling of getting away to the left. It may not curve very much in the air, but you know that the moment it touches down it is going to bounce away further into the rough or greenside trap and cost you that one shot or two shots which is the difference between winning and losing.

Many good players wrongly try to counteract this by weakening the left-hand grip to the point where only one knuckle is showing. This has exactly the opposite effect to that intended, in that the left hand becomes so power-less that it doesn't stand up at all to the power of the right hand and any tendency to hook is aggravated. Some players have also tried to counteract any tendency towards hooking by adopting a very straight back-and-through type of path to their swing, almost cutting across the ball and producing a fading action. This is very much the way in which I used to play the game, with a feeling of total left-arm dominance, swinging the club high in the backswing, using exaggerated leg thrust and hip action and working at a very high finish. This is certainly one way of playing and will no doubt continue to be used widely. The feeling, for this kind of player, is very much one of separating arms and legs in the throughswing, the hips shifting forwards and then turning while the arms go very much up and out towards the target. The danger here is that the hips will tilt and block excessively through impact, the right shoulder will drop and you are left from time to time with an equally disastrous shot which pushes violently out to the right.

Let's therefore get away from that idea and see how the good player can confidently hit the ball using his right hand without this fear of the ball getting away to the left. I presume now that you will have read everything that has gone before in this book relating to the grip, posture and the swing. Let's recap the feeling of standing tall with the bottom out and let's recap also the way in which the arms turn on the backswing and the way in which they turn on the throughswing. Let me repeat again that the throughswing can and indeed should perfectly mirror the backswing so that the arms turn on the same plane, right elbow down in the backswing and left elbow diagonally down in the throughswing.

It is now the feeling in the right hand and the right wrist which you need to work at. Learn to 'set and hold'. Set the right wrist angle early in the backswing, almost at the moment of takeaway, so that it cocks back on itself. As you work through impact, the right wrist moves back into a hitting position identical with the wrist position at address, but you resist any release all the way. Now look very closely at what happens to the back of the right wrist. Take a normal swing and look at your wrist action at three stages. First look at it at address, second look at it at the top of the backswing and third, look at it at the end of the follow-through. You will see the natural angle at address; you will see the cocked-back 'set' position at the top of the backswing, and you will see that the right wrist is again back on itself at the end of the swing. But what you probably also do if you hook the ball is that somewhere along the line through impact, you let that wrist straighten out so that you are in effect releasing the right hand past the left hand. Club golfers to an extent have to be told to do this to get the club face squaring up, but their problem is different from yours. Address the ball, looking at the right-hand position. Set it fully on the backswing and then have the feeling of holding this position right through the shot. The force of the club head will in reality slightly straighten this wrist set, but you resist it all the time, feeling as though you pull with the arms rotating. Have the feeling of holding the right wrist in that way through to the end of the swing without it flapping through straight and the left wrist in turn loosening. It is obviously difficult to encourage the club golfer to do this because he will probably hold the

club face open. But for a top-class player this is the feeling you need to produce.

At the moment of impact, the right wrist is then in a strong position, delivering a really powerful blow, and also producing a really crisp contact. You should then have the feeling of the left arm folding away and I suppose if anything, have the very slightest feeling of the club face pulling across the ball at the moment of impact. In other words you may be able to feel the very slightest tendency towards fading the ball but with the right hand in command and achieving this feeling. The left arm then folds away as both arms turn but with a hint of a slightly upwards movement of the arms once the hips face the target.

What you should begin to feel is that the right hand is really in control of the club face. You should be able to control the club face by using the right hand and be able to feel that you can produce the slightest draw or the slightest fade on the ball. What a good golfer is looking for is a ball that leaves the club face and to anyone watching looks as though it is straight. At the moment of impact he knows, and can control, whether the ball has the slightest tendency to move to the right or move to the left. For the top-class player we are talking in terms of a ball which moves 3 or 4 feet in the air with a short iron, 10 to 15 feet with a driver. It is more that you can feel which way it wants to go rather than a spectator being able to see it move.

Learn to hit the ball hard with the right hand, setting it and holding it through impact and knowing instantly that ball leaves the club face whether you have produced a perfectly straight flight or one with the merest suspicion of a drift to the right. Experiment with the feeling of the right hand until you can safely feel that it controls the club face rather than having to be submissive with the left doing all the work.

The easiest way of learning to counteract the tendency to hook is by holding the club face off with the right hand. Go on the practice ground, aim yourself perfectly parallel to the target line with a driver, then simply stand up and try to hit the ball as far right as you can. Don't do it with anything other than a feeling of the club face being held off – open through impact. For a while you won't do it; you'll still hook it. I did. It takes some time until you can hold the right wrist in that position. Have patience and don't cheat by opening the stance or compensating in any way. Aim at a target and be determined to fade or push everything away to the right of it, without aiming right. In this way you undo fear of the left side of the course and learn to resist any overreleasing with the right wrist. Then all of a sudden it happens and you begin to feel the ball with the palm of the right hand. At this point you become more conscious if anything of the right side of the course. Now you keep the same position with the wrists and feel the left side of the upper body really pulling on through to face the target.

THE TOPPED SHOT

Let's now move from one extreme to the other. The last shot was the one for the really top-class player. This is the one which affects the long-handicap golfer. His problem is that the contact with the ball is difficult. It is quite easy to produce what looks like a classic swing but which doesn't have the accuracy to come down in the right place. Most club golfers are nothing like as accurate as they imagine through impact. You can easily come down an inch behind the ball, half an inch above the ground or too near to or too far from your feet. You have to get the feeling of making the club head strike exactly the right spot. The player who tops the ball usually hasn't mastered the feeling of depth judgement and simply can't get the club head down behind the ball accurately. Check that you really do look at the back of the ball. Don't tip your head excessively to the right, but just focus on the back of the ball and not on the top of it.

Secondly, make sure that you are relaxed. If you get tense, you are likely to breathe in, lift your whole rib-cage and not get the club head down to the ground. So relax. The next stage is to make sure that you really do understand how the golf ball gets airborne. The loft of the club makes it rise, and all you have to do is to ensure that the club head brushes the ground on which the ball sits. If you top the ball then the odds are you are consciously or subconsciously trying to lift it. In trying to lift it and in trying to get under it, you probably lean slightly back on the right foot and lift the club head through impact. Instead of getting to the bottom of it with a nice U-shaped or even a V-shaped attack, you catch the ball around the middle. The more you try to make it rise, the more it wants to run along the ground. If you do have a tendency to top the ball, think of hitting down and through it, ensuring that your weight is on the left foot at the finish but without picking the club up excessively in the backswing. It still has to be a turning action, but combined with a downward attack for any shot where the ball sits on the ground. Remember that you cannot get under the golf ball. The ground gets in the way. Only on a tee shot or with a very grassy lie can you hit the ball with an upward attack. Everything else has to be a slightly downward one.

THE PUSHED SHOT

Club golfers often aren't quite sure what constitutes a push and a slice. A slice is a shot which bends away to the right and may in fact start left of target. A push is a shot which starts out to the right and keeps heading straight there. In many ways it is often linked to the player who hooks the ball, often the good player. Golfers who hook often instinctively stand off to the right of target and then start pushing the ball out there rather than letting it hook.

The first checkpoint for a push is alignment. I should think 50 per cent of golfers aim their feet off to the right of target instead of standing parallel to the direction of the shot. It doesn't necessarily mean they hit the ball right; often they will turn on it and hit the ball left. But it seems to be some sort of optical illusion which sets people off to the right in the first place. So very simply, check that. As a second point, you may well push the ball out to the right if you play the ball too far towards your right foot at address. You will get the same effect if you sway excessively to the left through impact.

In either case your weight is well ahead of the ball at impact and you make contact with the ball before the swing has come round to be on target. This sort of action is often associated with fairly strong, well-hit irons but frequently with a tendency to take divots and have a rather steep contact with a fairway wood and possibly also to sky dives. Here the player needs to check the ball position, keeping it ahead of the centre of the stance. He also needs to ensure that the leg action is a free turn through impact rather than a lateral shift to the left. The player can be too much on the left foot by the end of the swing and needs to concentrate on keeping the head still through impact.

The next, and I suppose most common reason for the push is insufficient leg work. The legs simply do not turn through to face the target at the end of the swing. Let's review very briefly what should happen with the leg action. In the backswing you turn so that the weight in the feet naturally transfers towards the heel of the right foot and the ball of the left foot. In the throughswing the weight should turn through in the opposite direction, in other words moving back round onto the left heel and through onto the toes of the right foot. By the end of the swing the hips should face the target, balancing on the left *heel* and big toe of the right foot. The player who pushes the ball will frequently turn correctly in the backswing and then never get the left leg and hip out of the way in the throughswing. The weight tends to stay on the ball of the left foot through impact, so that by the end of the swing the player is either balanced – or more commonly slightly off balance – on the ball of the left foot and the ball of the right foot. At this point the hips now face well out to the right of target and that is where the shot goes. Very often the left leg is also bent instead of turning through to be fairly straight.

This sort of action often comes from the player who doesn't give himself space at address. He may well have the legs too bent in a sitting position at address, not having room for the left leg to work freely through impact. Instead of the left leg being able to turn and straighten through impact, it

How not to do it! This time the typical action of the pusher, blocking hips and legs, leaving them facing off to the right

can only stay bent unless the player rises up excessively through impact. The correction here is one of standing up tall at address, sticking the bottom well out and ensuring that there really is room for the left leg to work freely. Work at a good turn through, checking that the hips really are facing the target at the finish. This player should exaggerate the feeling of holding the follow-through for at least a count of 5 seconds. Even if the arms have to recoil down, the player should try to balance with the hips on target until the ball stops moving. The player who pushes the ball will almost certainly get through to the end of the swing and then want to spring back with both arms *and hips*. If he doesn't hold the finish the legs and hips usually revert to being lazy. The feeling here should be of finishing the swing with the balance point, when looked at from the direction of the shot, being over the left heel. The left leg should be straight but the hips sunk down on this straight left leg, weight on the heel and not the ball of the foot, left hip shifted slightly left.

Left and below To correct a push – and in some cases a hook – clear the hips through to the target. Hold the finish. If you let the arms down, keep the legs still until the ball lands

THE SHANK

I suppose the most disastrous of all bad shots is the shank, the ball that flies off the bottom of the hosel instead of off the middle of the club face. The basic cause of this is simply that the through-swing comes down perhaps 1½ inches too far from the feet. Instead of contacting the ball from the middle of the club face it comes off the neck. The instinctive thing players do to correct this is to stand further from the ball. This is often the wrong adjustment to make. If you tend to shank, check that you really do have the ball in the middle of the club face to start with. Set up to the ball in your normal way with the ball in the middle of the face. Now have a look round from behind. You may find the ball is much more towards the neck of the club than appears from your normal address position. This is something of an optical illusion and can be the sole cause of problems.

The second cause of a shank is similar to the one I have just described. Instead of using the legs properly so that the weight turns onto the left heel

in the throughswing, it is all too easy to leave the weight on the balls of both feet through impact. The player loses balance, falling very slightly out towards the ball. Instead of the swing coming through in the right place, it comes out too far from the feet. The player who does this will almost certainly be off balance at the end of the swing. Instinctively he wants to move further from the ball, but in so doing is likely to move forward and off balance through impact.

The correction very often is to have the feeling of standing in closer, sticking the bottom out to give space. The address position must feel balanced and lively, and then ensure that the feet and legs work properly in the down and throughswing. The great check point here is to stay balanced at the end of the swing for a good 3 or 4 seconds. Players often say that if they do a good shot they produce a good finish. For this kind of player the thought must be exactly the opposite. 'If I can produce a good finish, then I will produce a good shot.' The feeling from the top of the backswing needs to be to push the weight backwards onto the left heel and to ensure that the left knee and left hip get out of the way. Once again the balance position must be the left heel and never the ball of the foot.

Check whether you really do get the ball out of the middle of the club face. Even good players can get into slight difficulty by not really middling the ball. It is only when you have the odd disaster that you realize things have got out of hand. A good practice routine is to put a mark on the back of the ball, either with a chalk or a felt tip pen, and then to hit shots, monitoring where the ball leaves a mark on the club face. You may find that the marks come all over the face and do edge back towards the heel.

POOR DISTANCE

We all want to hit the ball further. I suppose even those of us who are amongst the world's longest hitters would really like to squeeze another 10 yards out of a drive! For the club golfer one of the greatest thrills of the game is to hit the ball a really long distance, consistently outhitting his opponents. Almost every Wednesday of the year I play a Pro – Am with 2 or 3 amateur golfers and the one thing they would all love to do is to drive the ball like a professional. Usually we don't drive from the same tee as they do, but I can still feel them watching me, making a comparison and, if they aren't very careful, trying to hit the ball harder and harder through the round of golf to squeeze out maximum length. Unfortunately the harder they try to hit the ball, the more the body comes into play, the right shoulder starts becoming dominant, and if anything the ball will start slicing and actually lose length.

Let's have a look at the way of producing the maximum possible distance. First of all, you need to understand that a ball which has a cutspin – a slicespin – is not going to run when it lands. So what most club players need to do is to try to get a ball which will if anything bend a little from right to left, so that it runs when it touches down. Secondly, you need to understand just how very loose and relaxed top golfers are when they hit the ball. Hitting a ball a long way is very much more a question of acquiring a knack than of tremendous physical strength.

Obviously when you get to the world's longest hitters, we are all strong and do some sort of physical training to keep in peak condition. But to be a long hitter by club standards is far more a question of timing, good hand action and a feeling of freedom. I think the greatest thing for the club player is to learn that you have to let the club head swing right through at speed. Cast aside any thoughts of thrusting in power with the right shoulder, or kicking in power with the legs, or trying to muscle the ball away with any part of you. Just think in terms of the club head and trying to swing it – and I mean the club head not the whole club – at real speed. Pick up your driver, or whichever wood you drive with, holding it as loosely as possible in the fingers, and just play around with it until you get the feeling of the head itself. Just make it feel ridiculously loose and relaxed and just whoosh the club backwards and forwards, swishing it around with your wrists until you gradually feel you start to swing the club back and through. Let the arms turn and fold in the way I have described, again paying particular emphasis to getting the left arm out of the way as you swing through. Now just lengthen the swing in each direction, all the time having a feeling for that club head. In the initial stage, let the hands and wrists be so loose that you actually feel the club almost move in your hands. Don't be afraid of the club. It won't bite.

The great secret now is to be able to tee up a ball and to hit it with total inhibition. Swing the club back, making a full, smooth turn, and then whoosh it through, knowing, of course, that the shaft of the club is going to land safely on your left shoulder and not crash around the back of your head. Waggle your hands and wrists at address and just feel absurdly, ridiculously loose. Now try this with the ball, watching the back of the ball and really letting fly at the thing. Don't try and steer it but just be as loose as you possibly can. If you can start to feel the left arm getting out of the way, you should have the feeling that you can produce tremendous club head speed with the right hand, combining it hopefully with balance and a fairly controlled finish.

The next stage is to go out on the golf course and do the same thing. Most players are so terrified of hitting the ball crooked that they won't wind up and have a go at it. Save every old golf ball you ever find, whether it has a chip out of it or is scuffed and dirty. They are useful pieces of ammunition to use and if necessary lose! Long hitting is very much a question of freedom and relaxation. I have never yet seen a club golfer who has held the club so loosely and been so relaxed that he has actually let go of the club through impact. But I've seen an awful lot who grip the club so tightly and who try to hit the ball so hard that in so doing they can never really get good distance.

The art of putting

I AM GOING TO START the sections on the short game by looking at putting. The putting stroke is the basis for many of the other shots around the green.

THE CHOICE OF PUTTERS

First of all let's look at the kind of putter you should use. As a very simple starting point, when you grip the putter, you should set your hands to the side of the club, palms facing and the thumbs down the front of the grip. For this reason nearly every putter has a grip with a flat front. Certainly don't go for anything with a rounded grip.

Secondly, you need to look at the lie of the club. This will largely depend on whether you stand up well to the ball or whether you crouch down. I am going to advocate a stance where you have the feeling of standing tall, with the hands and wrists held fairly high. I would therefore suggest, unless you have other very fixed ideas about putting, that you have a club which has a comparatively upright lie.

The third consideration is the loft on the putter. The club golfer is often surprised to know that putters don't have a perfectly vertical face. Most putters are made with a loft something between 3 degrees and 5 degrees. If you play on courses which have excellent, fast rolling greens then you can probably do with a putter with relatively little loft. If you play on poorish greens you may find a more lofted putter is suitable, allowing you to push your hands a little further ahead of the ball at address without producing a negative loft to the club. Some players constantly change their putters, with the idea of having a light putter on fast greens and a heavier one on slow greens. I am not sure this is necessary, but certainly you may find that putters with a slightly different loft encourage a slightly different action. As to the weight of putter, I think a light putter can cause the club player difficulties. Even on a very fast green it can be difficult to control. Players who tend to have a slightly jerky action often think that a lighter putter will help them. I am not so sure that this is the case; very often by using a fairly weighty putter it will slow the action down and produce smoothness.

As far as the length of putter is concerned I would suggest for most men a putter of about 34 inches to 35 inches and for most women a putter of about 32 inches or 33 inches. A lot of golfers under 5 feet 8 inches in height to my mind use putters which are much too long. If you use a club which is long, it encourages you to hold it too near the top of the club, often with excessive bending in the left wrist. It is better to have a putter which you can hold with a fairly straight and relaxed arm position. So experiment with the length of putter. It is true that if the putter is long you can simply hold it further down the shaft. You may, however, have the hands too far down, losing the benefit of the flat-fronted grip, and also of the slightly curved top to the grip which steers the hands into the correct high-wristed position. Experiment a little and try out putters of different lengths.

Lastly on the question of putters is the design and balance of the head. If you look at an old-fashioned blade putter you will see that the head of the club is attached to the shaft in just the same way as a standard iron head. Most putter manufacturers have worked at altering this design with the idea of giving a larger 'sweet spot' with which to hit the ball. The sweet spot is the ideal striking point in the middle of the club face where the club head twists the least and should therefore give the most solid hit. To check on the size and position of the sweet spot, start by dangling it from the top between the left thumb and index finger. With a small coin or tee peg start tapping the face of the putter, beginning at the toe and working towards the heel. As you tap towards the toe you will feel the putter head twisting. As you work back towards the middle of the club face, it should then feel as though the putter wants to move straight back and through, and as you get towards the heel you will again feel a twist. Ideally you want a putter which has a fairly large striking area where you don't feel any twist. The old-fashioned blade putter may only have a sweet spot of about half an inch; the heel-and-toe putter or a centre-shafted putter is likely to have a much larger sweet spot. Most players probably don't hit the ball as truly from the centre of the club as they imagine; the larger the sweet spot, the more forgiving the putter will be.

There are three other points to consider about the sweet spot. Most manufacturers put a line on the top of putters to help alignment. Check that this line is in the middle of the sweet spot and is perfectly square to the club face. Secondly, do bear in mind that if you alter the lie of the putter at some stage, the sweet spot can change and any line on the top of the putter may not necessarily then be correct. Thirdly, really do check that you line up with the ball opposite the sweet spot. Just as with the long game there is often an optical illusion. When you look down at the ball from your setup, you may not get an entirely accurate idea of where the ball is positioned.

THE GRIP

Putting styles and stances vary enormously. Most good golfers will have certain set ideas about the golf swing, but as far as putting is concerned there are many different ideas as to what is right and what is wrong. With the grip, however, you will see that perhaps 90 per cent of tournament professionals follow the same kind of guidelines.

Firstly, you must have a grip where the left hand is to the left of the shaft and the right to the right of the shaft, palms facing. In the long game, you will find a number of good players who have the left hand predominantly on the top in a strong position. But with a putter this would be entirely unsuit-

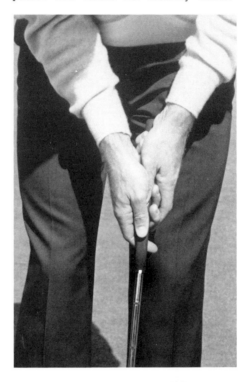

The reverse overlap putting grip, thumb down the front of the club, left index finger down the back of the second and third fingers of the right hand

able. In putting it is crucial that the palms are facing each other and square to the target-line. I would also suggest that the pads of the thumbs should be at the front of the grip, whether you like to run both thumbs straight down the shaft or whether you have the hands in a slightly more open position. The majority of professionals, myself included, adopt the reverse overlap grip. This is an adaptation of the Vardon grip, with a slight difference in the positioning of the thumbs and palms, and now with the index finger of the left hand riding down the outside of the grip rather than the little finger of the right being outside. Some players have the left index finger virtually covering the little finger of the right hand. Others prefer to run the index finger more down the back of the first three fingers. It is just a matter of personal preference but, whichever the choice, it does mean that the left index finger helps to give a feeling of pushing the putter back in a controlled way.

Whether you hold the putter tightly or relatively loosely, again is one of personal preference. There are indeed some players who say that they grip a putter extremely tightly, though on the whole I would suggest that good players have a relatively loose and sensitive type of grip, with even pressure in both hands.

When you set up to the ball with this type of grip, the shaft of the club should be sitting at a fairly upright angle. This in turn brings the left wrist up into a firm, high position rather than allowing it to drop down and relax as it does in the long game.

THE ADDRESS POSITION

Address positions vary enormously with putting. Some players have the ball right opposite the left foot and others opposite the right foot. Some stand open and some stand closed. Some stand tall and some stand low. All this conflicting advice doesn't help the player who is trying to establish some sort of method.

I would suggest as a starting point that you try to stand up fairly tall, so that your arms can hang relatively straight as you hold the putter. The elbows are then relaxed back into the sides, so that the wrists are arched up and not dropped and relaxed. One of the generally accepted keys to good putting is to keep the left wrist firm through impact even though, as I am going to explain, putting can be seen as a relatively right-handed action. If you crouch over the ball too much the left wrist is likely to be bent at address,

At address the elbows are back into the body but with the wrists arched up, palms of the hands to the side of the club. The ball is positioned just opposite the left heel or fractionally inside it, weight just favouring the left side

Far right: This emphasises the arching up and over of the wrists to encourage firmness in the wrists throughout. A low wrist action would produce a wrong, wristy stroke. Although I feel I stand up tall the head is horizontal. It can then swivel, not turn and lift

It is vital to have the eyes directly over the ball, both seen from this angle . . .

. . . and from this. Here I am dropping the ball from between my eyes to get it in the right position!

the wrists may well get very low and if anything this encourages a wristy action. Standing up tall, both arms can hang relaxed.

In standing up tall, however, your head should still be tipped over into a relatively horizontal position. This means that as you look at the ball and then at the hole your head should swivel rather than turning and lifting. Ideally you should have your eyes directly over the line of the putt, possibly fractionally inside the line but certainly never outside the line. It is also best if you can get the line along your eyes parallel to the putt. I would suggest that the overall posture for putting should feel much the same as with the long game, with an impression if anything of standing up fairly tall, bottom out, lower back straight and legs relaxed with comfortable balance. The arms should hang really loosely, although with the proviso that the left wrist is now arched up rather than dropped down.

THE PUTTING PATH

Start from a square stance, feet, hips, shoulders and eyes parallel to the putt. My own feeling of putting is that you should do much the same as in the golf swing. Take the club back on the inside, again setting the right wrist very firmly in position at address and letting it bring the putter head naturally back on the inside, low to the ground. The club face turns to follow that natural curve without any feeling of trying to keep it aimed directly at the hole. Make a nice, low, slow stroke on the backswing, from there taking the putter straight through to the hole with the right hand set in the same position as at address. To me, the through-swing does *not* mirror the backswing; the putter doesn't move away on the inside and turn as it goes through. Have a feeling of the putter coming back low on the inside but then straight through and slightly up during impact. Let it be a right-handed action.

I used to think that the putting stroke with a short putt should be very much a straight back-and-through action. I don't in fact now believe that this is really the case. Certainly some players

One of my favourite putting exercises. I trap another club between my elbows and body, encouraging the feeling of moving the arms, shoulders and wrists as a whole firm unit. It develops the feeling of keeping the elbows in and wrists arched up

With the club trapped by my elbows ideally the club shaft moves back and through parallel to my putt. If it does, so in turn do the shoulders and most importantly the putter. It encourages a feeling of the putting stroke being as a unit from the shoulders, a really good, up and down, pendulum action

1

2

3

1

2

3

feel that the putter moves back and through in a straight line for putts of up to, say, 8 feet; but even here in reality there is usually a little movement on a slightly inside curve on the backswing. Keep the right elbow in and what feels to be a straight path should bring the putter in just the right amount on the backswing. Then on a straight path in the throughswing.

THE PUTTING STROKE

Once you have a good grip and address position the putting stroke is just a shoulder movement. It's a pure shoulder rocking motion with just the tiniest feel of movement, though not really noticeable, in the wrists. It is very difficult to hit putts consistently well with the hands and arms, not day after day and week after week. By contrast, if you use the shoulders you can get a repetitive pendulum stroke.

A great exercise for this is to trap a club shaft or cane between your arms and body. Practise the shoulder pendulum with the idea of rocking shoulders and club shaft smoothly back and through on line. It stops the right elbow wandering away in the backswing or the shoulders turning off line in the throughswing. The shoulders rock, the wrists stay as a unit and this brings the club head on up, keeping it square, towards the hole.

The basic action if initiated from the shoulders is reasonably reliable. But for the tournament player it does lack an element of feel. A shoulder action alone can become rigid, perhaps a slight scooping with no real hit or touch.

Having built a reliable pendulum stroke from the shoulders the good player should add just a suspicion of hand action, even for the short putts.

To be able to use the hands and wrists in this way the wrists *must* be arched up. The hands then hang over and down and any wrist action works more or less straight back and through on target. If the wrists are wrongly held low it would go round. Arch the wrists but still comfortably. This locks them and only allows them to hinge in one way.

The right wrist is obviously slightly set at address. Even for short putts my feeling is of just adding to this a touch, a *feeling* more than something visible. My feeling is of hinging the wrists *very* slightly, not really in the backswing, but just setting them and creating this lag to start the throughswing. This means you keep the club head travelling back for a moment while the wrists work into reverse and forward to the target. The movement is minute, but it does give a fluid change of direction, popping the ball away crisply. This added feel in the hands protects against any tendency towards dragging putts left. You need just a suspicion of lag in the hands. Good players will understand what I mean. It protects against hitting the putt too early, letting the club head get ahead of the hands.

As the swing goes through, the right

1

2

3

4

I like to think of putting as a right-handed action – and practise one-handed to encourage the stroke. My right elbow stays into the waist throughout, bringing the putter slightly inside on a curve in the backswing and then through and straight up to the target beyond impact. It is just a very small version of the golf swing itself, keeping the angle in the right wrist constant through impact. There is a slight hinging in the right wrist going back

This shows the right hand moving the putter straight through and up beyond impact, the putter face still aiming directly on target – never being pulled or turning to the left. There is a slight hinging of the right wrist going back. For the top player this almost happens after the throughswing starts. It resists any tendency to straighten the right wrist. So, as with the golf swing itself, hinge and hold the hinge. It is a question of feel rather than a movement that actually shows

wrist maintains its slightly set position – either the position from address, or where a touch of wrist action is added, with this new angle.

I am sure this minute hand action is more a question of placing emphasis on the hands than real movement as such. I don't believe the difference can be seen but it can be felt. To feel what I mean try two putting strokes. In the first, swing back and through smoothly, concentrating on a feeling of changing direction to the action with the hands. In the second, concentrate on the club head and just think of bringing *it* into reverse. My impression is that the first is correct – the slight lag I mean – where the second can almost bring the club through too early. It probably won't show, except to the very trained eye. It is one of those 'Should I do this, or should I do that?' situations, where the feeling can be so different, and the spectator can't detect the change.

To develop the stroke, work with the right hand only. Feel the hand working the putter face through and up to the target, and then experiment with a little freedom in setting the right wrist in the backswing, and eventually with creating this slight lag by setting it to start the return. Whichever position is created, hold it through impact.

In taking the club back the shoulders are the key. You have to have a trigger movement, something to start it away smoothly. I bounce the club up and down behind the ball when I am ready to go. Just a couple of times to avoid becoming too static. It is hard to move from a completely stationary position. The club comes up off the ground a fraction for a split second and then everything goes from the shoulders. This movement just before the takeaway is crucial. You must take control of the putter, supporting it in your arms and hands, *hanging* it from the shoulders. The club has to be above the ground for a split second before you start it back. Watch any good putter and you will always spot a slight lifting movement somewhere. Without this, you are in danger of sitting the putter on the ground, not really supporting its weight, and then gathering its weight and swinging it back in a slightly jerky fashion. Hold the club lightly but do support it.

The feeling of the strike is a slightly upward one – low and slow on the backswing – and then moving through maintaining the slight wrist break and the right wrist position. The shoulders rock, the wrists stay as a unit and this in itself brings the club head on up, keeping it square. The club head must hit the ball at a consistent depth for reliable feel, but never brushes the ground, always staying just a fraction above it.

HEAD AND EYES

With a short putt I very definitely keep my head still and at all costs never look up to see where the ball is going. More short putts are ruined through looking up too soon than anything else. With a 4-foot putt or thereabouts you are very definitely conscious of being able to see the ball and the hole at the same time. It is crucial here to keep both the head and the eyes still. This encourages you to produce a stroke with a definite finish, maintaining the head position until the ball drops. Listen for it to fall (in reality you see it out of the corner of your left eye). Don't even move your eyes. Keep absolutely stationary. This will help you build a repetitive stroke. If you look up at all early, the stroke usually moves off line.

As I get back to a putt of perhaps 8 to 10 feet I very definitely again keep my head still until the ball really is on its way. If under pressure at the end of a tournament I would certainly try and keep my head absolutely still until I either hear the ball drop in or it has obviously missed. I would try and exaggerate this as much as possible so that if I do weaken and look up at least the stroke is completed. In practice I keep the head still at this length but try to be aware of whether the ball drops by seeing it out of the corner of my eye. In a tournament I just stare down

1

2

at the ground at the point where the ball was and ignore totally what is happening to the ball. If it does miss my caddie will give me information about what happened.

I cannot stress enough this feeling of really staying still on the short putts.

PERFECTING THE STROKE

I have explained what happens in the putting stroke with the short putt. Now let's take it a stage further and go through the routine which is going to make you a good putter.

One of the crucial things is to get the putter head square to where you are going and to sit the putter flat on the ground. If you have the toe or the heel off the ground then the putter doesn't sit correctly for you. Sit it flat on the ground and check that the putter face really does aim at your target. Most players don't aim as well as they imagine, so from time to time walk round behind the putt while holding the putter and check that it really is on line.

Now before even doing this I suggest you have two or three practice swings. For a 4-foot putt I would suggest you go through this routine. Grip the putter and set yourself up just inside the line of the putt itself. The next move is important. Don't have

5

3

4

6

7

The complete putting stroke:
Eyes directly over the ball, wrists arched up. A rocking, pendulum action from the shoulders, adding a suspicion of wrist hinge and then holding it firmly through impact. Low, slow and slightly inside on the backswing, club face following, then through and up to the hole and a stationary finish

your two practice swings as though aiming at the hole. Take those practice swings aiming parallel to the line you are going to putt on. All you are doing is rehearsing the stroke. If instead you aim the practice swings at the hole, you are likely to aim the putt itself out to the right. And don't just do practice swings on pressure putts. It may confuse your alignment. Stick to the routine.

Right, now you have had two practice swings and you are then going to set the putter head down behind the ball. If you follow my advice about gripping the putter loosely, what you will do is to set the putter behind the ball; at this point the putter head is probably resting on the ground. The weight of the putter is probably supported by the ground. The next step is an absolutely key movement in putting. Grip the putter, however loosely, but then make absolutely certain that you lift the putter off the ground so that you gather its weight in your hands. You can then set the putter head back to touch the grass, but you must retain control of it by supporting it yourself. You are now perfectly in control of that putter and can move it back as slowly and smoothly as you like. The slower and smoother you swing it, the better.

If by contrast you do the wrong thing and set the putter head to the ground, resting it there and then take the putter away, you will be gathering it into your hands and swinging it at the same time. This is quite wrong and results in too long a swing which is likely to be jerky. If you watch virtually any good putter you will see that small mannerism of lifting the putter marginally from the ground, taking perfect control of it and then being able to swing it back smoothly. It is a key move which is often ignored and won't necessarily show up to somebody watching you.

The depth of contact with a putter is

The putting stroke from behind:
In this practice routine I am putting along a chalk line. With right elbow in, the putter moves slightly inside on the backswing. The putter then moves through and up to the hole, the line on my putter head following the chalk line to the hole

1

2

3

4

5

no less important than in the long game. You should have the putter moving low to the ground in the backswing and then low to the ground as it strikes the ball, on good greens certainly with a feeling of hitting the ball at the bottom of the swing or even slightly on the upswing. The putter must stay low to the ground through impact but must not scuff the ground. Only on bad or very slow greens or very grainy ones do you need any feeling of hitting down into the back of the ball and even in this case there must never be any question of scuffing the green at impact. You will see pros from areas with grainy greens – Japan, Africa – using a downward stroke and in their case making slight contact with the ground, but always just beyond and never right at impact. This may sound fairly obvious but it is surprising the number of people, including some professional golfers, who will have a practice swing with a putter and allow themselves to scuff the ground. Work at a good depth of contact where the

putter is almost as close to the ground as possible through impact but always just above the ground.

SHORT PUTTING DISTANCE

Good short putting is almost all about developing a perfect stroke. You can spend hours on the practice green simply repeating this stroke and trying to roll the ball smoothly. Direction may seem to be all-important but it is also necessary to get the right sort of strength to a putt. If the green is absolutely perfect you can roll the ball fairly slowly so that it just dies into the hole. Many people think that this is the ideal way to tackle a short putt. If the ball is moving slowly the argument is that it has a chance of tipping in from the front and also from both sides of the hole. This is fine when the greens are perfect. But if faced with greens which aren't in tip-top condition it is awfully easy to miss short putts simply by not hitting the ball firmly enough. The last

To encourage a good stroke chalk a line or peg a length of string on the green, practising your stroke along it

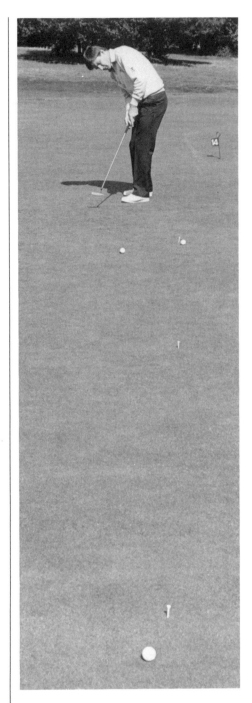

Long putting is far more a question of good feel for distance than anything else – but combined with reliable reading of the greens. The stroke remains the same, though of course longer, concentrating on striking the ball purely (never catching the ground) and developing feel in the fingertips to produce accurate length. Practise to different targets. Get it right *first* time

6 inches or so of any putt are crucial because at this point the ball takes up any imperfection and can easily wobble off line. If the green isn't perfect you want to make sure that the ball has reached the hole before it starts wobbling. I would suggest that the best way of approaching short putts is to hit the ball sufficiently firmly so that if the ball does miss it will travel 12 to 15 inches past the hole. In this way you have maximum chance of the ball staying on line. Then get confident and practise the really little ones and your holing-out will improve.

Where there is a substantial break from one side or the other you need to judge the line of the putt in conjunction with the speed. If you are bold, you can ram the ball firmly at the back of the hole, hardly allowing for any borrow; the ball will run fast and straight, holding its line. On the other hand, you may need to allow 2 or 3 inches to the side of the hole if you are going to trickle it in slowly. Different players will see a putt in quite different ways. Some see it firmly at the back of the hole; others see it as a slow trickler. The main thing about deciding which approach to have is to be positive and not to get caught between the two.

The situation of the game may dictate the way in which you approach the putt. If, for example, you have a putt for a half in a match it doesn't really matter what happens if you do miss. You may now like to hit the ball firmly to the back of the hole, not being concerned about how far it runs past if it misses. By contrast, in a stroke-play tournament you may prefer to allow for the borrow and take the putt more slowly for safety.

Practise short putts with both kinds of approach. It is all too easy to stand on the practice green ramming the ball at the back of the hole with little fear of failure, and then on the course to approach putts in quite a different way. Understand that there are two approaches and practise both.

LONG PUTTING

Good short putting is very much about making a reliable stroke. Long putting is far more a question of having good distance judgement and reading the greens well. Assuming you have read the green and decided, for example, to aim for the right or left, I would suggest that you have this idea of the line of the putt firmly in your mind but think more than anything about the distance you are going to produce. In reality on most greens you probably won't be more than a few inches out with direction but can so easily leave the ball 4 feet short or run it 8 feet past. Good distance is the key to getting the ball close.

Here again a repetitive stroke is important, particularly in getting the right depth as the putter comes through. If your depth is inconsistent then the strike is going to be inconsistent and so too is the distance. Keep the putter low to the ground without any tendency to scuff it. I would then suggest that you have a couple of practice swings in which you very definitely try to rehearse the sensation of the ball running to the hole. You will probably want a slightly wristier action if anything with a long putt and definitely need to get good feel in the right hand so that the putter head almost becomes your fingertips. Experiment with the feel of a little lag, just setting the wrists a touch in the backswing or almost to start the downswing, the hands feeling to lead into impact.

Having chosen an exact aiming point, set everything towards that. Then very largely forget it and work at distance. Aim to pass the hole with every putt but by no more than 2 feet. It is then a question of feel and practice. Don't just hit one long putt after another from the same spot. Vary the points you aim for to practise distance judgement and feel. You have to get it right the first time and not the second or third or fourth. The stroke is important, just a longer version of the short putt, but perfect control of the ball is really what we are after.

READING GREENS

Having developed a stroke with short putting and good distance judgement with long putting, it is essential to know whether to aim left or right of the hole and to decide on the correct degree of borrow. Broadly speaking, you are looking for the slope of the ground and

On most courses, particularly modern ones, the majority of greens are higher at the back than at the front. Look for this information as you approach the green. Sometimes the back is a matter of inches higher; sometimes feet. If the green looks dead flat from the front check whether it runs down to the back. On a modern course it is unusual and is going to be a special feature of the hole. On an old-fashioned course it may just follow the contour of the ground. But let's assume the back of the green is higher. Every putt from the right side of the green is likely to fall from right to left, and every putt from the left of the green is likely to be left to right. View every putt armed with this information and this assumption. If your reading of the putt confirms this, all well and good. If not, ask yourself why, and look again from other angles. The same follows even if only putting slightly across the slope. Think of anything slightly right of the flag whether short or past as right to left, left of the flag as left to right. Obviously it isn't infallible but it is a starting point for gaining an instinct for reading greens. Watch golf on the television, equipped with this information, and you will soon find yourself instinctively knowing the overall break of putts. In this way you will soon learn to read the putt on the correct side each time; quantifying the amount you allow obviously takes practice and experience

simply trying to gauge how much to the left or right you need to allow for any slope.

As you approach the green look at the overall lie of the land. Is the whole green sloping from right to left or from back to front? You can get a good clue to this 10 or 20 yards from the green. If faced with a long putt, look first at the green from the lowest point, from where the slope above you is going to be the most obvious. If you look from a higher spot downwards, the slope won't show up as much. This should give you an idea of whether you are going across a slope and also the degree of the slope. Next view the putt from perhaps 6 feet behind the ball, looking first at the overall lie of the land and crouching down lower to see any imperfections. I would suggest you then also look at the putt from the side – and preferably the lower side – to reinforce your ideas about the slope and also to see whether you are going uphill or downhill. Don't necessarily think that the uphill or downhill aspect will be obvious from behind the putt. It can be deceptive. Again if you look from the lower side of the slope you see much more than from the higher side. Last, if you are a good tournament

player and meticulous or if you are a club player with some uncertainty about the putt, do have a look at the area around the hole. At this point the ball is going to be travelling at its slowest and any imperfections in the slope of the ground have most effect. See what is going to happen within the last 2 or 3 feet of the roll of the ball. You may also get a clue to the slope of the ground from the way in which the hole is cut. Is the depth of soil greater above the can on one side than the other? If so this is likely to be the higher side.

With this overall information to hand look again at the putt from behind the ball then quickly assess the overall slope. Let's suppose that we have a putt which breaks from the left. I would suggest that you allow for the slope in one of two ways. On a fairly slow putt or one where there is relatively little borrow, choose a spot to the side of the hole and level with it. Concentrate on hitting the ball straight to it; think of it as a straight putt to this spot. It is almost as though you choose this spot, putt to that point and ignore the hole itself. Certainly what you mustn't do is try to steer the ball round in a curve. Treat every putt as a straight putt to a spot.

Do remember that when you have the flag attended, you can ask your caddie to stand on whichever side of the hole you prefer. You can't actually put him to a point where you specifically aim at his feet, but at least by having him on the higher side of the hole it does give you more of a reference to aim for. Bear in mind with both long putting and short putting that where you allow for a break, it is much better to keep the ball on the higher side as long as possible than to let it get below the hole. At least if the ball is above the hole it always has a chance of turning and rolling in. Once below the hole it can never turn back up the slope.

Reading greens and aiming correctly has to be precise. There always has to be this combination of line and length. It is meaningless to ask a caddie for a line without exchanging ideas on speed. His idea of 'right lip' may assume you ram it hard; yours may be to lag it. If reading the putt yourself be clear of your approach and if you read putts well, don't suddenly look to a foursomes partner or caddie for assistance if they are unfamiliar with your approach on length.

Tournament players have to be precise. Most major championships are won or lost on the odd putt. On fast, championship greens you can't simply aim for the hole if the putt looks virtually straight. I read greens to the extent of looking for a short putt as centre, right half, inside right or right edge. It is that crucial on a fast green. When aiming like this I look at the back of the hole for the exact spot – other, of course, than when it is right edge. Outside the width of the hole, many tournament players think in terms of the width of a ball or hole for making the allowance. It is visual and an internationally understood language between players and caddies.

When the break is substantial or the green fast it can be meaningless to aim at a spot level with the hole and way outside it. Look now for a curved path for the ball, choosing an aiming spot say two-thirds of the way along this path. Now see the putt as a straight putt to this point, from where it dies on down to the hole.

One of the problems with putting is that you don't always get proper feedback. You may miss a putt and not know why. Did you pull it, misread it, close the club face or were you unlucky? Sometimes you just don't know. In play, a caddie can't stand directly on your line. But when he attends the flag get him to watch how reliably you start the ball on line. If your direction is poor check that you really are concentrating on an aiming spot, rather than steering the ball round a curve. In practice, get a caddie or playing partner to check your stroke and to give you feedback as to how the ball starts and rolls. Only in this way can you know if the stroke, your reading of greens, or both need improvement.

Good reading of greens only comes with experience. As you start playing more courses and under different conditions the subtleties of reading greens become apparent. Not only is there the overall slope of the green to master, but also changes in texture, different growths of grass and so on. It is a continual learning process. Look at the grass itself. Most British courses have a fine-leafed, bent grass that sits straight up and has little bearing on the putt. In Asia, Africa, Southern Europe and America the grass is broader leafed; it doesn't just sit up but lies flat, usually in the direction of the setting sun or of the nearest water supply. Look along the grain of grass and it looks pale and shiny; look into the grass and it looks dull. The effect is like the mown stripes on a classic English lawn! Dark and you are going into the grain for a slow putt, pale and you are putting with the grain for a fast putt. The grain, in some parts of the world, can have more effect than the slope. A putt in South Africa can literally run *up* the slope with the grain; in Japan the grass is so thick that you can hear the ball run through the grain! And be prepared in hot countries for a substantial growth during the day. The grass gets thicker, the putt slower and you may find Bermuda greens in America where the grass gets burnt off one side of the hole and almost overhangs the other. Learn to adapt quickly. Examine the grass on the green and fringe carefully, feeling the texture with your feet and experimenting to understand it.

Learn to assess greens quickly. Look for a plateau green that may drain quickly and be fast, a basin green gathering water and being slow. Beware of a green with adjacent large trees. If they are to the south of the green it may remain in shadow all day and be slow. But also look for telltale signs of roots near the surface which may drain moisture and make the putt fast. A new or relaid green may play quite differently from any other. Look too for an overall slope to a course, perhaps away from a mountain or down to a river. Pick up clues like this as early in the round as possible and read every green with this in mind. Take time in practice rounds to read greens. Don't just putt to the hole, but practise to different points on the green. If limited to the practice green just experiment over and over again, choosing a target, reading the putt and getting perfection first time.

Pitching and chipping

THE LONG GAME is the exciting part of golf but in reality it is often excellence at the short game which helps most with good scoring. There is a whole range of different kinds of shots around the green and I want to take you through as many as possible. The sequences show my own approach to various situations with key thoughts for the advanced player and tournament golfer. The amateur must read through the text for further information on developing these shots and other more basic shots round the green.

Before starting on describing the shots I want to talk about choice of clubs. The first choice of club for most golfers is going to be the putter. Look at any shot near the green and simply ask yourself whether you can putt the ball. If you are 2 feet or 3 feet off the edge of the green and the grass is short then the putter is probably the easiest club to use. But if you go back a few feet don't think there is anything amateurish in taking a putter. Look at the ground you have to run the ball over. It doesn't need to be absolutely flat and perfect for the putter to be the right choice. As long as it looks fairly predictable you can probably still get the ball running better with a putter than trying to chip or pitch over it. The ball may bobble about a bit but it will probably still run fairly accurately.

Another consideration is the way in which the ball sits. If the ball sits up nicely with grass beneath it then it may be fine to run or pitch the ball. But if the lie is bare, even sitting in a tiny depression or possibly even a slightly difficult lie, the putter may be the most accurate club to use. You don't have to find the bottom of the ball but simply

have to hit into the back of it. You can pop it away from a poor lie without risking an awkward contact with the ground. The strike is going to be easy and you can probably judge distance accurately. Look also at shots where you have to go up or down a bank in terms of whether you can take a putter. Don't imagine that a bank in front of you means you have to loft the ball over it. The easiest way of getting up or down a bank is just to run the ball. The putter has many uses round the green so experiment with it.

The second choice if you can't putt the ball is to get the ball running. Many players find it far easier to judge length with a running shot than with a pitch. If you run the ball with, for example, a 6-iron, the ball will be touching down fairly quickly and then running most of the way. You can probably judge this distance by looking at the ground in front of you far more easily than you can judge it through the air with a wedge. So the second choice for most people is to run the ball. Only when it is obvious that you can't putt the ball or run it should you look to the wedge and assume that you have to carry the ball all the way.

THE SHORT CHIP – GRIP AND SETUP

The short chip from a few feet off the edge of the green is one of the most important shots for scoring. If you can chip the ball really well you have every chance of holing it; if you chip badly then you are going to waste shots needlessly. I use a variety of

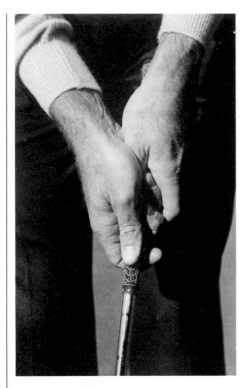

Left With short chipping I use a similar reverse overlap grip as for putting, hands to the side of the club, left index finger down the back of the fingers of the right hand, but not as far down as with the putter

1

Right These two frames show the similarity between the short chipping and putting address positions. The hands are again brought into an arched position, elbows in. If the left hand isn't brought into this position the left elbow simply won't tuck in correctly. Weight is a touch further to the left in chipping, ball back and hands therefore slightly ahead

2

clubs around the green and may play a short chip with a 4-, 6- or 8-iron. I would suggest for the club golfer sticking to one club – possibly the 6-iron or the 7-iron – and learning to use it well. The basic principle of short chipping is to make it as near as possible to putting.

In order to chip properly there are several key moves you need to make. First of all you will see that most good players grip the club in much the same way as they would the putter. I adopt what is virtually my putting grip, doing the reverse overlapping grip, index finger of the left hand down the outside. This isn't essential, but what is essential is that you get the hands to the sides of the club, thumbs down the front. Very definitely *not* having the left hand on top and the right hand beneath. Keep the palms facing in the same way as you putt.

The second key move here is that you must also alter the lie of the club by bringing it up so that it sits towards its toe. This is the kind of lie that you use with the putter and it is fundamental that you do the same thing with chipping. What most club golfers do in chipping is simply to use their normal grip and go down the shaft of the club, keeping the wrists low in much the same way as they would for the long

game. This is entirely unsatisfactory. What happens if you get this low wrist position is that it encourages you to use your hands and wrists and this generates power. The last thing you want in this kind of shot is a loose wrist action. You therefore have to bring the club up so that it sits a little towards its toe, the left wrist now coming up into a slightly arched position from where the wrist will stay firm with perfect control on the shot. The taller you are the more upright your club sits in the first place. The shorter you are the more noticeable the change you will need to make. This then helps you to get the eyes directly over the ball as in putting.

The next key move is to make sure that you have the ball in the right part of the club head. With the club sitting slightly up on its toe, it is this point on the club which brushes the ground. You need the ball positioned fractionally towards the toe and need to strike it slightly towards the toe. This gives feel, not unwanted power. If you strike the ball off the middle of the club face or at all towards the heel, it may rush off with too much speed. From the toe you get a soft, dead shot, particularly useful for the really short chip onto a fast, tournament green.

These two frames show the similarity between putting and chipping from this angle – elbows in, wrists up, the reverse overlap grip. Perhaps the most important lesson is just how close I am able to stand to the ball when chipping. Just as when putting I aim at having the eyes directly over the ball. This requires a conscious – or for most really good players, unconscious – movement of sitting the club more upright and so slightly on its toe. The ball is therefore played slightly towards the toe of the club

The Short Chipping Stroke

In this shot I am playing a tiny one from just off the edge of the green, in this case using a 6-iron to loft the ball forwards about 5 to 6 feet and running it another 20 feet or so to the hole. I am using the reverse overlap grip, elbows in, wrists arched up as in putting. This brings the club up to a far more upright lie than normal, the club balancing slightly on its toe and the ball correspondingly played towards the toe of the club. This allows me to stand in close to the ball and to get my eyes directly over it. Using the toe of the club will give masses of feel, but with a deadened hit from the toe to produce a short, controlled shot.

The stroke is played with the same rocking of the shoulders as for putting, but with a little more hand action. With the wrists arched in this way you can let the wrists hinge in the backswing, and still swing the club in a comparatively straight path. Having the wrists arched in fact limits the wrist action to the right amount, the end of the club meeting up with the inside of the left wrist if the hinge is fairly free. And then you hold the hinge in position without really letting it return. The last thing you want is the club head passing your hands. You can either have a main thought of the right hand, hinging the right wrist and hitting through with the right – I quite often do this if I want to hit it a touch harder – or think of the left. With the very short one I almost think of hinging and then hitting with the left, perhaps just slowing down the strike a shade and shortening the throughswing a fraction. The ball is just nipped away, taking the ball, skidding the club head across the grass for a moment but definitely with no divot. Holding the wrists off gives a solid contact.

The advantage of this action is that it allows you to make a longer swing, easier under pressure, while still producing a very tiny shot. Sometimes you just have to loft the ball a yard or two out of the fringe, before landing it on a very fast green, running it say 10 yards. With this grip and wrist position you get a dead hit, real control. With an ordinary grip you get so much hinge and release, and great difficulty in keeping the shot small enough. I use the same action with 4-, 6-, 8- or pitching wedge, just looking at the degree of run needed. The same stroke with a 4-iron might run it 25 yards and with a pitching wedge 10 yards. I consider the carry and run needed, but having chosen the club, look at the overall length for judgement. Only with the trickiest of little shots with the wedge, onto a very flat green, do I make the main thought the landing spot. In practice I keep making the same stroke, working through the four clubs, and always spending time on the very short ones. These are the ones requiring a really good action under pressure.

1

4

2

3

5

6

1

2

5

6

This shows the chipping action with an 8-iron. The ball is just behind centre, hands ahead, weight favouring the left foot. Elbows stay tight into the side, back and through, rocking from the shoulders. The strike is slightly downward, taking the ball, then skidding the club on the ground before allowing it up again

The main fault of the club golfer is that he becomes wristy. Usually this comes from standing too far from the ball, holding the club with its normal lie and the wrists dropped instead of arched. This already sets up much too much hand action. Get the club sitting up on its toe, elbows back into you, forearms out and wrists up. Adopt the reverse overlap grip, left hand in a weak position round to the left of the club. This will bring the left elbow back into your side and allow you to chip with a putting stroke. Keep the elbows tucked right in and rock from the shoulders. Experiment first with no wrist hinge, keeping the wrists arched. Play the ball from the toe of the club until the contact feels soft. Practise

3

4

lining up balls no more than 1 inch apart and strike them away one at a time until you do take them off the toe. Experiment with one club first, say a 7-iron, and then gradually add a little wrist hinge and learn to work with a variety of clubs for real control. As with putting, any wrist hinge is very slight for the short chip – far more a question of emphasis on the hands to change direction than making a very definite movement that shows. Think positively and work, not just at getting the ball close, but at getting it in the hole.

One other tip for the club golfer. Sitting the club with the correct lie is probably the most important key to improvement at chipping. I probably only have the ball about 10 inches from my feet for this shot and my eyes very definitely directly over the ball. It is for this reason that club golfers often find a chipping club useful. It is not really the design of the head or the length of the shaft of these clubs which make life easier but the fact that they are set up with a different lie. Having got your hands to the side of the club, left wrist up, do make sure that the swing doesn't become stiff in the arms. Try to have the arms hanging down so that the upper arms and elbows feel tucked into the side. You can then produce a simple back-and-through stroke like a putting stroke without the arms ever leaving the side. If by contrast you incorrectly get too far from the ball, the arms are going to swing away from you, leaving the body and looking ungainly.

LONGER RUNNING SHOTS

Running shots with anything from 4-iron to pitching wedge also have their part to play round the green for a longer distance. You may need to use these shots on seaside courses when the ball needs to be kept below the wind, or on dry heathland courses where the ball will run quite merrily. Other situations lend themselves to running shots. You may have over-hanging trees to negotiate or a two-tier green where the ball has to be run up the bank onto the upper layer, pitching being more risky. In this situation I would again use my 4-, 6- or 8-iron or pitching wedge rather depending on the trajectory I want. The club golfer is possibly best to stick to a 4-iron for a very low shot or a 7-iron as his general-purpose club. At this stage, to add leverage I now go back to my ordinary Vardon grip rather than the putting grip. You will remember that I stressed having a grip where the right palm is very much behind the club. Any golfer who has a fairly strong grip, with the left hand well on the top or the right hand well underneath, will certainly need to adapt that grip for most of these finesse shots round the green. A strong grip is going to tend to lose loft and get the ball taking off with too much speed. So if you do have a strong grip, certainly weaken it for this shot and for the pitch shots which follow. Ensure that the line between the thumb and index finger of the left hand

1

2

5

6

To play this 30-yard running shot with a 6-iron I now use the ordinary Vardon grip for added leverage, hands well down the shaft, eyes directly over the ball, weight well on the left foot and the hands ahead of the ball. This presets most of the wrist angle I need. I swing the club back and through from the shoulders, just letting the legs ease through if they need to. The wrist angle is added to very slightly in the backswing, hinging and setting the wrist, not cupping it, maintaining this wrist angle through the ball. Back and throughswing are much the same length, feeling a slightly downward contact, with just a minute divot beyond the ball, but the club coming out and up to mirror the backswing

points up no further right than your right ear and make sure that the right hand is predominantly behind the club, and the line between the thumb and index finger up towards your chin. You should be able to feel that the right hand controls the club face and that whatever you do with the right palm you in effect do with the club face.

It is a good discipline to practise these running shots for anything from 15 yards up to 60 or 70 yards. For the advanced player they can be developed even further into a real punch-and-run shot for windy conditions. In the address position, set the hands slightly ahead of the ball, so that the ball is roughly in the middle of the stance. The weight must be comfort-

3

4

7

8

ably balanced on the balls of the feet ensuring that the bottom is out, the knees flexed but the legs back and out of the way of your hands and arms. The upper arms will still be close to the body and relaxed, the wrists gradually becoming firmer the shorter the shot and the more control you want. With the ball a little further back in your stance towards the right foot, you may now need to turn the feet slightly left of target to keep the ball flying straight. This is very much a question of trial and error and varies from one player to another. One word of explanation about the stance. If you do turn the feet slightly to the left, this is just a question of withdrawing the left foot slightly and also turning it out a little

more. At the same time check the position of the right foot. This should point straight in front of you or may almost need to be turned very slightly towards the target. Many players get into difficulty by turning the right foot out for running shots and pitching and so not being able to get off the foot through and beyond impact. For the short running shot you may like to have the hands well down the grip of the club. There is no harm getting to the bottom of the grip and almost getting your right index finger onto the metal of the shaft. This is usually an easy way of cutting down the swing and getting good control. As the shot gets longer you can ease back up the club to produce a little more momentum.

For the club golfer I would suggest that you play these shots with a feeling of being fairly firm in the wrists, never loose. You will automatically set some wrist angle at address, firstly by having the wrists dropped slightly and secondly by having the hands forward slightly. All you really need to do is to maintain this kind of angle in the backswing, and in the throughswing, feeling that the swing is done predominantly from the arms. Again, as with short chipping, the upper arms should stay in so that there will be some necessary leg movement through the ball rather than a stiff, pendulum action from the shoulders. Think very much of the club head, producing a neat, saucer-shaped arc and small divot, just letting the legs move in sympathy with this. If you do this shot with a 6- or 7-iron you should find distance judgement comparatively easy and for shots up to 30 yards or so the feeling simply needs to be of swinging the club back and through for much the same distance and with much the same speed as you would swing a putter. Judgement should be fairly easy and require relatively little thought. You can then alter the trajectory of the shot by tipping the hands forward a little more at address to turn the club face over slightly, getting the ball down on the ground sooner with a greater proportion of run.

For the advanced player, I would suggest building in some hand action which will obviously increase as the length of the shot increases. At address you already have wrist cock built in, with the wrists down and the hands forward. You should then add to this wrist cock as the length of the shot dictates, by setting the right wrist back on itself in much the same way as I have explained for the full swing. For short shots this setting is obviously slight but gradually increases as the length of the shot increases. The important point then – this is what is often almost impossible for the club player – is to hold this setting of the wrists through impact, just releasing it very slightly with the right hand but never to the point where the right wrist straightens through impact. The club player trying this invariably actually straightens the right wrist with disastrous results. If you can produce this

A pitch and run:

This shows a low pitch and run about 25 to 30 yards from the green, played with a pitching wedge. I am not trying to float it in, mainly because there is nothing to go directly over and no fixed reference point for judging distance. In this case I have a slight ridge in front of me; I am trying to land the ball on the top of this and then run it to the hole. You can use this shot when there is a lot of undulation right in front of you, when you can't land it in this because it is too unpredictable, but you still want to run the ball to the hole; perhaps if the green is very fast and hard, wet and skiddy or with a double-tier bank to negotiate.

The ball is played fairly centrally in the feet, Vardon grip, weight favouring the left foot and stance slightly turned to the left. The wrists hinge on the backswing, holding the club face slightly shut, holding this same position through impact to punch the ball forwards, but then pulling the hands to the left in this same wrist position just at impact. This gives a kind of sliding action through impact to impart a touch of cut spin but combined with a punching, rather than floating, trajectory. It also allows you to hit it aggressively, particularly important from a tight lie.

Holding this wrist angle through impact is crucial on this shot and the longer punches and pitches. At impact the hands and wrists are ahead of the club head but also obviously 'inside' the club head – in other words closer to your bodyline than the club head. Beyond impact the arms and body pull away to the left, keeping the hands ahead of the club head, but most importantly keeping them left of the club head. The hands will come round level with the body, the club head remains outside it. The wrists stay set, left elbow tight to the body, adding spin to the shot

1

5

9

2

3

4

6

7

8

10

11

12

1   2   3

6   7   8

The 100-yard pitch with a pitching wedge: My full pitching wedge shot would be 115 yards. To produce this slightly shorter than full shot I grip down the club an inch or so. I then play the shot in much the same way as an ordinary short iron, positioning the ball slightly ahead of centre and with my hands as normal just ahead of the ball. As usual I want to feel the backward setting of the right wrist in the backswing and so set it first as preparation before the swing. I then start the swing with this feeling of an early, backward wristbreak, quite a sharp wrist set, and ensure that the angle is held through impact. The overall feeling is one of an arm action, resisting too much movement with the legs. I then hit down and through the ball, head and body still

correct use of the hands for the running shots you should be able to get tremendous feel. Once again it is worth experimenting with your contact with the ball for the relatively *short* running shot. The middle of the club face gives you power; moving up a little more towards the toe may give you more feel and control for the short ones.

LONG PITCHING

Whenever I look at books or articles about pitching I always think there is too much generalization, as though there is just one shot. In fact there is a whole variety of pitch shots and the

4

5

9

10

11

way you play a shot of 80 yards bears little resemblance to the method you have to use for 10 to 20 yards. I am therefore going to look at a full range of shots, starting with what is the easiest for most people – the long pitch.

I aim to hit a full pitching wedge 115 yards. That is with a full, smooth swing but without pressing for all the length I can get. To me it is an easy, full swing. For most club golfers the length with a full pitching wedge will be more like 90 to 100 yards. So at this distance I am simply thinking in terms of a full swing, playing the shot in just the same way as I approach the other short and medium irons. The contact I want with the ball is still just the same, with no

feeling of gouging out great divots or an excessively downward attack. There is certainly a ball–divot contact but the attack is still relatively shallow and the club is taken through to a full finish.

One of the simplest ways of adjusting distance downwards by up to 15 yards is simply to grip the club a little shorter, going down the club progressively 1 inch, 2 inches and 3 inches. The feeling of the swing and contact will remain identical. The change is easy to make and the results accurate.

From here we then need to work down through shorter distances – for the good club player from around 80 to 85 yards back to 50 yards where full shots with the sand iron can take over.

In this range still grip down the club by about 3 inches and you may find, particularly if you are not tall, that you can keep going down the grip of the club and still shorten the shot even further without much change in the action. But at some point we certainly have to shorten the swing and begin to produce a real pitching action. What mustn't happen, and I can't emphasize this enough, is for the full swing simply to become looser and slower with the feeling of 'dolly dropping' the ball a relatively short way. Medium- and long-handicap players tend to do this. There is no such shot in golf! Every pitch must have a sufficiently short and controlled backswing to enable you to accelerate slightly through impact.

So for this range of 50 to about 85 yards (say 100 yards for the tournament professional) the action requires a shorter backswing to produce more finesse. I use a slightly narrower width of stance than I use for the long shots, the ball around the middle of the stance, my arms hanging down, upper arms into the side and the hands slightly ahead of the ball at address. The right wrist is already set in a slight angle, and we increase this wrist break in the backswing, right elbow staying into the side, limiting the length of the backswing as we need a shorter shot. This is obviously a matter of subjective judgement but do bear in mind that the swing probably goes further than you imagine. The shorter the swing you need, the earlier the right wrist has to be set back on itself. In the downswing and throughswing it is essential that the setting of the right wrist is maintained so that through impact the right wrist never straightens. The swing is taken through to a fairly short, punchy finish, the forearms very definitely never crossing over but with the right wrist remaining set back through impact. This will mean that at the end of the swing the left wrist too will be in the same position it held at address.

For the club player I would emphasize that the end of the swing is short and controlled, and this is one shot where the left arm really can stay firm beyond impact without any feeling of turning and folding away. You need to stress firmness to get away from any tendency to be loose and sloppy

1

2

5

6

9

10

3

4

A pitching wedge at 100 yards:
The action here is almost identical to the full shot with a short iron, using a square stance, normal ball position but just shortening the swing very slightly. The club doesn't quite reach horizontal and is therefore not quite parallel to the line of flight at the top of the backswing. Don't confuse this as being a swing on a different path. It is simply slightly shorter. From here I still feel the plane of the downswing dropping and I attack the ball well from the inside, moving on through to a slightly shorter finish than for the full shot. Through impact there is a definite feeling of holding the club off, pulling the club face slightly across the ball, without actually attacking it out to in. This means that I am pulling hard round with the left side, wrists still set, to impart a little cut spin. It shows up in the way the left elbow draws away behind me and the slightly round body position of left elbow and club shaft. The break in the right wrist held through impact is still very apparent at the end of the swing. Set the wrists, hold the wrists all the way and turn on through with the left side

7

8

11

12

through impact. The advanced player can produce a softer finish and still keep control. Again let me emphasize the way in which the arms stay close to the body in these shots for a compact action, despite the feeling of a firm finish. Even with the left arm staying firm beyond impact don't have the feeling of pushing the arms out and away from the body towards the target. The left upper arm can still stay close to the body, providing the legs just ease the weight through smoothly onto the left side.

Once more, as with the running shots, you may have to make an adjustment to the setting of the feet. By playing the ball a little further back in the stance towards the middle of the

FOR THE ADVANCED PLAYER

1

5

The advanced player should with shots of this distance be able to feel the shot as very much a right-handed action without the club golfer's tendency to straighten the right wrist through impact. The right wrist is set back on itself in the backswing and it very definitely holds the degree of wrist cock as it strikes the ball. The palm of the right hand and club face work in harmony. If you want to hold the club face back or slightly open then you can feel this in the palm of the hand. If you want to feel a slight drawing action and the tiniest bit of closing of the club face, then again the right hand should be able to ease this through. Providing the right hand is set behind the club shaft at address, pitching can be a right-handed action, the left hand obviously giving support and never of course breaking down through impact. Where I explained to the club player that the left arm should stay firm through and beyond impact, the good golfer will often allow the left arm to soften and break slightly beyond impact. At this point if you are trying to keep full loft on the club face, the left arm isn't actually going to turn and fold beyond impact. The elbow may now almost break outwards and behind you, an action which we will see becomes more pronounced with the shorter pitch.

Good pitching is all about judging distance. Professional golfers as a rule select clubs almost entirely by reference to distances paced out and plotted in practice rounds. I like to know specific distances down to perhaps 50 yards; from there down it is visual. I would suggest that you practise pitching to various targets, knowing the exact distance of each so that you can then repeat the action on the course with considerable precision.

A 70-yard pitch with the sand wedge: My maximum with the sand wedge is 90 yards, using a loft of 57½ degrees, so this is slightly shorter than my full swing. I now use a slightly narrower stance than for the full pitch, weight favouring the left foot and hands ahead of the ball. My feeling again is of an early setting of the wrists. In the downswing I sink slightly into the shot with the legs as opposed to staying up through impact with the fullish pitching wedge shot. The contact I aim for is to get the leading edge down into and almost under the ball, the bounce of the flange bringing the club out and up from impact. Backswing and throughswing mirror each other for length, so although the right foot is fairly still through impact, right side back, the hips must come through quite crisply to allow acceleration through the ball

9

2

3

4

6

7

8

10

11

12

1

2

3

7

8

9

70-yard pitch – sand wedge:
In this shot I am aiming at pitching the ball right at the flag – in fact slightly left of it to allow for the wind – and hoping to stop the ball quickly on the green. I am gripping down the club slightly, stance a shade open, and standing in close to the ball. This is the nearest I get to an up-and-down kind of action, creating quite an upright swing to hit down and impart backspin. The club does now work up and down, but notice how just before impact the attack is coming from the inside, the arms still having plenty of space to swing past my body. Without in

any way attacking the ball from 'out-to-in' there is this definite pulling to the left action at the moment of impact to impart cutspin. It is very clear here just beyond impact. The hands have pulled left, hidden by the body, club still out in front of me. The whole unit of left elbow and wrist stays constant to the end. The left side of the body and left shoulder work hard through impact to create this pull away and cut spin. The left shoulder works back and up, keeping the right shoulder passive for an inside attack, combined with spin

feet there may be a tendency to catch the ball in an in-to-out direction and so push it right of target. If this is the case, the line of the feet may need to go a little left of target, turning the left foot out but ensuring that the right foot is straight in front and certainly never turned out at all. Last, for the club player and advanced player alike, it is essential to watch the ball really well through impact without any tendency to look up and see where it is going.

MEDIUM-LENGTH PITCHING

Shots of about 30 to 50 yards can cause problems. Often this is because players use a pitching wedge instead of a

4

5

6

10

11

12

sand iron, making life more difficult than they need. Many pros in fact use two sand irons in their set, one for bunker shots and one for shots round the green. The added loft of the sand iron gives you a ready-made shorter shot than a pitching wedge. Don't be put off by the name of the club, the weight of it or the flange on the bottom of the club head. The sand iron is really a far more useful club round the green than a pitching wedge.

The difficulty with these medium-length wedge shots is that most people swing the club too far back and then feel that too much power is created. They slow down through impact, and as a result of this, let the right wrist flip the club head through, producing a

fluffed shot or a thin shot. For most players, the easiest way of working in the range of 35 to 50 yards is to use the sand wedge, starting at, say, 50 yards with a fairly full swing, going down the grip inch by inch and simply producing a shorter distance. The maximum with a sand wedge can vary from 50 to 80 yards, depending both on the strength of the player and loft of the club. For the longer-handicap golfer the danger with a sand wedge is that the club is heavy and if you don't get a good contact, with this full swing the ball travels an alarming distance. Emphasis must be on watching the back of the ball, ensuring that the weight really does get onto the left foot through impact and producing a very

1

2

5

6

9

10

3

4

7

8

11

The 30-yard pitch:
Here we start getting down to the shorter pitches – the shorter the shot the more difficult they often become for the amateur. I am now playing this with my sand iron, from a narrow stance, ball back in the feet, hands ahead of the ball and the weight favouring my left foot. The shot requires a bit of wrist break to get suffi-cient length, cocking the wrists backward, rather than upward, in the takeaway, and then holding this wrist break through impact with firmness in the left wrist. The club is swung through smoothly with a combination of a shoulder rocking action and arm action, but with the upper arms very definitely staying close to the body throughout

definitely downward attack into the back of the ball – ball and divot – which should see it pop up. Any tendency to try to lift the ball must be curbed. The right hand must be kept behind and never beneath the club at address. Remember that you cannot get under the ball so hit down and the ball will come up.

For the club player the danger is one of producing a loose, slow, full swing where the club head decelerates into impact. All these shots must be played with a short enough backswing to allow for acceleration through impact. The method used must be identical to that of the pitching wedge for the longer shots, setting the hands down and forward a little at address so that the wrists are pre-set, adding a little to this wrist set in the backswing, transferring the weight through onto the left foot through impact and then stopping in a firm, punchy position, wrists firm, left arm firm, left upper arm still close to the body and the eyes firmly focused on the spot where the ball was.

If the action through impact is firm enough the left wrist should still seem almost arched as it was at address. It is this holding of the wrist cock through impact which is generally the most difficult thing for the club player to understand and to feel. Let's go through it slowly again.

At address the hands are slightly down and they are slightly forwards. This gives you two dimensions of the wrist cock already set. You set the upward wrist cock by having the hands low; this is the one that will show up when looking directly at the player from the other side of the ball. Having the hands forward sets the right wrist in so that the wrist is slightly back on itself. The important point with all of these short finesse shots is that the right wrist angle must never change through impact and the right wrist must never straighten. Now in the backswing the wrist cock is added to, not any more of the upward wrist cock onto the thumbs, but the backward wrist set of the right wrist. For a fairly strong shot with the sand iron the wrist is almost going to set right back on itself. This will mean that the left wrist is naturally going to arch a little more by the top of the backswing. In the

throughswing your weight will be transferred onto your left foot, back into the heel of it, the arms swinging down and keeping that pre-set wrist action through the ball. The good player will often uncock the right wrist *slightly* a moment before impact, but he will never let the wrist straighten. The club player is much better to think of setting that wrist angle and then to maintain it absolutely solidly through the ball. Once more you have a firm unit of the left forearm, left wrist and right wrist which must not buckle before or as the ball is struck.

I like to feel these shots to be very much an arm action through impact, but again with the proviso that there is just enough leg action to keep the body moving through and to enable the left upper arm and body to stay pretty much together. Excessive leg action tends to lead to an overly steep attack on the ball, often with wedge shots sprayed away to the right and left. Too little leg action, which is likely to be the fault of the club player, often doesn't enable the wrists to stay firm enough through impact.

SHORT PITCHING

For all but the very fine player the shorter the shot the more difficult it is to cope with. Books by tournament professionals often suggest that the short pitch of 15 yards or so is just a very small version of the long pitch. To them, and indeed to me, I suppose that is really what it is. But for scratch amateurs and club players alike the small, delicate shot over a bunker is the one which can be a nightmare. I am going to look at these shots in several different ways and also working with a variety of lies. You aren't going to play the shot from an easy, lush lie in the same way as you are going to tackle one from a tight lie or a slight divot hole. So let's work through them one by one.

I am going to deal with all these shots first for the club player and by this I mean anyone other than a really top-class golfer. I am then going to look at the shots in a more advanced way. Once again, work through the shots patiently and don't try to play the advanced player's shot if in reality it is

In these short pitches we begin to see how the loft on the club face is held through impact. The club face still faces upward beyond impact, *not* turning into a toe-up position as it would by now in the long game. Instead of the left arm stopping, with the club head passing the wrists through and beyond impact, the left arm keeps moving and begins to break the other way, left elbow hugging the body, back of the left wrist, right palm and club face now looking upwards

1

2

quite unsuitable for you. The basic principles of short pitching are that you want to get almost as much loft on the club face as possible, again using a sand iron. You want to hold that loft through impact so that the ball pops up softly and you want to be able to produce a slow, constant speed through impact which sends the ball the correct distance. You are far better with short pitching to feel some sort of method which gives you really short shots which you can then lengthen, rather than having the feeling of being overpowered. The shorter the shot the more impossible it generally becomes. Hitting the ball 6 or 7 yards over a small bunker or bank is for most people far more difficult than hitting it 30 yards. So concentrate on really short shots.

I would suggest you adopt a method for short pitching which has as few moving parts as possible and certainly minimal hand and wrist action. The easiest way to do this is to use the sand iron, holding the club several inches down the grip, again making sure that the grip is relatively weak, right hand very definitely behind and not beneath the shaft. The left hand too should be to the side of the shaft, again in a weaker position than you would hopefully use in the long game. Set the club with its full loft, the shaft straight up towards you. Don't tip it forward or you lose loft. Keep the hands low, dropped at address. This presets sufficient cupping in the wrists to enable you to swing without having to add to it.

Let's tackle this first from a good lie. Feel at this point that you virtually lock the elbows into the side of your body, with the wrists firm and the grip quite tight. Possibly turn both feet very slightly in the direction you are hitting, opening the stance, the weight if anything favouring the left foot. The idea of the swing is now to move the club back and through in a smooth, shallow, wide arc, simply brushing the ground on which the ball sits. There should be no twisting or rolling of the wrists, the wrist action feeling passive. The backswing should be kept simple, just easing the club head back perhaps 4 or 5 feet, with no pickup in the wrists. In the throughswing there must be emphasis on keeping the wrists firm and returning the club face to the ball with its full loft. To do this the feeling I would suggest is that you keep the elbows, and in particular the left elbow, tucked into the side, working arms and body as a unit, and allowing the legs to move. In other words you don't get a stiff, pendulum action from the shoulders but you actually keep the upper arms well in. This means that at the end of the swing there will have been a noticeable leg movement, the club now swinging straight through to the target, with the club face held under and up as it strikes the ball. The wrists will remain passive. Providing the upper arms have stayed in and the body has worked, the shot won't look rigid but will simply look neat and controlled. If it looks rigid and feels awkward then the odds are the legs aren't playing their part. Try the same exercise I suggested for the long game with the towel trapped between elbows and body to feel the arms and legs working in harmony. Correctly this takes emphasis off the hands and wrists and will stop any tendency to flick at the ball and try and help it up.

All you should be trying to do in this spot is to brush the ground on which the ball sits. The deeper the cushion of grass the easier the shot becomes. With a little cushion or on a bare lie the depth judgement needs to be more accurate.

The way I suggest you approach this shot in play is to have two or three practice swings – the tighter the lie the more you need – feeling that the sole of the club very definitely brushes the ground. It shouldn't just tickle the grass but you should actually feel and indeed hear the flange of the club almost bouncing on the ground itself. Once you have the depth judgement firmly in mind choose a definite spot to land the ball on, look back at the ball, visualize that target you want to hit and execute the shot.

One of the most difficult points for the club player here is to keep the head still and to stay looking down. Often it is not just a question of lifting the head because you want to see where the ball has gone, but of actually lifting the head almost before impact to try to see where you are going. You need to visualize the landing spot so that as you look down at the ball you have a clear picture of the shot in your mind. The shorter the shot the more difficult it often is to resist looking up. With longer shots you know that you can stay down 2 or 3 seconds and still look up to see the ball flying through the air. With short shots there is almost a feeling of having to look up early or you miss seeing the flight. The best discipline here is to stay looking down at the ground until you actually hear the ball land on the green the other side of the bunker.

Once you can grasp this basic action you should be able to work slightly more at club face control through impact. I would suggest for most club golfers having a sand iron with at least 60 degrees of loft. This may not give you quite the distance I have suggested for the longer pitch – so that you may need to use your pitching wedge more – but it can be so helpful in this kind of short shot situation. The more loft you have on the club quite simply the easier it is to get the ball popping up well. Let's look at the way in which the club face works through. You set it at address with full loft and

1

5

2

3

4

6

7

8

The 10-yard pitch with a sand wedge:
Here I am using the heaviest club in the bag to produce a really short, delicate shot. Emphasis throughout is on slowness combined with crispness, almost having to hold the club head back with quite a positive feeling to keep the shot short enough.

At address I grip well down the club, knees slightly bent and wrists fairly low. This brings the hands in close to the body, elbows and upper arms glued to my chest so that everything works as a unit. In the takeaway the hands and arms work away in much the same manner as an ordinary swing. The backswing is short, from there making the throughswing accelerate while being reasonably slow. As I accelerate the wrist set if anything increases, almost a flailing. I take it back and as the body pulls

through the hands are almost left behind. There is a definite restraint in the wrists, never letting the club head catch up. The wrist angle is held, the hands being both ahead of, and inside the line of, the club head beyond impact. Again I am pulling away to the left with body and arms to add cutspin, keeping the elbows tight to the side. The left elbow drags away behind me, keeping the wrist angle, and most importantly keeping the back of the left hand, palm of the right and the club face looking upwards beyond impact.

The contact is one of bouncing the flange of the club down in behind and beneath the ball, not taking a divot with the leading edge, but denting the ground with the flange.

as you come through you very definitely want that loft retained. The club head almost slides beneath the ball and works through into an open face position where it looks up beyond impact. To do this the left arm isn't going to turn and fold away as I have described in the long game; it doesn't bring the club face round into a toe-up position. It works through so that the left elbow almost drags out behind you beyond impact, the upper arm still into the side, club face upwards in the finish. Practise making short shots in this way, really watching the club face as it reaches the bottom of the swing and easing it up into this open-faced angle. Now sit the ball on a really good, lush lie and gradually feel that you can almost set the club slightly more on its back and still ease it between the ball and solid ground. Slide and slice it under for the ball to pop it up. Any tendency to use the wrists through impact or to turn the wrists, closes the club face and doesn't give you enough elevation.

The short shot from a tight lie
Players are often afraid of using a sand iron from a tightish lie. The fear is that the leading edge of the sand iron is slightly off the ground and so won't get the ball up. When correctly played the feeling is of holding the club down through impact, the flange of the club if anything making a slight impression in the ground. A pitching wedge, by contrast, has the leading edge as its lowest point and can cut or dig into the ground on a short shot in an unsatisfactory way.

So, providing you have a sand iron which doesn't have an absurdly large flange, it should be quite workable to do precisely the same shot as I have just described from a tight, dry lie. All that this means is that the ball sits tight to the ground without any cushion of grass beneath it. You need now to execute the shot in exactly the same way as before, but with perfect depth judgement, really ensuring that the sole of the club is held down through impact. It dents the ground rather than taking a divot. Again have two or three practice swings and very definitely listen for the sole of the club to bounce slightly on solid ground. The shot is no more difficult, except that you have to

judge the depth within a minute fraction of an inch. You should still not have any feeling of using the hands and wrists but must simply keep the club face working through with full loft, elbows into the sides of the body, wrists firm through impact and the club face looking upwards at the end of the swing. Don't be afraid of the shot, just work at good depth judgement and watching the ball intently. Force the club down, dent the ground with the flange and the ball pops up.

Once again, the shorter the shot the more difficult it will feel. For a really short one ensure that the length of backswing and throughswing mirror each other, the club head probably staying within your peripheral vision throughout so that the backswing never becomes long and loose and wristy. The shorter the shot and the tighter the lie the firmer your hands and wrists need to be.

The short shot from a poor lie – advanced short pitching
In both of the other shots I have described I am assuming that the whole ball sits above the ground. In other words you can actually meet up with the bottom of the ball by scraping the ground with the club head. You don't have to think of a particularly downward contact and don't have to use any wrist action. The method is identical for club golfer and tournament player. Once you get the ball in a lie where part of it is in a little divot hole or depression you have in effect lost the bottom of the ball and cannot easily meet up with it. This is where the shot becomes particularly difficult and where we have to move to a far more advanced method. The good player in the single-figure handicap range wouldn't find this shot particularly difficult from 30 yards or so, but will often find it extremely hard to play with a shot of perhaps 10 yards. The reason very simply is that you need to get a degree of wrist cock in the backswing to get a steep enough attack into the ball but mustn't then release this wrist cock in the downswing. Most people also find it extremely difficult to set the wrists early enough in the backswing and to feel ready to come down again without swinging the club too far. What in

effect you need to do in this kind of shot, for perhaps 10 yards, is to set the wrists really early but keep the swing extremely short, maintaining that wrist cock down and through the ball. The low-handicap amateur should only attempt this when a poor lie makes it essential. The top-class player may use this as his normal short-pitching method, producing quite exceptional feel from good lie or bad. This is an advanced shot but let's have a look at it.

The setup is going to be much the same as before, bringing the feet a bit closer together and getting the weight if anything a little more on the left foot to encourage a slightly steeper up-and-down action. The hands are held down and forward which will begin to set the right wrist back on itself. If the lie is particularly nasty you may find it easier to balance the club towards its toe where the rounded part of the toe of the club may eat into the depression a little more easily than does the leading edge of the club. Now the feeling must be to cock the wrists, setting the right wrist back on itself as slowly as possible and almost with the minimum of arm action. The left arm may even soften and bend to get the club up steeply. The shorter the shot the more difficult this is to achieve. You set the right wrist back on itself and in turn the left wrist will almost arch back a little, not being cocked up onto the thumb. The wrists are set and what you now need to feel is that you transfer the weight onto the left foot, take the club down into the ball and then draw it out the other side, maintaining the arched left wrist and the set right wrist. You don't just produce a U-shape into impact, but must produce a slow, V-shaped contact. In other words you have once more created a unit from the elbows down which is held absolutely rigidly through the ball and beyond it. With a 30- or 40-yard pitch from a poor lie you simply accelerate and take ball and divot, with a crisp strike. With the really little one the contact must be a slow in-and-out V-shape with no release or acceleration.

At the moment of impact the wrists are passive, and initially feel quite firm as you develop the shot again with the right wrist set back on itself. You want now to produce a nice V-shaped attack so that you get steeply down into the back of the ball and then withdraw the club out again the other side with an equally steep return. This *must not* be done with the wrists. You mustn't flick at it but must be able to get this V-shaped attack even with a locked wrist position. The way in which you do it is literally to ease the club down and ease it out again, drawing the wrists up as a unit.

At this point I want to explain what happens to the left arm. The right wrist is back on itself and the left wrist is arched and as you draw the club up again beyond impact, the left elbow has to lift and break away behind you so that you will almost have the feeling of it poking out behind your body, moving into a fairly acute angle. For the good player this kind of arm movement probably happens fairly instinctively in certain cut-across pitch shots and in the bunker shots, but in this kind of very difficult short pitch you may actually have to work at the feeling of the arm making this movement. In other words you lock the whole position from the elbows and wrists down and then draw the thing up from the left elbow. This should then enable you to move the club ridiculously slowly into impact and out of impact with the wrists remaining perfectly locked and set.

This, as I have explained, is a very advanced shot. It requires a degree of setting of the wrists in the backswing and then very definitely holding that angle through impact. It is only necessary to use this action once the lie is poor and you have actually lost some of the ball below ground level. Really top tournament players, however, will often use this type of action for a short pitch even from a fairly good lie. Letting the arm move in this way enables you to get a crisp up-and-down action without any danger of the hands and wrists becoming loose through the ball. For all but the very top-class player – and here I mean real tournament professionals – it is far better to make the shot from a straight-forward lie, whether grassy or tight, one which you execute with absolutely no wrist action at all. Don't do the difficult shot when the easier one will work and look at this advanced shot as one which you only have to use in an emergency.

THE CUT SHOT

In the next chapter we are going to look at bunker shots. As a prerequisite of being able to play good bunker shots you need to be able to hold the club face open through impact to produce maximum loft on the ball and a little extra cut and stop. I am going to suggest to any club player that you learn to do this from grass with a short pitch shot so that you can transfer the skill to shots from the sand.

Let's look first at the design of the sand iron. By far the easiest type of sand iron to use is one which has a rounded leading edge. I would suggest that club players also look for a club with plenty of loft, one with 60 to 64 degrees, enabling you to play these shots most easily. When you play a normal little pitch you hold the club with its full loft but with the club face in a square position. This means that the leading edge and the bottom groove on the face will be aimed at your target. To play a cut shot and impart extra spin you need to get the club face opened. This in itself is very easy for the advanced player but can be very difficult for the club golfer. Let's look at exactly what we do. The club sits with its full loft, the shaft straight up towards you. You now need to rotate the shaft, still with it pointing straight up towards you, so that the club face turns away to the right and the effective loft is increased. Having done this you now grip the club.

For the club player there are three key points to opening the club face. First of all it may feel uncomfortable. The grip on most clubs is not round but is egg-shaped and as you open the club face the egg-shaped part of the grip comes in a different point in your hands. It may feel funny. One way of getting round this discomfort is to have a perfectly round grip on your sand wedge. As a second point the club face looks awkward because it is now turned away to the right. This is where a club head with a rounded leading edge has an advantage; it doesn't look as awkward and will still in fact give you the feeling that the club face is on

FOR THE ADVANCED PLAYER

An advanced downhill pitch: here I am playing the most advanced of all small pitches, using a sand wedge from a treacherous downhill lie for a shot of no more than 10 to 15 yards. The tournament golfer should also use the same approach from a divot hole or slight depression. But is advanced — for scratch golfers and professionals.

I start with the club face open, hands way ahead of the ball, weight on the left foot. Now we really do see wrist break. The club is picked up, cupping the wrists, with almost no arm action, to get the club head up steeply and clear of the ground. I now want a V-shaped attack into the ball, sharply down into the ball, following down the slope for a moment, and then drawing the club up again. The wrists set and cup quite sharply, the angle is held down into and just beyond the ball, before being pulled up again with a very narrow return, drawing it up with a pronounced lift from the left elbow. This gives a crisp V-shaped attack for a *short* pitch from a difficult or downhill lie. From a divot hole, experiment further by tipping the club onto its toe to find the bottom of the ball more easily

3

6

1

2

4

5

7

8

A short pitch from the rough:

This is a small pitch, again played with a sand wedge, lofting the ball about 5 yards from heavy rough. I need to get the ball up quickly and to stop it quickly. I have to get it up and out but am then faced with a ball which is hard to stop – firstly because of a slight slope down to the flag and secondly because shots from the rough generally run more than you expect.

The shot is very definitely *not* played with wrist action or a steep up and down action. The whole essence of the shot is to make a wide, shallow swing with passive wrists. The club face is laid back open, from a grassy lie letting the hands get a touch behind the ball to add loft. The stance is particularly wide and solid, opened round to the left, both to allow for the open club face and to enable the legs to stay still throughout the swing. The knees are well bent, allowing me to bring the hands down into a low position. This low wrist position presets a considerable degree of cupping in the wrists, so that if any wrist action is added in the backswing it becomes a cupping rather than setting.

The legs stay very still through the swing. The club is moved away in what feels a very wide, shallow path, holding the club face open and, if anything, letting the right elbow move away from the side more than in any other shot. There is definitely no wrist action of any kind. The wrist will now show an upward cupping, an angle which is created almost entirely – if not entirely – by having the wrists dropped at address. The wrist angle at the top of the backswing is *not* the result of an early wrist break. It is simply the cupping at address taken back by the arms. The club face is held open, using a dead wristed action, wide and shallow feeling. The wrists feel very dead – nothing at all from them. They are then held like this through impact, holding the club face through with plenty of loft, slicing and sliding it under the ball to pop it up with height and stop

1

2

5

6

target. As a third point do realize that when you open a club face there is danger of the socket, i.e. the neck of the club, swinging round towards the ball so that the ball is no longer in the centre of the club face. We will see in bunker shots that the most common fault of all for most club players is hitting the ball from the socket instead of the middle of the face. So whenever you open the club face do ensure that the ball is kept in the middle of the face or even more towards the toe.

The feeling in executing the shot should be much the same as with the standard short pitch. The club golfer should keep the elbows into the side, feel that the swing needs no wrist action at all, and should work at sliding the club head beneath the ball. The first stage here is to practise the shot with a good cushion of grass between the ball and solid ground. You then have plenty of room to play with so far as the depth is concerned. Try to get the feeling of holding the club face open so that it almost lies on its back as it passes between the ball and the ground. The ball should then pop up with good height and you in turn

3

4

7

8

should be left with a finish where the left arm and left wrist are firm and the club face faces up to the sky.

The thing you will begin to notice here is that the ball tends to drift away to the right. Not only does the club face have more loft but it also faces off to the right. You in turn must offset this by turning your feet and whole stance, including the club, round to the left until the bottom groove on that club face is still aimed at your target. The swing will then go more or less straight back and through in the direction you want to hit and the ball will pop up with good height in the right direction. It is well worth practising these shots for a very small distance, as little as 4 or 5 yards, just getting the feeling of the club head working beneath the ball and the ball coming up with really good height. From an exceptionally grassy lie the club can almost pass right beneath the ball. As the lie gets tighter and the cushion of grass is less, so the shot becomes more difficult to play. Now the depth of contact has to be judged very finely and once again, as with the standard short pitch, you should have a couple of practice swings to ensure that you get the right depth, listening for the sole of the club, or this time almost the back of the club to brush the ground at the bottom of the swing.

1

This shows another short sand wedge pitch from fluffy rough, bending the knees and widening the stance to get the hands low at address. The lower the hands the more the cupping of the wrists is already set. The club face is held open at address, using a wide, shallow arc with passive wrists, and really sliding the club head beneath the ball through impact. The frames beyond impact show how the club face is held open, left elbow dragging away behind me while keeping the palm of the right hand, back of the left hand and club face looking upwards. Aim for a crisp, aggressive feel to the shot, wrists passive to cope with this little one under pressure

8   9

2

3

4

5

6

7

10

11

12

This shows a 30-yard lob pitch from a normal lie, trying to get the ball up and down quickly with the sand iron. The stance is wide and open, the legs staying quiet, not adding any power, and yet the open stance allowing me to turn through. For the lob I still take the club back and up on the inside; if you take it back outside you won't get enough distance. The club face is held open, relative to me at address, bottom groove at the flag. I then make a fairly sharp up and down swing, setting the wrists, holding the wrists and then bouncing down into the back of the ball to get it up. The club face is still held open all the way, attacking it from the inside, bouncing the sole in and out, rather than taking a divot with the leading edge. Again there is a pulling across action at the moment of impact, left elbow dragging out behind me, wrists still set

1

2

6

7

11

12

13

3

4

5

8

9

10

14

15

16

FOR THE ADVANCED PLAYER

This shows the tight lie lob with a sand iron. Same setup as for the normal lie, but with more weight on the left side. This gives an instant feeling of an even steeper action. It becomes a short, sharp stroke, gradually building up speed and really zipping it through into the bottom of the ball. This is a difficult shot. You need to set the wrists very sharply, holding the set quite forcibly, with a most definite bouncing in-and-out feeling with the flange. It comes down and in steeply behind it, through with a very short divot – in reality just bouncing the flange and denting the ground – and then out again: a real V-shape. It's a short, fast, clipping action, holding the wrists and working at a crisp, controlled feeling 2 to 3 feet beyond the ball

1

4

5

8

9

2

3

6

7

10

THE LOB PITCH

Once you can get the feeling of this open club face you can develop the shot for slightly longer pitches, keeping the club face open and extending both backswing and throughswing, the main use of the shot being to lob the ball up steeply over an obstacle and then land it softly the other side. The good player can then adapt this open-face shot to produce a longer lob pitch. This time the feeling of working the club face through the ball will be identical, combined with cocking the wrists in the backswing and then holding this wrist angle through impact. The really advanced player will be able to work with this shot simply by feeling what happens to the club face. He can concentrate on the club face, holding it open through impact and almost cutting across the ball with an out-to-in action just at impact to impart greater backspin. His left arm and hand will probably work instinctively. But let's just check what happens so that the player can be absolutely sure he's on the right lines. The club face is held open through impact. In turn the back of the left hand will be up through impact and the left elbow must be allowed to be drawn away behind the body in sympathy with this club face action. Any tendency to allow the left elbow to fold and break inwards or to let the left wrist break is going to allow the club head to pass the hands with loss of control.

With this 30-yard sand wedge from thick rough I want a particularly steep attack, letting the left elbow bend and soften to get the club up quite quickly. The hands are held low at address, cupping the wrists to produce this steep up and down action. Once more we see the action of the left arm through impact, staying tight to the body, pulling away behind me to hold the club face open

1

2

3

4

5

6

7

8

These then are the basic shots to be used round the green. The club player's choices should be to putt the ball, then run it and then pitch it. He should as far as possible keep the wrists firm in each shot, keeping any wrist action out of the movement as far as possible, only using wrist action from an appallingly bad lie or where the length of the shot means that extra power has to be generated. With every one of them the head has to be kept still, resisting any temptation to look up too soon in the hopes of catching sight of the ball before it lands. For the advanced player, the key to almost every shot is to let the finesse and feel be done by the right hand, setting the wrists early in the backswing and then maintaining this wrist unit through and beyond impact.

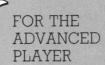

FOR THE ADVANCED PLAYER

A tiny chip from heavy rough. This shows just how the wrists are set in the backswing and then almost set more to keep the hands leading as the downswing starts

1

2

3

4

5

Bunker shots

I SUPPOSE bunker shots give almost more trouble for the club player than any other kind of shot round the green. This is often not helped by the sand irons that players use. Don't necessarily buy the sand iron that goes with the rest of your set of clubs. Look for something which has plenty of loft, at least 60 degrees for most club golfers, and has a rounded leading edge, the leading edge being ahead and not behind the hosel. You should also check very carefully the lie of the club. I often find players using clubs where the lie of the sand iron is too upright. If you look at a set of clubs, you will see that the shaft of the club gradually gets more upright the shorter the shaft. Many manufacturers make what I believe is a mistake by working up through the 8-, 9-iron and pitching wedge and then up again with the sand iron. My own feeling, and one I know most tournament professionals agree with, is that the lie of the sand iron should be the same as that of the pitching wedge if not in fact slightly flatter. For one thing your feet may be shuffled into the sand and so slightly below the ball and as a second point it is one of the few shots where if anything you sink down at impact with the hands slightly dropping. If you do have a club which sits too upright, opening the face becomes awkward and uncomfortable and you are likely to find the heel of the club wanting to sit down into the sand. So not only check the loft of your club but also have the lie checked.

THE SHORT SPLASH SHOT

I am going to start by looking at the sort of shot you would play from beside the green, beginning with one from a good lie. Again, be patient and learn the basic shot where the ball sits above the sand. You can then use this shot and adapt it for everything else. I would suggest, as a starting point, learning a shot of approximately 12 yards. If you can do a shot of this length fairly reliably it will serve as a fairly general-purpose short bunker shot. As you acquire more skill you can then learn to adapt the distance upwards or downwards. But learn one shot first and I would suggest you put a target out at 12 yards for your practice sessions.

The idea of the shot is to splash through the sand, popping the ball out with the sand. The aim is to enter the sand perhaps 1½ inches or so behind the ball and then to splash out of the sand a couple of inches beyond the ball to a fairly full finish. Start with the club head an inch or two behind the ball, almost as close to the sand as you feel you can without touching it, and look at the area of sand just behind the ball. Concentrate on looking at this rather than the ball itself. This should ensure that you get into the sand in the right place, but do remember that it isn't a chopping down into the sand; it is a splash through and out the other side.

Make sure that you have the club face slightly open and at this point I would suggest that you re-read the section on opening the club face on page 184. Open the club face, then grip it. Keep the ball towards the middle of the club face or even the toe, certainly making sure that you don't get the ball towards the socket as you open the face. Make sure you have a suitable grip with the right hand behind and never beneath the shaft. The ball should be positioned fairly well forward in your feet, perhaps as far forward as your left instep from a good lie. The club shaft should come straight up towards you, not with the hands pushed ahead of the ball. This gives you maximum loft on the club face. The whole idea of this shot is to take a fairly full swing and then to keep the club face open as it splashes through the sand. The feeling should be one of taking what feels almost a three-quarter or fairly full swing, keeping the timing as slow and smooth as possible. If you feel you can swing the club ridiculously slowly, it will penetrate through the sand and out the other side. If you rush at the shot the club digs into the sand, it compresses the sand together, the sand builds up resistance and you won't be able to get the club through. The slower the club head moves the easier it travels

Right This shows the sand iron held open at address for the splash shot. The club has been turned in my hands to increase the loft, keeping the shaft straight up towards me, *not* with the hands pushed forward. I have then turned my whole stance round to the left to keep the open face and swing aiming at the target. Ensure that the ball is kept in the middle to toe of the club face

1

2

5

6

The bunker splash shot:
Here I am playing a splash shot of about 15 yards from a good lie, club face held open at address and through impact. At address I try to feel the texture of the sand with my feet, using a fairly wide stance, knees bent but with fairly firm pressure to keep balance, and to control the depth of swing and contact. I focus on the back of the ball and area of sand up to about 2 inches behind it. This helps to bring the sole of the club down behind the ball. The feeling of the swing is very much a U-shape, keeping the right elbow in and allowing the left arm to soften and bend a touch. With the wrists held low at address there is a degree of cupping to the wrists

already built in. The backswing is a combination of turning, lifting the arms and adding to the cupping of the wrists. In the downswing the feeling is of splashing the sand forwards, holding the club face open through impact. This is really the only shot where I actually have the feeling of the right wrist straightening through impact. It very definitely holds the club face open, while releasing the cupping and almost adding a little flick to pop the ball up. In this way the sole of the club just bounces down and is brought up, popping the ball up with plenty of height and without a heavy contact. The club golfer does, of course, have to hold the club face open without risking any wrist release until the basic action is mastered

through the sand. Right, now the swing itself is going to be full and very slow. The wrists should cock in the backswing in just the same way as they would in a fairly full shot. The weight is going to be fairly evenly balanced, if anything still slightly favouring the left foot.

What happens through impact with a bunker shot is absolutely crucial. You want to hold the club face open and this means that you must retain the wrist cock as the club head is eased through impact. In other words you have set the wrist cock in the backswing and then you have to hold this through impact. If you release the wrists so that the right wrist is allowed to straighten it will either dig the club

3

4

7

8

head down into the sand behind the ball or, if you watch the ball itself, will probably thin it into the face of the bunker or across the green.

The wrist cock has to be set and held. Now again let's look at how we do this. The right hand starts behind the club in the correct grip, never letting it drop beneath. As you come through impact the club face has to be held open. What this means is that the back of the left hand is going to be upwards through and beyond impact. If you look at a good player playing a bunker shot, the impression is that he swings with what is in effect just an ordinary full swing. What you will see, however, is that the club face is held open and the left elbow will very

definitely break out, not fold in, and will therefore move out behind the player in the follow-through. In this way he is holding the club face open and keeping it open almost to the end of the swing, cutting slightly under and across the ball through impact for additional cut and backspin. The good player probably does this instinctively and by working at the club face and what happens to this the left arm responds accordingly. For the club player and even for the single-figure handicap player it may be necessary to work quite carefully with what the left arm and left wrist do through and beyond impact to see just how the club face can be kept open and the slowness through impact maintained. If

there is any tendency to release and uncock the wrists through impact there is likely to be a sudden flicking of the club head through impact, producing much too much speed to the shot.

By the end of the swing the weight has certainly got through onto the left foot. The good player does this instinctively. The club player almost always needs to emphasize this movement onto the left foot to ensure there is no tendency to hang behind the ball and to try to lift it. So for the club player the general rule is to look about an inch behind the ball, swing as slowly as possible with a full swing and to finish on the left foot, holding the club face open throughout.

Tempo is one of the most difficult

9

10

11

12

FOR THE ADVANCED PLAYER

This shows the move for the advanced player of actually allowing the right wrist to release and straighten, a feeling of almost slinging the ball up and out with a perfectly timed flick of the wrists

I have emphasized, in learning bunker splash shots, keeping the wrists firm and passive through impact. The very good golfer should learn to add a feeling of wrist release – a slightly flicking, slinging action – at impact. Timing is crucial,

making this still quite unsatisfactory and impossible even for most single-figure handicap players. In the backswing, allow the wrists to cup. Hold this angle until a split second before impact, and then allow the right wrist to straighten. Tweak the ball up and away, feeling that this added hand action pops the club head in and out quite sharply and really does help the ball up with greater height.

things for most people to produce in a bunker shot. Often panic sets in and this tends to produce a quick, chopping action. Do make sure that the swing is kept very slow, and I would certainly always recommend having a couple of practice swings outside the bunker to rehearse the swing and calm yourself down before actually playing the shot. If you do tend to hit the ball much too far in a bunker then the odds are that the swing is too fast and the hand action is loose and flicky through impact. A good concept is to imagine that you are swinging something ridiculously heavy – so heavy that you can only swing it very slowly. Imagine a pickaxe, for example. You could only swing it in a slow, laboured fashion and in many ways this is what the bunker shot will initially feel like.

DIRECTION IN BUNKER SHOTS

We have looked first at a basic 12-yard bunker shot from a good lie, where the ball sits above the sand. I have suggested that you open the club face to give yourself extra loft but let's now see how this open club face affects the direction of bunker shots. If you simply stand square to your target and open the club face I think it goes without saying that the ball will pop away to the right. What you need to do is to turn your whole stance and then the club round until the bottom groove on the club face seems to aim on target or fractionally left of it. I emphasize this more than the leading edge itself because the leading edge of the club

is probably rounded and you may not necessarily know where it is aiming. So look at the bottom groove. The easiest way of lining up in a bunker shot is to open the club face, not be too fussy about where you are aiming and then gradually shift round to the left until you can see that the club really is going on target. The feeling I then have is of swinging the club virtually straight back and through on a line from the ball to the target, holding the club face open and adding cutspin to the shot by allowing the left elbow to draw away through and beyond impact. The ball will then pop up in the direction you want quite easily.

I want to explain at this point the phrase 'hitting out-to-in' in a bunker. Swinging out-to-in basically implies that you swing across the line of the shot to add extra cutspin and backspin. I feel there is a lot of confusion about what good players actually do in a bunker and my own feeling is that most club golfers who get into difficulty in bunker shots do so because of an exaggerated idea of swinging across the line in a bunker. Let me explain what happens. If we take a line from the ball to the target you can see that by aiming my club face directly along that line, I now have to set my body and my feet a bit to the left of it. If you look at most really good bunker players, they swing the club virtually straight along that line. The feeling may be of being very slightly out to in in relation to this line, and certainly we add sidespin by holding the club face open and pulling it slightly across the ball through impact. But in practice I don't believe most of us do go outside the line unless we are trying to put on exceptional backspin for a very short shot. Those good players who do swing out to in only swing very fractionally out to in *in relation to this line*.

What I believe happens is that players, and indeed unfortunately people who teach golf, look at the line across the feet and think in terms of swinging out to in in relation to this line. In this way the player is given the feeling of swinging excessively across the body, letting the arms leave the side in the backswing and trying to bring the club across past the left foot beyond impact. Under no circumstances whatever do good bunker players play their shots

1

2

3

5

6

7

9

10

11

4

This shows the important direction of stance and swing in the splash shot. Having opened the club face I turn the stance into an open position, the bottom groove of my sand iron aiming at the flag or fractionally left of it. The line marked in the sand shows the line of the shot. In reality I am simply aiming left to allow for the open club face. There is no exaggeratedly out-to-in feeling. The club is simply swung back on the same path as an ordinary short pitch, still moving back slightly on the inside of the line of my feet. It is similarly attacked in this same direction, holding the club face open, and cutting under and slightly across the ball at the moment of impact to add spin

8

This shows the direction of my feet, the ball position and direction of my splash through impact. My feeling, let me repeat, is of a cut-across action through impact but without any feeling of taking the club outside on the backswing

12

like this. It would be an entirely diffi-cult and unnatural feeling and in my opinion trying to do so is why so many club golfers hit the ball off the socket. They are taught to swing out to in across the ball in a most unnatural way. Really it is a confusion in terms as to what we mean by swinging out to in. Remember that if it is at all out to in, it is out to in in relation to the ball target line and never, never out to in in relation to the line of your feet and body. Personally I think the club golfer can forget any feeling of swinging out to in and should simply aim the feet left, keep the shoulders virtually square, and bring the open club face to aim on target. He should then swing back and through on this line. If you do hit bunker shots which you believe are thin and which go into the face of the bunker, ask yourself whether what you are in fact doing is catching the ball off the socket. If this is the case, check the position of the ball in relation to the club face and make sure your club goes straight back and through and not out to in.

FOR THE ADVANCED PLAYER

This view of the splash shot shows how the club is still swung back inside the line of my feet, not out-to-in following the line of the feet. My feeling is that backspin and cutspin are imparted through impact by holding the club face open and drawing it inside and across the ball. The action of the left elbow can be seen, pulling back into the side, rather than folding in as in the long game. For players like myself this happens simply from feeling the club face is held open. For many players the movement may at first need to be a conscious one to keep the club face open and impart proper spin. For the advanced golfer, compare this with the sequence on pages 180/181. Beyond impact the slight releasing, almost flicking action of the right hand can be seen here, adding that little extra pop up action – possible with sand beneath the ball, but not, of course, with the ball tight to the ground

1

2

5

6

VARYING DISTANCE

Exactly the same bunker shot can be adapted for shots down to perhaps 7 or 8 yards – a really difficult one – and up to distances of 25 yards or so. For the club golfer, however, I would repeat that I think you are better to learn consistency at one level before trying to be too clever and vary the distance.

For the advanced player there are several ways in which you can adjust the length. My own feeling is that you should *not* try to do this simply by varying the amount of sand you take. I think it is too hit-or-miss. My own feeling is that I take exactly the same amount of sand and play very much the same shot for everything from say 8

ment players we get to the point where we almost do it instinctively. Sometimes that little longer shot will be produced by squaring up the club face a touch. Sometimes the bank you have to go over won't allow you to do this and you just have to generate a little more club head speed.

The main thing is to practise bunker shots of all distances, starting with a reliable 12-yard shot and then working up and down yard by yard, aiming at different targets. For the advanced golfer, I think you can also experiment with the feeling of looking at the back of the ball or looking at the sand slightly behind it. Looking at the sand behind the ball will probably if anything help to keep the shot short enough for the tiny one, where looking at the ball itself may be more meaningful with the slightly longer shot.

For the club golfer I would suggest that the very short shot of under 10 yards is almost too difficult to attempt. If anything you can make the swing even slower than usual, perhaps concentrating on a spot a fraction of an inch further back in the sand than for your usual shots. But don't be too fussy on what is a very advanced and difficult shot. To produce the slightly longer one, working up to 20 or 25 yards, I would suggest doing much the same as normal but now, if the bank in front of you allows, squaring up the club face so that the ball tends to travel forward a little more.

BAD LIES AND THE BURIED BALL

The ironic thing about bunker shots is that professional golfers nearly always play under tournament conditions where the bunkers are immaculately raked. Every caddie has to leave the bunker in pristine condition after his player has extricated himself from the sand or the player can face a monetary fine. As such we are faced with bad lies in the bunker far less frequently than the club golfer. As the lie becomes worse so the shot can become more difficult. What you need now is the combination of loft on the club face with a fairly steep attack into the sand behind the ball to force the

yards to 25 yards, simply shortening and slowing down the whole action for a really tiny shot and then perhaps squaring up the club face a shade and speeding up the delivery through the ball a little for the longer shot. Mainly I would suggest that you vary the distance by feel more than anything else, in just the same way as you would vary length for the pitch. For tourna-

For this plugged ball, explosion shot I am using a square club face, ball further back in the stance than for the splash shot. The hands are now forward at address, sacrificing some loft but helping to force the ball out. I pick the club up sharply in the backswing and then really move my weight through to the left to drive through the sand and ball. Notice the weight transference, my knees really bending to the left to take me through – my head and shoulders being allowed to move quite noticeably compared with the trees behind me

1

4

5

8

9

2

3

6

7

10

11

In this very short splash shot I am still electing to use a fairly full swing. The club face is open, the stance very open and the sequence shows in detail how the club face is held open through impact and beyond, showing this important move of allowing the left elbow to pull backwards through impact. The finish appears fairly full, but in reality the wrists stay firm to keep the club face open and impart backspin

1

2

6

7

10

11

ball out. Let's look at the ball sitting in a progressively worse lie. What I do to practise is to gouge out a line in the sand, shallow at one end and deep at the other. At one end I have the ball sitting up perfectly on top of the sand. I play my ordinary splash shot going in about 1½ inches behind the ball. The ball pops up, lands and runs say 4 feet. Next the ball sits a little bit down, the equivalent of sitting in a very shallow footprint or its own pitch mark. Here I would play the shot exactly the same, still with an open club face, still going in about 1½ inches behind the ball and still trying to ease the club head out the other side of the sand. Now the ball will pop out in exactly the same way but on touching down will run, say, 5 yards.

Next as we move along the line to something deeper, I will play the shot in exactly the same way, still with the club face open, still splashing right through the sand. I know the ball will carry out in much the same way as before but will run say 8 yards. Last, let's take a ball sitting right down into the sand. Once again I play exactly the same shot as usual, club face still open. This time the ball will splash out as before but will now run perhaps 10 to 12 yards. So in each of these situations I am tackling the shot in just the same way as normal but knowing that the ball will run more when it touches down. My own feeling for strong tournament players is that you can play each of these shots with an open club face, still get the club head through the sand and out the other side, and still get a good amount of height. It is the run that varies. Each of these is still really a splash shot.

THE EXPLOSION SHOT

For the club golfer the above approach can be difficult and it can be hard to make yourself really get the club face through the sand and out the other side. For the club player an alternative to using this splash shot throughout is to use what we would now call an explosion shot. In an explosion shot you begin to swing the club up and down more steeply, blasting down into the sand behind the ball but moving well through onto the left foot and forcing the ball out with the sand. The splash shots I have explained above still have a degree of real finesse and a good player has control over where the ball goes. Once you get to an explosion shot you are really saying to yourself that the lie is so bad that what you want to do is to force the ball out at the expense of finesse. This would be what you would do if the ball buries in a really bad pitch mark or is in a fairly deep footprint. The club player can no longer splash the club head through and indeed even for the professional golfer there are some lies which are so bad that you cannot easily get to the bottom of the ball without an up-and-down chopping action. At this point you may find it easier to play the shot with a square or even slightly closed club face, although for my own preference I still try to keep the club face open. Club players may find a square club face easier to maintain through impact, rather than having an open face which opens away even further as it meets the sand. So keep the club face square, keep your weight on the left foot and the ball fairly well back in the middle of the stance. Keep the weight if anything favouring the left foot, pick the club up fairly steeply with your hands and wrists in the backswing, transfer the weight really well to the left foot through impact and force the club head through the sand as though trying to blast it out onto the green. Get the weight through onto the left foot and trust the ball to come out.

It should now pop out of the sand quite easily but give you very little control of the precise distance. If the lie is very bad it doesn't really matter how hard you hit. The odds are the ball will only carry about 10 yards, possibly running another 10 yards on land.

THE UPHILL BUNKER SHOT

In some situations around the green you can find yourself on an up slope, either in a fairly low bunker or with the face of the bunker in front of you. If faced with a fairly low bunker with an uphill lie I would suggest that you lean into the slope so that you keep your body in a vertical position. In other words, lean on your left leg and let the left leg bend. The easiest way to play this shot is then to produce what almost amounts to a short pitching or chipping action, taking the club head fairly straight back from the ball and hitting into the ball and sand. I myself would do this by looking directly at the back of the ball but the club player is probably going to find it easier looking about an inch behind the ball. The feeling now as you take the sand is that if anything the club is going to go too deep into the sand and the blow on the ball tends to be cushioned too much. If anything you will have difficulty in getting the ball far enough. Bear this in mind and really convince yourself that you want to get the ball past the flag. It is all too easy to leave these shots short.

On a steeper lie in a low bunker you may feel difficulty in taking any sand behind the ball because in effect the sand is below the ball and not behind it. In this shot you will definitely need to look at the back of the ball itself and concentrate on the equivalent of a ball–divot contact, this time being very definite about striking the ball and taking a bit of sand beyond it. This shot will no longer feel like a bunker splash shot but will be far more like the ordinary little pitch. Again distance can be hard to control and you need to be bold enough to get the ball all the way there.

Under the face

Club golfers tend to find shots from under the lip of the bunker far harder than they should do. I am not talking about one where you are on a flat lie at the bottom of the bunker with a high face in front of you. To negotiate that is a question of opening up the club face as much as possible and really holding it open through impact. No, what I am referring to is the one where you are on an up slope in the sand below the lip. Obviously there are shots which are impossible and the bank over-hangs so much that you would have to get the ball up completely vertically to get it out. If you are faced with one like this then you have to improvise and come out sideways. But assuming the shot is playable the thing to do here again is to lean into the slope of the bunker, so that you shorten your left leg and manage to stand vertically. You need to get well up the face of the bunker to be ahead of the ball, weight very definitely favouring the left foot. Keep the club face square, not open. The angle of the up slope gives you all the height you need.

The shot should now be played by taking the club virtually straight back from the ball, not lifting it, looking at the back of the ball or perhaps ½ inch behind and beneath it and then really whacking into the face of the bunker, keeping the weight on the left foot throughout. You aren't going to get a follow-through because the club head simply jams into the sand in front of you. Drive into the face of the bunker and the ball will pop out and upwards. In some ways it is an easy shot because it doesn't matter how hard you attack it, the ball isn't going to travel far. One point I would empha-size in the shot from under the lip is that this is the one time when you might enter a bunker from above, usually of course a breach of etiquette. There is always a slight chance that the ball might not come out and the last thing you want to do is to have it land

1

Under the lip: the club golfer's nightmare

2

3

6

7

This shot is a really easy one to execute. The upslope encourages height. Get up the slope ahead of the ball, lean into the bank, take the club away with a fairly wide takeaway and really whack into the back of the ball.

Don't be afraid to hit hard. However hard you hit, the ball isn't going to travel forward very far. Just hit in horizontally at the ball, pulling the club head up beyond impact from the left elbow

10

4

5

8

9

in your own footprints. So in a really steep bunker work yourself down the face of the bunker to ensure that you keep up ahead of it on the bank, taking care not to ground your club in so doing.

PLAYING FROM WET SAND

Different textures of sand can require different sorts of contact. If the bunker looks wet and fairly well compacted I would suggest in fact that you can play the shot in exactly the same way as normal and the sand will probably not set up as much resistance as it appears. As soon as you walk into the bunker and set your feet at address you should get some idea whether there is any give in the sand.

If on the other hand the sand is frozen or you feel there is no depth to the sand, a different approach is required. Where there is no depth of sand there is no point trying a splash shot as all that happens is that the sole of the sand iron is going to bounce on the solid surface and shoot the ball away with insufficient height. Here you have to manufacture little pitch-type shots with the sand iron, in much the same way as you would play the shot from a bare lie behind the bunker. You need to set as much loft on the club face as you feel you can, playing the shot with firm wrists, ideally bouncing the club down and up again with a V-

1

2

5

6

9

10

3

4

7

8

The downhill splash shot is played with the ball further back in the stance than on a flat lie, a wider stance than normal, right shoulder held higher so that the shoulders almost follow the slope. Both this and having the weight on the left foot encourage a steep back and downswing. Keeping on the left foot, pick the club up sharply with the wrists, stay well on the left foot and splash down and through the sand and ball. The whole weight really does finish on the left foot – hence the wide stance – keeping the club head travelling low and wide out beyond impact. Even with an open club face the ball comes off lower than normal, so choose a sensible route out and expect the ball to run on landing

shaped attack, but still maintaining a good angle in the wrists. I would suggest that you look back at the section on short pitching from tight lies to see how this shot is executed.

THE DOWNHILL BUNKER SHOT

Perhaps the most difficult of all bunker shots is the one where the ball just runs into the back of the bunker and leaves you with a ball sitting on a down slope, still with the face of the bunker in front of you to negotiate. Do bear in mind that once you have the ball on a down slope you are going to get less height to the shot and may be faced with one which is virtually unplayable. Don't expect to get the ball up quickly and even if you do get good height it isn't going to stop easily on the green. The ball is probably going to run as far if not further than it carries. My own feeling with bunker shots is that I try to keep the same level with the club head as it goes through the sand beyond the ball. The difficulty with the downhill lie is that there is in effect no sand directly in front of the ball but lots of sand to negotiate behind it. You need to produce a fairly steep up-and-down action where the club head rises well in the backswing, then gets down into the sand behind the ball and very definitely is held down beyond impact as the ball starts on its way. To play this shot you need to get the wrists cocking early and suddenly to get sufficient steepness in the backswing. I play the shot with a wide stance, the weight well on my left foot and with the right shoulder held high at address. This helps to get the swing moving up and down the slope, with the added feeling of picking the club up sharply, to make absolutely certain that you don't catch the sand behind the ball. It is well worth having a couple of rehearsals of the backswing to ensure you are going to get it up and down sufficiently steeply. I keep the club face open, ensuring that the club head goes into the sand about an inch behind the ball. The last thing you want is to catch too much sand behind the ball. For this reason you should play the ball quite well back in the feet, with the feeling

FOR THE ADVANCED PLAYER

This downhill shot is in itself an advanced one. For the very skilled player it is a shot where in reality the right wrist can be allowed to release and straighten. This keeps the feeling of following down the slope, and if released at just the right moment can almost scoop and tweak the ball up with the tiniest flick of the right wrist at the ball. You literally do help the ball up with the right hand, holding right palm and club face upwards under and through the ball. Again for the advanced player it is a shot with low wrists at address, presetting some upward cupping, adding to this in the backswing, holding this angle just long enough and then releasing it with precision timing. But basically this is only an approach for scratch players and professionals!

of leaning out from a slope. The swing is now one which goes very much up and down beyond the ball through impact, working hard at maintaining balance as you do this. As with all bunker shots, and indeed with every shot, the wrists have to be set in the backswing and, for all but the very advanced golfer, very definitely held through impact, without the right wrist having any tendency to flick and straighten through impact. At the end of the swing you may almost feel yourself going on down the slope from a really steep lie. Keep your eyes firmly on the back of the ball, or sand just behind it, don't expect miracles and allow for the ball to run. Aim for a sensible route out where you don't have too steep a bank to negotiate and where you have sufficient green to play with, for the ball to run perhaps 10 or 15 yards on landing.

THE LONG BUNKER SHOT

The golden rule with long bunker shots is not to be too greedy. If you want length from a bunker make sure you really do stand to gain something. It may be worth going for length if you can actually reach the green or if by getting out a certain distance it puts you in a position where you can just reach the green with your next shot. But don't take risks unnecessarily and, as we will see with all recovery shots, choose a sensible route back to safety rather than attempting something which even Seve wouldn't risk! In some countries fairway bunkers give you a really good chance for getting length. They hardly have any lip and you can even take a long iron or a wood if the lie permits. But on most championship courses in Britain, and indeed elsewhere, the fairway bunkers are relatively punishing and you have to look carefully at the face of the bunker in front of you to see what loft you need. American players often find our bunkers in Britain deceptive on

their first visit and try to take a club with too straight a face which simply won't get the elevation. Look at the bunker shot from the side and really do gauge what height is needed.

Next look at the lie. If the ball sits down at all in the sand you need to produce a contact which is the equivalent of a ball–divot contact on grass. This kind of shot would be played exactly like a normal iron shot, making absolutely certain that there is no question of taking any sand before the ball. You want a clean, but slightly downward attack, taking the ball with a little bit of sand beyond. This time the danger is in a slightly fluffed contact which won't get the length you require. With a lie like this I would always be hesitant about taking a medium iron and certainly a long iron, unless there really is no bank in front of you.

If on the other hand the whole of the ball sits above the sand, you can pick the ball off almost cleanly, but again paying particular attention to the height you need. If the bunker is one of those low traps with nothing to negotiate then you can in effect try to catch the ball slightly cleanly or almost thinly for maximum distance. It may help you to look slightly higher up on the ball than normal, making absolutely certain that you don't graze the sand.

In this way you should get maximum length, if at the expense of a little height, and may almost get the ball flying as far as, if not slightly further than, a shot from the grass. The danger here for the really good golfer is in catching a 'flyer' which goes a little further than you expect and may run a little more on landing. If you have a lie like this, and much face in front of you, you can't risk a thin shot but need to try to pick the ball off perfectly clean, again avoiding the risk of catching any sand behind the ball. Long shots from a bunker are always very slightly hit-or-miss even for the very good player, the slightest contact with the sand taking the sting and distance out of the shot.

The 60-yard bunker shot (overleaf):
In this shot I am aiming for a slightly downward attack, ball and then sand, just like taking a divot from grass. I play it very much like an ordinary pitch, setting the feet firmly on top of the sand, no shuffling in, looking at the back of the ball and starting with the club head fairly close to the ball and the sand. I use very little leg action, setting the right knee in with a little flex and turning and pulling against it. My main thought is on a perfect strike, definitely no sand before the ball or distance is lost, with the eyes really focused on the back of the ball intently

1

2

5

6

3

4

7

8

9

10

13

14

11

12

15

16

The finesse game

1

5

I HAVE NOW COVERED the long game and most of the short game. There are, however, several other shots you need to master for good scoring. The good player needs to be able to bend the ball from left to right or right to left, needs to be able to cope with all sorts of sloping lies and also needs to be able to hit the ball with extra run or extra stop. I often think that the best discipline for a potential champion is to go round the golf course with two or three clubs, learning to manufacture all sorts of shots, however ridiculous they feel, cutting up the ball with a 5-iron, punching it low with an 8-iron, bending it this way and bending it that way. All world-class golfers have wonderful ball control and tend to be very experimental in what they can do with the ball. Hold the club face open, use the wrists. Stiffen up your wrists, stand in close, stand a long way from the ball. In effect the potential champion should try everything in a search for feel and versatility. I am therefore going to look at some shots for the very advanced player, but will also go through the basic shots that the club golfer will need.

THE UPHILL LIE

Hitting from a fairly gentle up slope is usually no problem for the club player. The up slope in effect adds to the loft of the club and makes it all the easier to get the ball airborne. You may find a 3-iron difficult from a flat surface, but be able to get good loft from an up slope. I play shots from any kind of an up slope by leaning slightly into the bank so that my body is still held in an upright, vertical position. This means that I am in effect hitting into the slope, bracing myself against it. From a fairly gentle up slope you almost have to make no swing change at all, other than to set the weight on the left leg to stand vertically. Your feeling through impact will now be one of striking the ball and then very definitely going through a bit more ground beyond the ball than normal. The ball will usually fly with slightly more height than usual but with very little other change in flight. Whether you push the ball to the right or tend to pull it slightly to the left will depend on how you transfer your weight at impact. If you tend to hang back on the ball at all through impact, which is what may well happen with a fairway wood or very long iron, you can find the ball being pulled slightly left of target. If on the other hand you exaggeratedly transfer the weight onto the left foot through impact, in an attempt to keep balance, you may find the ball push away to the right. Trial and error with these shots will tell you your own tendency. For the club player, the shots are possibly more likely to go to the left and for the top player more likely to go right.

As the lie becomes steeper, it becomes more difficult to take a long club. You now have to hit into the slope

2

3

4

6

7

8

From an uphill lie I lean into the slope, bending the left knee slightly to achieve this and really bracing myself against the slope. The feeling through impact is of driving through onto the left foot to keep ahead of the ball, my left knee being allowed to bend out towards the target to keep the weight moving forwards. As you can see from the silver birch tree behind me, my weight really does move on forwards, the feeling at impact being of punching into the slope. This keeps the ball flying more or less as normal. If you hang back at all through impact the ball is likely to fly left; if you sway forward too much it may push out to the right. Take plenty of club and attack the flag

and will find with a steeper lie that you probably cannot work the club head through the ball and then through enough turf beyond it to reach a full finish. You are in effect going to be playing a kind of punching shot into the slope. At this point the longer clubs, and certainly the fairway woods, become far more difficult if not impossible to play. The feeling now has to be one of a firm backswing combined with a punching attack into impact with little follow-through at all. The weight has to be kept on the left foot through impact, leaning into the slope and resisting any tendency to fall back onto the right foot. Once again the direction of the shot will depend on your weight distribution through the ball – pushing right if you sway forward excessively, pulling left if you hang back.

In pitching from an up slope I follow exactly the same principle, leaning into the bank and punching the club

1

2

5

6

9

10

3

4

7

8

This is a short, uphill pitch of 20 yards, played from a fairly steep upslope, 5 yards or so from the green. The danger here is that the upslope can increase the effective loft of the club, often taking the ball higher than you imagine. Convince yourself of the importance of passing the flag. The sand wedge gets too much height; I am using a pitching wedge. Move to a 9 or 8 from a steep slope if in danger of leaving the ball short.

My feeling is of the weight being almost totally on the left foot, leaning into the bank to squeeze the ball up and off it. You can't use a descending blow but have to get enough forward momentum, feeling a horizontal or even slightly upward attack into the ball. Set the wrists as usual, strike the ball crisply and then, beyond impact, keep the wrists set as a unit, pulling the left elbow sharply up to bring the club on up the slope

horizontally into it. The steeper the bank the less follow-through you are going to produce – the bank obviously gets in the way. But even so there must be a feeling of accelerating firmly into impact and never quitting on the shot. With an uphill pitch near the green, do bear in mind the loft of the club tends to be exaggerated. A short pitch from an up slope with a sand iron often produces too much height, leaving the ball short of the target. You may need to come down a club or two to produce the same shot as normal. A 9-iron from an up slope will give the trajectory of a sand iron. Be confident and make sure you get the ball to the target. Chastise yourself mercilessly if you don't get there!

Standing below the ball tends to encourage a flatter plane of swing with shots moving right to left. For any player trying to flatten the plane this side slope is a good training ground.

I grip down the club an inch or so, allow the swing to take up its slightly flatter plane and aim away to the right to allow for the ball to both bend and kick to the left. Balance on any sloping lie is important, resisting, of course, any tendency to fall back onto the heels. The good player can, naturally, counteract this tendency to let the ball move left, swaying into the shot and really holding the club face off if needed. With a really strong action like this it is possible for the tournament player to move the ball left to right.

Club players should allow for the bend to happen; scratch golfers should learn to resist and counteract the slope, taking whichever approach seems more satisfactory

1

2

6

7

STANDING BELOW THE BALL

Shots from below the ball usually cause little problem for the club golfer. With the ball above your feet the plane of your swing should naturally become flatter and more round the body. You may like to grip down the club a couple of inches to overcome the feeling of being a long way from the ball. With the ball about knee level, let's say, your feeling is going to be one of swinging the club round your body, collecting the ball and then round your body again. For the club golfer who tends to swing the club in too much of an up-and-down plane, this often brings out the best in his swing and indeed is a good position from which to practise. If anything the ball will now be pulled or drawn away to the left, with much the same length of shot as from a normal lie. The only thing the club player needs to do in this shot is to ensure that he uses a

3

4

5

8

9

10

good grip with the right hand behind and not beneath the club and to aim away to the right to allow for the bend to the left. Most club golfers don't allow enough to the side on side slopes. Really do aim away to the right. The chances are the ball will also be landing on ground with the same side slope; the ball is not only going to move to the left in the air but is also going to kick left on landing.

For any player who tends to hook the ball this can be the most difficult of the sloping lies. I would suggest that you learn to counteract the side slope. Particularly, for example, if faced with a side slope and a side wind, I would very definitely ensure that the right hand is kept up behind the shaft of the club and try to hold the club face fractionally open through impact. The good golfer should certainly learn to hold approach shots into the green from bending left, setting the wrists and holding them sufficiently through impact for a straight flight.

STANDING ABOVE THE BALL

Standing above the ball is if anything more difficult than standing below it. Particularly for a tall player like myself, you can feel alarmingly close to the ball. With the ball below you it means you have to bend your body over more, still keeping your weight on the balls of the feet but ensuring that you keep good balance throughout. This is going to produce a much higher, more upright plane of swing and bring out the worst in anyone who tends to slice the ball away to the right. You mustn't fight this natural change to the plane. What you do need to do is work at very firm balance through impact. The weight if anything tends to be pulled down the slope and so more onto the balls of your feet, meaning that you have to work firmly back onto the left heel through impact to get a solid strike. Anyone who comes off balance on a flat lie is going to find this a

Standing above the ball tends to bring out the worst in the club player's swing. You need to stand in close to the ball; it aggravates any tendency towards too steep a plane of swing and tends to pull you off balance towards the ball through impact. Compare the distance I am standing from the ball with the distance when I am standing below the ball – much closer now. My feeling is of ensuring I sit well back on the heels to keep balanced, really working hard to pull my weight backwards onto the left heel through impact and beyond to resist any movement out towards the ball. The ball is bound to fade away to the right, so do aim left of target, allowing for the ball to drift in the air and to bounce further right on landing

1

2

5

6

problem – many players find that they produce the odd shank from this lie by falling out towards the ball in the downswing. Keep the ball right in the middle of the club face, maintain your balance and aim well left of target to allow for the ball which bends, drifts and then bounces away to the right on landing.

As with the shot from below the ball, do make sure that you allow sufficiently to the side. I suppose with a 4-wood from this kind of lie, I might almost have to allow what feels like 50 to 100 yards left of the target to allow for the change in directions. Look too at the slope of the ground on which the ball is going to be landing. If you are standing on ground sloping in that direction, the odds are the ground round the green slopes in the same direction. Overcompensate if anything and keep the ball above the green. There is always the chance it can roll down the slope to the green. Once below it, the chance has gone.

3

4

7

8

1

2

5

6

A LONG SHOT FROM A DOWN SLOPE

From a hanging lie, in other words hitting down a hill, the first consideration is to make a good, clean contact with the ball without catching the ground behind it. The second consideration is the loft of the club. This tends to be reduced and the ball flies off lower.

On a down slope I play the ball further back towards my right foot, shift my weight to the left and hold the right shoulder higher at address. This helps to get the swing following the slope. I set the wrists more quickly in

the backswing and then concentrate on striking the ball and keeping the club head travelling down beyond the ball through impact. The ball will always fly off with a lower trajectory than normal – making the long irons and the fairway woods most difficult – with the ball also pushing and drifting away to the right. To allow for this you need to take a more lofted club than normal, aiming off to the left to allow for the right-hand drift.

The advanced golfer can probably play the shot quite easily. The feeling is of setting the wrists very early in the backswing so that the club comes up sharply and can get down the slope into the back of the ball. For the club

3

4

7

8

golfer, this type of action can be difficult and it really is essential to try to lean out at right angles to the slope, weight on the left foot, so that the swing can travel up and down the slope. The club head must be kept travelling down beyond the ball after impact, never with a feeling of trying to help the ball rise. By the end of the swing you may feel the weight is uncomfortably on the left foot; from a steep slope you may be almost walking down the slope after impact.

Balance again, as with all these slopes, is absolutely vital; so too are a couple of practice swings to rehearse the feeling of hitting down beyond the ball.

On a downslope the first requirement is to get a good contact, avoiding catching the ground behind the ball. Play the ball further back in the feet, weight favouring the left foot and the right shoulder carried higher to encourage a swing up and down the slope. Pick the club up fairly sharply in the backswing, with emphasis on setting the wrists early. Hit down and through the ball, with a feeling of the club head continuing down beyond impact. Weight really does move through onto the left foot – the head eventually coming forward too – but keeping balanced for as long as possible. Chase down after it.

The ball is going to take off lower than usual, making long irons and the 3- and 4-wood demanding, so take plenty of loft. Expect to see the ball drift away to the right and aim slightly left to allow for this

1

2

3

4

5

6

A low punchy shot with a 5-iron – the sort of shot you might use with overhanging trees in the way, to keep the ball low under the wind or to run the ball up onto the top of a two-tier green. The ball is played back in the stance, hands down the grip. There is a tendency to draw the ball, but if anything strengthen the grip, left hand over a touch. This acts to deloft the club a fraction, but also allows you to move onto and ahead of the ball through impact, holding the club face with reduced loft, while square to the target. Swing slowly and smoothly, turning the shoulders fully while making a three-quarter arm swing. Keep the hands passive and leading through impact. On this shot I might lose 30 to 40 yards of carry, making up for it to some extent with run. A useful shot for a blustery day

THE LOW PUNCHED SHOT

In certain circumstances you can't simply play a full iron shot into the green. You may need to set the ball off with a lower trajectory to get it running and bumbling its way to the flag. This may be necessary in windy conditions, with trees in the way or with a two-tiered green where you very definitely want the ball running up, rather than pitching, onto the top layer. The shot is played in an identical way to a long pitch, using anything from a 4-iron to a 7-iron and again making sure that the wrists are kept firm through impact. As with other shots where the ball is played back in the feet, the line of the feet may need to be turned to the left to keep the ball travelling on target. Once more, the club player needs to watch the positioning of the right foot ensuring that it is never turned out excessively but kept virtually square. Any tendency to turn it out inhibits the foot work.

PLAYING IN WINDY CONDITIONS

In windy conditions you need to guard against the swing deteriorating through a round of golf. You may almost feel the swing being blown inside out on a blustery day. You need to keep good balance and you need to keep good tempo. My main advice is to ensure that the end of the swing is absolutely solid and to exaggerate the feeling of holding the end of the swing until the ball really does touch down. If you can work at smoothness and balance at this end of the swing, you should be good through impact. It is very easy for the swing to become faster and faster, particularly when battling against a headwind. When hitting into the wind it is vital that you have a good idea of the distance you have to cover. Distance may be relatively meaningless in some ways in choosing a club, but if you have an accurate idea of how much green you have to play with beyond the flag and even beyond that, it can encourage you to be really bold in hitting into the green. Take plenty of club and swing as smoothly as possible, never with

any tendency to under-club and force the shot. Remember that the gap between iron clubs is probably reduced from 10 yards to maybe 7 yards and if you do over-club by the odd club, it is of less concern.

In a slight crosswind, the good player will usually try to hold the ball against the wind, slightly fading the ball into a right-to-left wind and similarly slightly drawing the ball into a left-to-right wind. These are shots for the advanced player, and I will explain later how to draw and fade the ball. But for the club golfer playing in a side wind, the main thing is to make sure that you always keep your club face going in the same direction as your stance and swing. In other words, if you have a right-to-left wind and are therefore going to aim off to the right, make sure that you really do aim the club face where you want to start the ball and then also set the feet and swing in this direction. Don't set the club to the flag and then try to push the shot out to the right. What you need to do is in effect to choose a new target and to try to hit a straight shot towards that, almost to the point where you forget about the flag and where you hope the ball will actually finish. Look at a new target, aim everything at that and really do mean to hit the ball to it. Let the wind then do the rest. If you feel you want to try to counteract the wind a little then you can certainly start to counteract the right-to-left wind by simply holding the club face open a touch at address, with the right hand a little more up and on the top of the shaft in your grip. Similarly, in a left-to-right wind it will do no harm in closing the club face just a touch at address in the hope of bringing it in fractionally closed through impact.

MOVING THE BALL FROM LEFT TO RIGHT

The good player needs to be able to move a ball in both directions. Tournament professionals usually like to hit certain greens with a slightly fading action, producing an iron shot which bends perhaps a couple of feet in the air but then lands softly with plenty of stop as it touches down. For the top-class player all it needs is a simple

FOR THE
ADVANCED
PLAYER

The intentional fade with a 5-iron: here I am playing to a target on a line just over the right-hand side of the tree. My stance is open, in other words aiming pretty well in the direction in which I want to start the ball. I use my normal grip, with the ball positioned slightly further forward and the club face aimed where I want the ball to finish.

In the backswing I take the club back in the usual way in relation to the direction of my stance. In the downswing and through impact I very definitely hold the club face a few degrees open, simply holding it off slightly with my hand action, delaying and holding back the right wrist slightly. In holding the club face open in this way the hips and shoulders turn through earlier in relation to the arms and hands, and continue to turn through, while the left arm breaks slightly out and up, with more separation from the body than normal. The corresponding frames at the end of the fade sequence and draw sequence show to the trained eye the difference, with far more separation between left arm and body in the fade than in the draw. The left side stays high in the fade; in the hook the right side will feel to come through higher

feeling of holding the club face very fractionally open through impact, again with a right-handed rather than a left-handed action. The palm of the right hand should give you plenty of control to do this. All the tournament player is aiming at doing is to hit what is in effect a straight shot but with a suspicion of a cutspin. To the spectator, unless he is absolutely behind the line of flight, the ball probably appears dead straight. But the player knows immediately the ball has left the club face that it will if anything spin right and never left.

He may in a similar way like to produce a slightly left-to-right shot with a drive on a very narrow hole, wanting a shot which once again will land and stop softly rather than running into trouble. This is done in precisely the same way, with no change at all in the technique, but just a slight holding off of the club face through impact. In layman's terms the right hand is just a little bit slower as it approaches impact and the club face held open just a degree or two.

But once you want to move the ball with what is a perceptible bend, you start having to do a bit more. Suppose you want to bend the ball round some trees at the corner of a dogleg. Now you have to ask yourself two questions. Where do I want the ball to start and where do I want it to finish? You choose the direction in which you want to start the ball and very definitely make sure you aim your stance parallel to that direction if not fractionally left of it. You can then set the club face slightly open, in other words to the right, of that direction, and to where you want the ball to finish. Once more ensure that the right hand is well up behind the club in the grip or if anything in a slightly weaker position more on top of the club. The right wrist is going to hinge back early in the backswing in exactly the same way as normal but will now very definitely approach impact in a slower, firmer manner so that the club face is held open through the ball, starting the ball in the direction of the stance and swing and then bending it away to the right. The shot will probably take off with slightly extra height and for this reason you may need one more club than the distance would normally dictate. The good player can also in effect add a shade to this cutspin by producing a slightly glancing blow at impact, almost drawing the club face across the ball with a slightly added right-to-left action. What one also feels, and may be noticeable, is that the relative speeds of body and arm action change slightly. The hand action is slowed down a touch and the hip and body turn is speeded up just a shade, so that the leg action appears and feels a little earlier. Hence the appearance with players who fade the ball of a slightly earlier and more pronounced spinning of the hips, body and arms separating beyond impact.

BENDING THE BALL RIGHT TO LEFT

Most tournament golfers start out life hitting the ball with a right-to-left draw. This is a powerful type of action which initially gives a lot of length. But although most tournament players can bend the ball well from right to left, they don't necessarily have the degree of control over the shot that they do with one which moves from left to right. The method I have described in the long game should give the player the feeling of being able to work the ball very slightly from right to left if he wishes, just tweaking the club face through into a very fractionally closed

FOR THE ADVANCED PLAYER

In this sequence I am aiming to bend the ball to a target round behind the trees. I aim my feet and swing out to the right on roughly the line I want to start the ball, the ball further back in the feet than normal to ensure an inside attack. I don't alter my grip (club players may need to strengthen it) but simply allow the arms to turn over rapidly through impact, left arm really folding into the body and so closing the club face. For a sharpish hook the feeling is of the left arm turning and folding, elbow down, palm up beyond impact, palm of the right hand and club face in turn almost downwards. A comparison between this and the fading action shows how in this the arms seem to work faster in relation to the legs, the left elbow staying far closer to the body through and beyond impact

3

6

1

2

4

5

7

8

position through impact, again giving a shot which to the spectator looks straight, but which to the player gives a feeling of a very slightly right-to-left spin. To get this feeling, the attack on the ball must always be in a circular path, attacking the ball naturally from the inside, though never with a feeling of being exaggeratedly in to out.

Now let's look at the way of bending a ball round an obstacle or really hooking into a crosswind. Once you want to get the ball moving from right to left so that the bend is apparent, you need to determine carefully where you want the ball to start and where you want it to finish. The stance and swing must be aimed in that initial direction, with the feeling of working the club face through so that a definite sidespin is put on the ball. What you are trying to do is to set the club face and swing at odds with each other so that the club face is closed in relation to the direction of the swing. The feeling you will probably need here is of attacking the ball with a more in-to-out direction of attack, playing the ball further back in the stance to encourage this. Then have a feeling of closing the club face through impact, and very definitely letting the left arm fold away beyond impact so that the arms rotate into a more round-the-body action. In other words you are producing a more circular attack on the ball, letting the right hand turn the club face in a slightly closing action where the right hand very clearly comes through into a palm-down position in the through-swing. Most good players can put far more hook on to a ball than they can cut. One of the disadvantages of a hook as a shot into the green is that the ball can also kick quite severely left on landing. The additional bounce away to the left can take the ball out of control. But if faced with an obstacle between you and the green and the option of bending the ball either right to left or left to right, the right-to-left bend is probably the one which is easier to play to get substantial movement on the ball.

If you are one of those players who find a right-to-left bend difficult to achieve, you may also need to adopt a stronger grip, right hand more beneath the club. I would also suggest that you look clearly at the way in which your legs work from the top of the backswing. It is very *easy* to attack a ball in an *out-to-in* direction and comparatively *difficult* to attack it in an *in-to-out* direction. From the top of the backswing, if you have any feeling of unwinding your legs prematurely, the right hip will come forward and almost be in the way of the direction in which your arms should be swinging. To draw or certainly to hook the ball, you will probably have to have the feeling of turning more in the backswing, of sitting back on the right foot and heel a little longer, very definitely starting the swing down with the arms, and then letting the club head pull your right foot through onto the toes so that the leg action feels a little more delayed than normal. For this reason you often see players who hook with what looks to be a slow unwind of the legs in relation to the speed of arms and hands. If you still find the action of a hooked shot difficult, go back to all my advice about the way in which the arms must rotate beyond impact and really let yourself have the feeling of an exaggeratedly flat, round-the-body type of follow-through, making sure that you achieve this through an arm and wrist action rather than trying to thrust in power from the shoulders.

PLAYING THE PAR 3s

The par 3s on any course should be relatively easy. Many golfers, however, play much better iron shots into the green on par 4s. This shouldn't be the case. After all, you know the precise distance of the hole, you can choose exactly the spot you want to tee the ball, not only giving yourself a good lie but giving yourself the view of the hole you prefer. I would suggest that you have a very definite approach to par 3s and in particular get used to teeing the ball up a suitable height. All you want to do is to tee the ball up to be the equivalent of a good lie. Don't tee the ball up to the thickness of your fingers as you would with a drive, or in effect you are tending to hit the ball much too near the top of the blade of the club. Tee the ball fairly well down so that you feel it is just like sitting on a cushion of grass. If you tee the ball too high there is also a tendency to feel the contact is too easy and if anything to look up too soon. I also believe that many players under-club quite drastically on par 3s, mainly because they cannot believe what club they need to hit a certain distance. They will look at a short hole of 160 yards and instead of taking a 5-iron or a 4-iron they will be tempted to use a 6-iron, bringing out the worst in their swing. Always take plenty of club to a par 3 and if the hole does appear difficult, be prepared to aim for the centre of the green rather than risking going too close to a bunker or any other problem areas.

PLAYING FROM BAD LIES

I tried to urge you earlier in the book to do all your practice from a good lie so that you encourage repetition in the swing. Obviously when you get onto the golf course you have to deal with all sorts of bad lies and may be unfortunate enough to find your ball from a perfect drive sitting in some divot hole or other little depression on the fairway. Although this is disheartening, you have to cope with the situation. The first thing to realize about almost all recovery shots or difficult lies is that you need a fairly steep, downward attack into the ball without having the feeling of an up-and-down, chopping action. In order to produce this sort of crisp, downward attack you need to allow the wrists to cock early in the backswing, with the feeling of the right wrist setting itself back at the very moment the club is taken away from the ball. To play an iron shot, or for that matter a wood shot from a slight depression, you need to move the ball back a little bit in the feet which will in itself help produce a slightly steeper attack. This tends to reduce the effective loft of the club so that your choice of clubs can be adjusted accordingly. In the backswing, work at keeping the head absolutely still, easing the club back with quite a sharp cocking back of the right wrist, as always making sure that you maintain this wrist cock right through impact. Any tendency to flick at the ball and let the right wrist straighten before impact is going to spell disaster and bring the club down either behind the ball or thinly onto the top of it. So set the right wrist back and keep the wrists firm through impact.

For the club golfer it is often easier to use a 5-wood or even a 7-wood from a bad lie than it is to use the 3-iron. The slightly rounded sole of one of these lofted woods can more easily fit into any divot hole or depression. In one extra piece of advice here to make the shot even easier I suggest you feel that you tip the club face forward into a very slightly hooded position which raises the back of the sole of the club off the ground. This can help to get the feeling of a crisp strike to the ball, without the sole plate making contact with the ground too soon.

Those then are the shots – or at least some of them – that you need for good scoring. The secret is to be versatile. Experiment and never stop learning. Golf is a continual learning process. Having reached the stage of winning an Open championship, I am still learning. Play around with clubs. Learn the extraordinary range of shots you can play with any one club. Hit it high, hit it low, bend it this way and that. Develop feel and wonderful ball control and with it the true art of good scoring.